The American Monetary System

The American Monetary System

A Concise Survey of Its Evolution since 1896

Robert A. Degen
The University of the South

Lexington Books
D.C. Heath and Company/Lexington, Massachusetts/Toronto

Library of Congress Cataloging-in-Publication Data

Degen, Robert A.
  The American monetary system.

  Bibliography: p.
  Includes index.
  1. Money—United States—History. 2. Monetary policy—United States—
History. 3. Banks and banking—United States—History. I. Title.
HG501.D44   1987   332.4'973   86—46363
ISBN 0—669—15827—5 (alk. paper)
ISBN 0—669—15828—3 (pbk. : alk. paper)

Published simultaneously in Canada
Printed in the United States of America
Casebound International Standard Book Number: 0—669—15827—5
Paperbound International Standard Book Number: 0—669—15828—3
Library of Congress Catalog Card Number: 86—46363

The paper used in this publication meets the minimum requirements of American National
Standard for Information Sciences—Permanence of Paper for Printed Library Materials, ANSI
Z39.48—1984. ∞™

89 90 8 7 6 5 4 3 2

For Eileen,
Cathy, and Barbara

Contents

Preface

This book explains how the American monetary system has developed since the turn of the century. An outgrowth of many years of teaching money and banking to undergraduate liberal arts students, it seeks to enhance the relevance and appeal of the subject by placing it in a larger framework of economic issues and developments than is typically done in money and banking textbooks. I have tried to achieve this by showing how the monetary system is integrated with recent history and how it has evolved.

The treatment is integrated in the sense that it discusses the banking and monetary system of the United States in relation to important events, theories, and policies of the twentieth century. It undertakes to show how monetary theory and policy interact with the broader economic problems of the country. It also recognizes the roles played by leading figures such as Paul M. Warburg, J.P. Morgan, Benjamin Strong, J.M. Keynes, Marriner Eccles, Milton Friedman, Arthur Burns, and Paul Volcker.

The treatment is evolutionary in outlook, following the lead of the distinguished economist and social philosopher Kenneth Boulding. A cardinal feature of the work is the adoption of this perspective and the demonstration of pronounced evolutionary changes over the past ninety years. I am convinced that an appreciation of these changes is essential to an informed interpretation of monetary matters, but that they have been largely neglected in favor of technical analysis and short-term policy discussion.

Dealing with the development of one subset of economics, the monetary system, as it interacts with a variety of other subsets, including economic history, macroeconomics, and international economics, necessarily raises questions of selectivity. Here the writer must make his judgments, knowing that others would almost certainly make somewhat different choices, and that he can make no claim of being uniquely correct. My general guide was to bring in topics from related fields when I thought that they were essential to the main story. For example, the gold standard is discussed at various points where it seemed vital to do so. I do not, however, attempt to delineate or compare different international payments arrangements, such as managed fixed exchange rate systems and flexible exchange rates. Similarly, while macroeconomic concepts are introduced, there is no attempt to provide an account of the microfoundations of macromodels. Only when the central theme, the evolution of the domestic monetary system of the United States, demanded did I reach into the adjacent territories of international economics and macroeconomics. Other fields drawn upon selectively at various places where they seemed particularly helpful in illuminating the "plot" include fiscal policy, developments in banking, political influences, and history of economic thought.

In attempting to explain how the American monetary system has evolved I have extracted essentials from the extensive literature in the field. The result resembles a small-scale map that shows the main features of a large terrain. It is intended to provide a context for understanding current and future monetary issues. A question that is certain to be raised is the degree of objectivity exercised in selecting and presenting the theories, developments, interpretations, and so forth that comprise the book. It would be foolish to claim complete objectivity, but it is not too much to assert, as I do, that I have conscientiously tried to write an account that professional opinion in the field of money and banking would consider essentially fair, reliable, and consistent with generally accepted understanding and interpretation.

The book is addressed primarily to two groups of readers. One group consists chiefly of undergraduate money and banking students who would read it as a supplement to their basic textbooks. In writing I have had my students over many years at The University of the South very much in mind. Because the approach taken is not narrowly focused but quite wide-ranging, the book may be deemed appropriate for other courses also, such as U.S. economic history, finance, and political science courses that deal with public policy. A second group of potential readers consists of persons who have some interest in and familiarity with economics in general and monetary policy in particular as a result perhaps of having taken one or more courses at an earlier time or by virtue of their careers. The subject is fascinating to me and I hope that some of the fascination has entered the pages that follow.

This project was undertaken while on sabbatical leave in the spring of 1983. The support of Dean W. Brown Patterson and the Sabbatical Leave Committee of the College of Arts and Sciences of The University of the South is gratefully acknowledged.

1

Conception and Birth of the Federal Reserve System, 1896–1914

Prologue

As a result of the long and painful Civil War, the slavery issue was resolved and national unity assured, setting the stage for economic growth on a grand scale. In the remaining third of the nineteenth century, industrial and agricultural growth was rapid, the railroad network was greatly extended, urbanization accelerated, and the population grew rapidly and spread across the country. While the outcome of the war provided a firm political basis for the march of economic development, it did not solve the problem of how to provide the nation with a satisfactory monetary system. Americans could build and run something solid or earthy, like a railroad, a steel mill, or a farm, but found a satisfactory monetary system to be elusive. Money seemed to be a perpetual national problem; it had been intractable before the Civil War and it defied satisfactory solution during the three decades (the "Gilded Age") that followed.

The National Bank Act of 1863, adopted as both a war measure and a reform of banking, provided a fresh approach to the banking problem by authorizing the federal government to grant charters to "national banks." These privately owned commercial banks could create a limited amount of national bank notes as circulating paper money, but the arrangement failed to provide an amount of currency appropriate to the nation's needs. During the Civil War the convertibility of paper currency into specie by the federal government was suspended, and the government issued irredeemable paper money in the form of United States notes, or "greenbacks." The country remained on a fiduciary or paper money standard until January 1, 1879, when the greenbacks were made convertible into specie as the gold standard was restored.

Despite the return to the gold standard, the question of the monetary standard remained unsettled as the advocates of silver money pressed for the adoption of a bimetallic (gold and silver) standard. They failed to achieve the goal of making silver a standard metal, but they succeeded in getting the government to add to the money supply by purchasing considerable amounts of silver. Finally in 1896 a showdown battle occurred between the defenders of the gold standard and the silverites in the presidential election between McKinley and Bryan. A review of this epic contest provides a good, as well as dramatic, point of departure for the events of the early part of the twentieth century.

Money—*The* Issue of the Presidential Election of 1896

The political storm over money began to build early in President Grover Cleveland's second term as the Panic of 1893 swept across the country, driving farm prices down drastically, closing thousands of banks and businesses, and causing severe unemployment. Groups favoring free silver and currency expansion, in existence since the 1880s, were joined by new converts to their cause. The demand for "inflation" to relieve the heavy burden of debt and revive the economy spread to others besides Populists; a swelling chorus of voices in the West and South joined in to make money the primary issue before the nation.

In 1893 and 1894 the government had to take emergency measures to keep the country on the gold standard. Under the Sherman Silver Purchase Act of 1890, federal purchases of silver bullion were paid for by the issuance of treasury notes legally redeemable in specie. The government could redeem them by paying out either gold or silver, but in order to adhere to the gold standard it paid out only gold, thereby reducing the gold stock by April 1893 to less than the $100 million considered as the necessary reserve. Cleveland, determined to preserve the gold standard, called Congress into special session in August, and at the end of October the Silver Purchase Act was repealed as the administration wished, although in the process the president's own Democratic party was badly split. The country at large also was split as westerners and southerners by the millions opposed repeal. They saw their sections of the country, largely agricultural and with heavy debts owed to the eastern financial and business interests, as suffering exploitation at the hands of the wealthy creditor classes of the East. In 1894, when the gold reserve again was deemed excessively low, Cleveland's secretary of the treasury, John G. Carlisle, acquired gold from private bankers by the sale of government bonds. The cost to Cleveland was high in terms of the bitter opposition of those favoring free silver; to many, Cleveland was a puppet of Wall Street. Economic conditions in 1894 were extremely bad in agriculture and in industry, with investment spending, consumption, and employment at low levels.

By 1895 the issue of free silver had become a great emotional issue, perhaps the most profound national question since the Civil War. Advocates of silver presented it as the monetary cure for the acute problems of the mass of farmers and workers, whereas gold was viewed by them as benefitting the rich bondholders and other creditors whose claims were worth more in purchasing power as prices fell. By 1895 many Republicans and Democrats were becoming sympathetic to the free-silver forces, thereby causing disaffection and dispute within the two major parties, both of which were led by supporters of the gold standard. A young Democratic congressman from Nebraska, William Jennings Bryan, who was soon to vault into prominence as a result of his role concerning the money question, took the view that his party did not owe much gratitude to its president; in fact, he observed that the Democrats should feel toward Cleveland as "toward the trainman who has opened a switch and precipitated a wreck."

By the time the Democratic national convention was held in Chicago during July 1896, the supporters of silver, with the 36-year-old Bryan as their leader, had gained control of the party. Bryan's famous Cross of Gold speech is credited with winning the presidential nomination for him. In it he gave eloquent expression to the frustration felt by large segments of the population. It is interesting that the concept now referred to as "trickle down"[1] was described by Bryan as the "leak through" approach of his opponents.

> Upon which side will the Democratic party fight; upon the side of "the idle holders of idle capital" or upon the side of "the struggling masses"? That is the question which the party must answer first, and then it must be answered by each individual hereafter. . . . There are two ideas of government. There are those who believe that, if you will only legislate to make the well-to-do prosperous, their prosperity will leak through on those below. The Democratic idea, however, has been that if you legislate to make the masses prosperous, their prosperity will find its way up through every class which rests upon them.
>
> You come to us and tell us that the great cities are in favor of the gold standard; we reply that the great cities rest upon our broad and fertile prairies. Burn down your cities and leave our farms, and your cities will spring up again as if by magic; but destroy our farms and the grass will grow in the streets of every city in the country.
>
> . . . If they dare to come out in the open field and defend the gold standard as a good thing, we will fight them to the uttermost. . . .
>
> [W]e will answer their demand for a gold standard by saying to them: You shall not press down upon the brow of labor this crown of thorns, you shall not crucify mankind upon a cross of gold.[2]

Following Bryan's peroration there was momentary silence followed by a great roar and a tremendous emotional demonstration. The enthusiasm was contagious, and gave the campaign an evangelical flavor.

The following excerpt from the "money plank" of the Democratic platform of 1896 shows precisely one of the alternatives offered to the country on this chief issue of the campaign.

> We are unalterably opposed to monometallism which has locked fast the prosperity of an industrial people in the paralysis of hard times. Gold monometallism is a British policy, and its adoption has brought other nations into financial servitude to London. It is not only un-American but anti-American. . . .
>
> We demand the free and unlimited coinage of both silver and gold at the present legal ratio of 16 to 1 without waiting for the aid or consent of any other nation. We demand that the standard silver dollar shall be a full legal tender, equally with gold, for all debts, public and private, and we favor such legislation as will prevent for the future the demonetization of any kind of legal-tender money by private contract.
>
> We are opposed to the policy and practice of surrendering to the holders of the obligations of the United States the option reserved by law to the Government of redeeming such obligations in either silver coin or gold coin.[3]

The split over the money question was less serious for the Republicans than for the Democrats, although there were defections from their party ranks also. The Republican party approached the electorate as the party that had put the country on the gold standard in 1879, was proud of having done so, and would defend the gold standard against the reckless and divisive Democrats. In his acceptance speech, William McKinley stressed both the money and tariff problems and asked the nation to unite behind the twin pillars of the gold standard and protective tariffs.

> For the first time since 1868, if ever before, there is presented to the American people this year a clear and direct issue as to our monetary system, of vast importance in its effects, and upon the right settlement of which rests largely the financial honor and prosperity of the country. It is proposed by one wing of the Democratic party and its allies, the People's and Silver parties, to inaugurate the free and unlimited coinage of silver by independent action on the part of the United States at a ratio of 16 ounces of silver to 1 ounce of gold.
>
> The mere declaration of this purpose is a menace to our financial and industrial interests, and has already created universal alarm. It involves great peril to the credit and business of the country, a peril so grave that conservative men everywhere are breaking away from their old party associations and uniting with other patriotic citizens in emphatic protest against the

platform of the Democratic National Convention as an assault upon the faith and honor of the Government and the welfare of the people. We have had few questions in the lifetime of the Republic more serious than the one which is thus presented.[4]

The Republican party platform, diametrically opposed to that of the Democrats but equally fervent and unequivocal, had this to say in its section dealing with money:

> The Republican party is unreservedly for sound money. It caused the enactment of a law providing for the redemption (resumption) of specie payments in 1879. Since then every dollar has been as good as gold. We are unalterably opposed to every measure calculated to debase our currency or impair the credit of our country. We are therefore opposed to the free coinage of silver, except by international agreement with the leading commercial nations of the earth, which agreement we pledge ourselves to promote, and until such agreement can be obtained the existing gold standard must be maintained. All of our silver and paper currency must be maintained at parity with gold.[5]

The election of 1896 resulted in victory for McKinley and the gold standard. McKinley received 7.1 million popular votes and 271 electoral votes to Bryan's 6.5 million and 176. Along with the ballots, the monetary die had apparently been cast in the shape of the gold standard; "apparently" because it took an exogenous development in the form of increased production from gold discoveries in the years that followed the election to eliminate serious doubt about the gold standard and so draw the teeth at last from the silver movement. That movement, having challenged the gold standard so passionately but unsuccessfully, virtually disappeared until its revival briefly in the 1930s.

The Gold Standard Act of 1900

> Money, which represents the prose of life, and which is hardly spoken of in parlors without an apology, is, in its effects and laws, as beautiful as roses.
>
> —Ralph Waldo Emerson[6]

As noted above, the country had been on a de facto monometallic gold standard since 1879, but it had not yet embraced the gold standard clearly and unambiguously. Under the Resumption Act (1875) which was effective January 1, 1879, the secretary of the treasury was required to redeem United States legal-tender notes in coin. As a practical matter this meant gold coin, because in 1873 silver ceased to be standard money; few silver dollars were in use, so Congress discontinued the free coinage of silver at that time. Still, the law did not unequivocally set the country on a gold basis, and the agitation for silver as well as the actual purchase of silver during the eighties and nineties raised some doubt as to the permanence of our adherence to gold.

On March 14, 1900, definitive legal recognition was given to the gold standard by the Currency Act of 1900, usually referred to as the Gold Standard Act. Two fundamental provisions of the act were:

1. The U.S. dollar was defined as 23.22 grains of pure gold and declared to be the standard unit of value. All money issued or coined by the United States was to be maintained at parity with this standard. Since there are 480 grains in an ounce, the price of gold was set at 480/23.22 = \$20.67 per ounce.

2. The secretary of the treasury was directed to set up a separate reserve in gold coin and bullion of \$150 million for use in redeeming greenbacks and treasury notes of 1890.

The act also provided for the withdrawal of the treasury notes of 1890 from circulation.

In 1900 Bryan and McKinley met in a rematch of the epic contest of 1896, with McKinley again triumphant, his popular and electoral vote margins larger than in 1896. The Democratic platform retained its 1896 position on money but gave it much less prominence. By 1900 the price level had risen from its trough of the mid-nineties, and the economy was vigorous. The Republicans were able to claim credit for prosperity and took pride in having made the gold standard secure. The two successive defeats of Bryan mark the end of the silver movement of the late nineteenth century. The basic reason for the triumph of the gold standard was the huge increase in the world supply of monetary gold after 1897. It is ironic that the gold standard was viewed as successful, because fortuitous increases in gold production resulting from gold strikes achieved the same results that the inflationist silverites had so ardently intended to bring about by the monetization of silver. In keeping with Emerson's simile, it appeared that money, whether gold or silver, could have beautiful effects provided it was sufficiently abundant.

The Heyday of the Gold Standard

The commercial world has become more and more committed to the gold standard through a series of historical events having little if any connection with the fitness of that or any other metal to serve as a *stable* standard. So far as the question of monetary stability is concerned, it is not too much to say that we have hit upon the gold standard by accident just as we hit on the present railway gauge by the accident of previous custom as to road carriages; and just as we hit upon the decimal notation by the accident of having had ten fingers. . . . Now that we have adopted a gold standard, it is about as difficult to substitute another as it would be to establish the Russian railway gauge or the duodecimal system of numeration.

—Irving Fisher[7]

In the three decades before 1897 the economy experienced a basically deflationary trend. The fall in prices is attributable in the early part of the period to a slower rate of increase in the money stock than in real income; after 1880 a fall in the velocity of money was important. During the period of pronounced distress from mid-1892 to mid-1896 the money stock failed to grow at all. In contrast, from 1897 to 1914 the money stock grew at a rate of about 7.5 percent per year, and wholesale prices increased at a rate of 2.5 percent per year. The gold stock of the United States, to which the money stock was closely linked, rose at an average rate of 6.8 percent per year.[8]

World gold production increased dramatically from the 1890s until World War I as a result of major discoveries (chiefly in South Africa, but also in Alaska and Colorado) and improved techniques of mining and refining. The gold stock of the United States grew more rapidly than did the world total; by 1914 almost a quarter of the total world gold stock was in the United States.

Today the basic money supply is most often defined as the public's holdings of currency plus demand deposits and other "transactions balances" in depository institutions. Several definitions of money are now in use, and in recent years their contents have been subject to change. For the early years of the century the definition is straightforward: prior to 1914, separate data for demand deposits and other (time) deposits are not available; the distinction between them was not then significant. The money supply for this period may be taken to be currency plus total deposits in commercial banks. From 1900 to 1914 the gold stock rose from $916 million to $1.9 billion, or by slightly more than 100 percent. The money stock rose from $6.4 billion to $16.1 billion, an increase of more than 150 percent. Thus the ratio of money to gold was about 7 to 1 in 1900 and 8.5 to 1 in 1914.

Let's examine the glittering standard more carefully. Gold provided the chief basis for the international monetary system from the 1870s to World War I, roughly forty years. Its remarkable prestige before 1914 would be quite understandable if based on a long and glorious history of success, but in fact the gold standard was something of a flash in the pan from a historical perspective. Great Britain adopted the gold standard in 1821 shortly after the Napoleonic wars. About fifty years later, other leading countries, including France, Germany, and the United States, followed suit, making gold the common monetary denominator and regulator of exchange rates and national money supplies. It is of the essence of the system that it be international, the participating countries being interdependent, with their prices and incomes linked through the gold standard mechanism.

Each country on the gold standard defined its monetary unit as a fixed quantity of gold, and then undertook to keep all of its money at parity with the gold monetary unit. For the system to function, the nations had to accept certain rules of behavior (the "rules of the gold standard game"). Gold could be coined freely, nongold types of money could be redeemed in gold, and gold could be imported and exported without restriction. The value of each currency in terms of another gold standard currency, that is, the rate of exchange, resulted (within narrow limits) from the relative gold contents of the currencies. Such stability of exchange rates is conducive to international trade and capital flows and thus to an expanding world economy. When imbalances in payments between nations occur, they are automatically eliminated by international flows of capital and gold. Modified versions of the gold standard developed later in which gold coinage was omitted, but the essential monetary control features of the system remained intact.

From the point of view of the domestic effects of the gold standard, which are of particular concern here, the central function of the gold standard is that it *controls the creation of money*. The quantity of gold *automatically* determines the money stock of the country, not with precision but within fairly definite limits. The money supply is tethered to the amount of gold. There is some give to the rope, but in practical terms an expanding money supply will normally reach the end of its tether in time to prevent an excessively large growth of money.

From 1879 to 1914 gold could be taken to the American mints and exchanged for gold coin without limit. Gold moved in and out of the country without restriction. In addition to gold coin, gold certificates (yellowbacks), that is, paper money issued by the Treasury representing gold coin or bullion held in the Treasury's vaults, also circulated. Unlike gold itself, however, the gold certificates (warehouse receipts) were not legal tender. Most of the country's gold was outside the Treasury, held by the general public and the banks. Of the $916 million total gold stock in 1900, 75 percent was outside the Treasury; of the $1.9 billion in 1914, 87 percent was outside the Treasury.

The amount of currency outside the Treasury grew by about $1.5 billion from 1900 to 1914. Of this increase, about $950 million or 64 percent was gold (coin and certificates) and some $400 million or 28 percent consisted of national bank notes. The other types of money, in particular silver and greenbacks, were essentially unchanged except for fractional coins that were only a minor part of the total. The Gold Standard Act of 1900 required the government to keep all of the nongold types of money at parity with gold, and all of the different types of money were in fact interchangeable at par with gold throughout the country. What stands out is that over 90 percent of the additional money came from either additional gold (the prime source) or additional paper money issued by the privately owned commercial banks with federally granted charters.

As noted earlier, the linkage of a nation's money supply to its stock of monetary gold under the gold standard is a cardinal feature of that system. To be more explicit about how total money and gold are related, it is useful to employ the concept of the monetary base or, alternatively, high-powered money. Before 1914 it consisted of currency held by the public plus vault cash held by the banks. It is called high-powered because every dollar of such money that is held as bank reserves can support several dollars of bank deposits, or is the base upon which the debt money of the banks (bank deposits) is built. The size of the multiple depends upon what ratio commercial bank deposits are to bank reserves, and what ratio bank deposits are to the amount of currency in the hands of the public. Changes in these ratios were of some significance during the years from 1900 to 1914, but it is clear that the growth of the money stock was due predominantly to the rise of high-powered money. We have noted that the lion's share of the rise of high-powered money was in the form of gold. Gold was the central core of the currency and thus of the total money stock. Since deposits were convertible by depositors into currency, and since currency was convertible into gold, the amount of gold was the foundation of the monetary structure. It follows that the larger the foundation, the larger the superstructure of total money.

Some Terminology and Institutional Features of the Period

"Scorecard here—you can't tell the players without a scorecard" was the traditional call of vendors in ballparks in the days when players had only numbers on the backs of their jerseys. This section identifies terms used on the monetary field of play early in the twentieth century.

Bank deposits were not considered by economists to be money, although the importance of bank deposits, via checks, to serve as means of payment was clearly recognized. A broader concept, *circulating media,* was used for the things that served as a means of exchange or payment. Money was one form of circulating medium, and bank deposits were another. The distinction lay in the extent of acceptability: money was *generally* acceptable, that is, acceptable by everyone, whereas a check required the consent of the payee.

The definition of money was very narrow; bank deposits had not yet received the respect or status attached to the term money.[9]

The money stock was classified into two groups, primary and fiduciary. Primary money consisted of a commodity which had as much value in non-money form as it did as money, gold coins being the quintessential example and the only type in use in the United States. Fiduciary money lacked inherent value, or at any rate full value, and got its value from confidence that it could either be exchanged for primary money or else be used directly to pay debts or buy goods and services.

From 1900 to 1914 commercial bank deposits plus national bank notes nearly tripled from $5.5 billion to $15.0 billion, while the number of banks doubled. With some 28,000 commercial banks by 1914, the United States had a great many more banks than any other country. Compared with banks in other major countries, ours were much smaller on average. They were mostly independent units doing mainly a local business and owned by residents of the communities where they were located. Another distinctive characteristic stemmed from the constitutional division of powers between the federal government and the states. It is usual to describe the U.S. commercial banking business as dual, because bank charters of incorporation are issued by the federal government to national banks and by state government to state banks. It would be more accurate to describe the scene in the early part of the twentieth century as a triad, since private or unincorporated banks constituted 37 percent of the banks in 1900. Between 1900 and 1914 the number of state banks more than tripled, national banks doubled, and the private banks declined by 40 percent.

Trust companies were a very important financial species in the period 1900–1914, although they were not new and had a track record in the panics of 1857 and 1873 that failed to inspire confidence in their longevity. The term comes from the function of trustee, fiduciary, or agent in various capacities, such as administering trust funds and serving as custodian for property held in trust. The financing of industry, especially the railroads, provided lucrative trust opportunities in connection with corporate securities. In addition, with the rise of a super-rich class, the families of mortal tycoons could ease the burden of protecting their gigantic nest eggs by engaging a professional financial curator. Of particular importance is the fact that the trust companies were also able to carry on a general banking business; they were in fact commercial banks in most cases and were so recognized in banking statistics, although technically they were not commercial banks.

For decades the trust companies, all of them under state charter, escaped government regulation for the most part. From the viewpoint of commercial banks, and especially national banks, they constituted unfair competition, because no reserve requirements were imposed on them in most states, they had tax advantages, and they could make mortgage loans not permitted by national banks. Some of the trust companies outside large cities were primarily engaged in banking, with trust business a fringe activity. National banks, prohibited from trust business, sometimes slipped the leash by forming separate affiliates, for example, the Bankers Trust Company in New York in 1903. With their greater freedom and high profit opportunities, the trust companies particularly, and the state-chartered banks also, grew rapidly. The trust companies proved to be a weak link in the chain during the Panic of 1907 when the Knickerbocker Trust Company fell and there were heavy runs on others. The shock of 1907 induced greater state regulation of trust companies, with the result that they gradually came to be treated on a par with state-chartered banks.

Private banks, or banks owned by individuals and partnerships, operated without a corporate charter from either the federal or a state government. In 1900 they were slightly more numerous than state banks and considerably more numerous than national banks. Their number declined substantially by 1914, and this process of gradual elimination continued until they became a negligible element by the 1930s.

Some of the private banks were large and impressive, but there were many small private banks that are a fascinating part of the country's development. A bank would appear in a new town as an offshoot of a shopkeeper's or a merchant's business because it was the safest place in town to store money. The "bank" might be a small part of the store. Some fifteen hundred or so of such small-scale banks were in existence by 1909. Usually as they grew they graduated into chartered banks in order to gain limited liability and additional owners. Banks too small to meet the minimum capital requirements for national banks could operate with state charters or as private banks. As Trescott points out, the private banks and trust companies filled roles that were proscribed for national banks.[10]

The Panic of 1907

> Panics, in some cases, have their uses; they produce as much good as hurt. Their duration is always short; the mind soon grows through them and acquires a firmer habit than before. But their peculiar advantage is, that they are the touchstone of sincerity and hypocrisy, and bring things and men to light, which might otherwise have lain forever undiscovered.
>
> —Thomas Paine[11]

In 1907 a blow usually described as either a panic or a crisis stunned the American economy. The two terms have been used interchangeably, but it seems helpful to differentiate between them and then to conclude that the country experienced both a panic and a crisis. A *crisis* connotes great danger or trouble with a decisive or crucial time or event which sooner or later resolves the difficulty; the outcome may range from highly satisfactory to disastrous. History is notched by crises: the Cuban missile crisis, the dollar crisis, the oil crisis, and so forth. *Panic* refers to a type of behavior at a time of crisis. The derivation of the word is quite lighthearted: the Greek god Pan, with human torso and the legs, ears, and horns of a goat, dashes from the underbrush playing pipes and startles passers-by. The modern connotation, hysterical fear, is deadly serious, and it is doubtful that many have Paine's view of its advantages. The phrase "hit the panic button" is associated with World War II when aircraft on bombing missions used a warning system by which crew members were notified of damage so extensive as to make abandonment imminent. A pilot who overreacted to a given situation could cause the crew to bail out unnecessarily by hitting the panic button. In a financial panic, fear of a collapse of the financial system leads to sudden huge withdrawals of deposits and a wave of selling various assets for cash. People bail out of a financial structure they fear will crash, and by doing so either cause the disaster or enlarge it.

The decade prior to 1907 was generally very prosperous. A mild two-year contraction that ended in 1904 interrupted the advance, but it was followed by an impressively strong and long expansion that featured industrial growth and was accompanied by rapid growth of the money stock as well as stock market speculation. By May 1907 the economy reached a cyclical upper turning point, and business activity entered a period of contraction of about a year's duration. The decline was gentle until October, when panic seized the banks, with the result that payments were restricted, that is, banks generally refused to pay out currency or specie to depositors on demand. Not only did banks fail but, of greater importance, the contraction of the economy greatly intensified. From 1907 to 1908 the net national product fell by 11 percent in real terms. The depression ranks among the more severe contractions experienced by the economy over the past century.

From May until September there was some decline in the money stock, but the public did not yet distrust the banks. In October banks came under severe pressure; the public ran on the banks, demanding currency in exchange for deposits, and the banks sought to increase their currency holdings so as to be able to meet their depositors' demands. With both public and banks scrambling for liquidity, the total money stock declined by 5 percent in five months. Prices collapsed on the stock market as banks called in loans used to finance security holdings. Interest rates on call money soared as high as 125 percent. Banks throughout the country withdrew currency from their balances in New York banks. The New York banks, fearing a greater drain on their reserves, may have panicked by prematurely restricting the convertibility of deposits into currency.

Among the financiers of the era, one towered above all the others, the Great Pierpont Morgan, as Frederick Lewis Allen called him. An image emerges of a financial Paul Bunyan, a vision not inconsistent with that of the greatest of the robber barons. Morgan was the embodiment of financial power, and whatever degree of justification (or lack thereof) might attach to his personal power, it was recognized as a fact.

For the first three weeks of October 1907 Morgan was in Richmond, Virginia, attending the triennial Episcopal Convention. He received numerous messages from New York as the panic developed but decided to stay in Richmond until the conclusion of the convention to avoid adding to a sense of alarm by an early departure. Upon returning to New York, Morgan devised a strategy to halt the financial collapse, and then directed a series of difficult and exhausting actions of implementation. The saying that "Wherever Macgregor sits, there is the head of the table" applied; wherever Morgan was, often in his opulent library, was the command center for the strategy by which this private individual dealt with a most urgent national problem. As self-appointed but generally recognized commander-in-chief, Morgan had his trusted banking subordinates bring him intelligence and provide help in evaluating the condition of financial institutions under attack, thereby enabling him to decide which units were too vulnerable to be defended, and when and where to effect a rescue. At critical times he called on financial allies and rallied them to the common cause. Morgan's outlook is indicated by an alleged incident in which a banker came to his office at 23 Wall Street and confessed he was disturbed by being below his legal reserve. Morgan replied, "You ought to be ashamed of yourself to be anywhere near your legal reserve. What is your reserve for at a time like this except to use?"[12] There were two weeks of chaos: loans were being called in large amounts, banks were suffering runs, and the stock exchange was demoralized.

Some major developments:

A run developed at the Knickerbocker Trust Company, a large bank whose investments were considered questionable. Morgan's men, including Benjamin Strong, who later became governor of the Federal Reserve Bank of New York, examined Knickerbocker's condition and found it too far gone for resuscitation. Its cash ran out, and it failed.

A run at the Trust Company of America was met successfully after Strong advised that the bank appeared to be solvent. Morgan, together with allies from the First National and National City banks, provided cash in the nick of time to avoid closure.

U.S. government funds were transferred to banks in New York by Secretary of the Treasury George B. Cortelyou to be available to the hard-pressed trust companies, and John D. Rockefeller made $10 million available for this purpose also.

The rush to sell securities to get cash caused stock prices to plummet. When the president of the Stock Exchange reported that the exchange faced closing as the result of a lack of money to buy stock, Morgan got the large banks and the Treasury to lend money, and the Stock Exchange stayed open.

Morgan himself bought bonds from the City of New York which required $30 million to pay off obligations coming due at a time when it could not raise the funds in the money market.

The uniquely powerful role of Morgan probably rested on the widespread belief that if his leadership failed, so would the whole financial world. Six years later the country set up a central bank to provide the kind of ultimate lending function that Morgan tried to provide as an individual. "He had been, as it were, a one-man Federal Reserve Bank."[13].

The restriction of payments by the New York banks was quickly emulated by banks throughout the country. Some states gave legal sanction to the restriction by declaring holidays, but in most cases the situation was simply accepted. During the last two months of 1907, substitutes for currency were issued, such as clearinghouse loan certificates used for interbank settlements, and banks usually supplied cash for payrolls. The restriction period ended in January 1908. Friedman and Schwartz, while recognizing that the bigger and stronger New York banks might conceivably have fended off restriction by heavy and prompt lending to their weaker brethren and by supplying the currency needs of outside banks, defend the relatively early restriction of payments. Weak banks failed, but such failures did not cause a domino effect, and few banks failed because of temporary illiquidity. "Restriction of payments thus protected the banking system and gave time for the immediate panic to wear off, as well as for additional currency to be made available."[14]

The shock of the events of late 1907 led to much reflection and eventually to major reform. One immediate response was a series of addresses at Columbia University designed to explain the crisis and to suggest principles on the basis of which the currency system might be reconstructed. The papers were published in a volume entitled *The Currency Problem and the Present Financial Situation*. Professor Edwin R.A. Seligman, a prominent Columbia economist (seventh president of the American Economic Association), discussed the crisis in historical perspective. Seligman reviewed eight U.S. crises of the nineteenth century and found their general features to be similar. During periods of expansion there developed an overcapitalization of anticipated earnings of growth industries through expansion of bank credit and new stock issues. This process went on until the high capitalization of assets was recognized as clearly excessive relative to actual earnings. A readjustment of values involving losses had to take place. If the financial world acted carefully and skillfully, the adjustment of values might be gradual and the economy could pass through its depressed period without the trauma of panic. But if confidence was shaken by some occurrence, a bank refusing credit, the failure of a prominent firm—even a rumor might be sufficient—then a crisis occurred. Seligman vividly summed up his explanation of the recent events.

> When we come particularly to the crisis of 1907, we find that the general causes were very much the same. The last decade has been characterized by the most unexampled prosperity in our history. The most striking initial cause is the prodigious increase in the gold supply. . . . The rapid accumulation of gold, much of which went into the bank reserves, enabled the financial institutions to expand their credit facilities manyfold, and as a consequence enterprise flourished in every direction. . . . Values were pushed up on all sides and the hopes of a prosperous community were capitalized with a recklessness born of unbounded faith. The pace was too rapid; the reaction was bound to ensue. In the late autumn of 1907 the revulsion was precipitated, with all the familiar accompaniments of an acute panic such as the collapse of several financial institutions, the sudden curtailment of loans, leading to the failures of some prominent business concerns.[15]

Seligman compared the American experience very unfavorably with that of Europe, where acute financial crises had been virtually eliminated. The lesson, on which all speakers agreed, was that legislative reform of our currency system was needed.

For a banker's view we have the observation of Frank A. Vanderlip of the National City Bank, later president of that institution. Having just been under the gun of the crisis, he understandably considered it "by whatever standard you choose, measured either by the direct financial losses, by the disorganization of industry, by the destruction of confidence . . . one of the great calamities of history.[16] Such overstatement reveals the distraught state of mind of (in Veblen's term) a "captain of finance." Vanderlip had some important insights to offer on the nature of the system. His comments on the psychology and behavior of the public and the bankers provide a remarkably frank explanation of how everyone looked out for himself. Even the most underdeveloped imagination would have little difficulty divining what happened to the hindmost.

> In a time of crisis two things are likely to happen. The public becomes suspicious of the banks and resorts to money as a store of value, converting

its bank credits into cash and hoarding the cash. At the same time, the
bankers are likely to become suspicious of one another as well as apprehensive of the probable demands on the part of their customers, and there
begins a scramble for reserve money. Each institution stands alone, concerned first for its own safety, and using every endeavor to pile up reserves
without regard to what the effort may cost the financial situation at large.

The result is an absolute immobility of reserves, and the effect upon
the general situation is probably far more disastrous than that produced by
all the private hoarding. . . . Many banks are carrying reserves far in excess of their needs. They will neither increase loans and thus build up their
deposit credits to a normal ratio to the reserve they hold, nor will they remit
their surplus reserve to their reserve agents in the financial centers, for fear
that they might be unable to get the money back again promptly if they
should need it.[17]

The Reformation

> America's leading manufacturing, transportation and commercial
> concerns years ago attained heights of economic efficiency which made
> them the envy of foreigners. None, however, envied us our banking
> system.
>
> —Edwin Walter Kemmerer[18]

It was clear from the Panic of 1907 that reform was overdue, but agreement
on need did not extend to the means required to achieve it. A stopgap remedy
was quickly provided by the Aldrich–Vreeland Act (May 30, 1908), but
more lasting reform came years later after much careful study, discussion,
and debate, in the form of the Federal Reserve Act (December 23, 1913).

The Aldrich–Vreeland Act, named for Senator Nelson W. Aldrich and
Representative Edward B. Vreeland, dealt with the problem of how to provide enough currency quickly to satisfy the demands of the public when it
wanted to convert large amounts of deposits into cash. To do so was critical
for the system, because if total currency (high-powered money) could not be
expanded rapidly, the withdrawal of it from the banks would deplete their
reserves and by a sort of reflex action make them reduce their liabilities and
so reduce the total means of payment (deposits plus currency) by a multiple
amount. "Short-period 'elasticity' in one component of the money stock—
currency—was therefore desirable in order to prevent undesired 'elasticity'
in the total money stock."[19]

Aldrich–Vreeland permitted banks to join together in groups to form
National Currency Associations which were empowered to issue emergency
currency. The banks would deposit certain approved assets (commercial paper and bonds) with the association; limits would be placed on the amounts

of currency that could be created. The notes were to be retired promptly once the emergency ended, a process to be encouraged by taxes on the notes. Aldrich–Vreeland was used only once. When the outbreak of World War I set off a run on the banks, a large amount of emergency currency was pumped out, very likely scotching a panic. A year later (June 30, 1915), Aldrich–Vreeland, no longer deemed necessary, expired.

A provision of the Aldrich–Vreeland Act authorized the creation of a National Monetary Commission which served as the incubator for the Federal Reserve Act. Aldrich and Vreeland were chairman and vice-chairman respectively of the eighteen-member congressional body. Through hearings and many special studies, the commission undertook an exhaustive examination of the monetary system and possible remedies for its deficiencies, and in 1912 issued a report recommending a plan of reform. Proposals for a central banking institution were highly contentious politically. A bill by Senator Aldrich that would have placed control of a National Reserve Association in the hands of bankers was rejected, although many of its features were later included in the Federal Reserve Act. Soon after his election, President Woodrow Wilson took an active interest in the preparation of a banking reform bill and called a special session of Congress in the spring of 1913 largely to deal with banking legislation. Fear of control by Wall Street on the one hand and too much government control on the other required reconciliation. Eventually the bill of Representative Carter Glass and a Senate version of it resulted in a compromise that received Wilson's signature on December 23, 1913, as the Federal Reserve Act. The legislative process was complicated and involved numerous political leaders, bankers, and academicians.

This major law established a new banking structure under the supervision of the Federal Reserve Board and twelve Federal Reserve Banks. It created a new system of bank reserves and a new form of paper money. It also improved the check clearing system, provided fiscal assistance to the Treasury, and served to mitigate the impact of Treasury revenue and expenditure flows on the banking system. The changes made by the Federal Reserve Act were varied and comprehensive, but taken as a whole, and as the considered national response to the urgent monetary problems of the time, its central function was, in the words of the Act, "to furnish an elastic currency."

Analyses of the monetary system typically focused on the related problems of an inelastic currency and a defective set of bank reserve requirements. The two are so intermingled that it seems best to consider them simultaneously. The problem of inelasticity was discussed in two main contexts, that of hand-to-hand currency and the broader concept of the money stock or supply (deposits plus currency). The inelasticity of currency was the more acute as well as the more clearly understood issue. Our earlier reference to the problem dealt with the matter in terms of the demand by the public for currency in exchange for deposits during a time of panic. A less serious but more frequent heavy demand for currency occurred annually with the autumn harvest and its shipment to market. The banking system had very little capacity to respond to either of these demands. The ratio of deposits to currency in the banks' vaults was high; more important, there was no feasible way of creating more currency when it might be required. It was obvious that currency needed to be made expansible or elastic to compensate for the relatively little currency available to be paid out by the banks to redeem their deposits.

Banks under the National Banking System were classified by the size of the community in which they were located, and their reserve requirements depended on their classification.

Banks in the large financial centers designated as central reserve cities had a reserve requirement of 25 percent in cash. Each $1,000 in deposits required a cash reserve of $250.

Banks in cities classified as reserve cities had a reserve requirement of 25 percent; half had to be in cash and the other half could be on deposit in central reserve city banks. Each $1,000 in deposits required a cash reserve of $125 plus $(.25 \times \$125) = \$156.25$.

Banks in small communities (country banks) had a reserve requirement of 15 percent; 6 percent had to be in cash and 9 percent could be on deposit in reserve city banks. Each $1,000 in deposits required a cash reserve of $60 plus $(.125 \times \$90)$ plus $(.25 \times \$11.25) = \$74.06$.

On the basis of these legal requirements, the ratio of deposits to cash reserves ranged from 4 to 1 for central reserve city banks to 13.5 to 1 for deposits in country banks, assuming that banks conformed exactly to the legal prescriptions. In fact, banks often held somewhat more cash and/or total reserves than the legal minimum, so that the stated ratios of deposits to cash reserves represent limits rather than rigid realities. For the entire system the ratio of deposits to cash reserves averaged about 6 to 1. For every dollar that depositors in a country bank wished to withdraw in cash, the bank legally had to have only 6 cents on hand. If it needed more cash it had to turn to its deposits in reserve city banks, which in turn would draw down deposits in central reserve city banks. The latter would need to sell securities, call in loans from stock market investors, and clamp down on new loans. For sheer perversity, the loans made on the stock exchange as "call loans" deserved a blue ribbon. Considered almost perfectly liquid because they could be called, when a large number were actually called simultaneously by many banks they might in fact be highly illiquid as a result of distress selling of securities and possibly the closing of the stock market.

The system had no outside resources on which to draw. The National Banking Act required banks to hold reserves, but the term was really a misnomer. Banks were legally prohibited from going below the average minimum reserve levels calculated over a week or two depending on the classification of the bank, and could be closed by the comptroller of the currency for violating the requirements. To gain liquidity in a time of stringency they could not avoid the necessity of contracting loans.[20] With deposits some six times cash reserves, when called on to convert $6 of deposits into currency the banks could readily enough pay out $1 from reserves, but they could not part with the remaining $5. The bulk of reserves were legally required to be held, and the money that constituted them therefore was not really available "in reserve." A military analogy illustrates the dilemma. If a general enters a battle with 100,000 men in the line and 25,000 in reserve, but then is prohibited by the commander-in-chief from committing them, they are not actually available to affect the outcome of the battle. The reserves did serve the function of limiting the total deposits that the banks could create but they did not, except marginally, provide a reserve available to meet extraordinary demands for cash.

Given the amount of currency in existence, it was impossible for the banks to satisfy the demand for currency during a panic. Could not *more* currency be created to fill the need? Before the passage of the Federal Reserve Act (and apart from the provisions of the Aldrich–Vreeland Act referred to earlier), the type of paper money theoretically capable of expansion was the national bank note. But national bank notes, "which should have furnished the elastic element in the country's hand to hand money, were notoriously inelastic."[21] To issue them the national banks had to deposit U.S. government bonds with the Treasury. Often the bonds were not available on terms profitable to the banks, and in addition the delay involved in depositing them and obtaining bank notes rendered this process quite impracticable. Apart from the question of favorable terms and the time element, linking the supply of currency to the amount of government debt was a primitive way of determining the amount of currency and was without justification in terms of the financial ends to be served. A link might more logically have been made to the national goat population which, according to a 1975 article in *The Wall Street Journal,* was closely related over many decades to the trend of the general economy! The point of course is that the size of the national debt was determined separately from and without regard for the currency needs of the nation.

The Federal Reserve System introduced new paper money in the form of Federal Reserve notes. The Federal Reserve Banks were required to hold a gold reserve of 40 percent against the notes, as well as collateral in the form of commercial paper, but the important point is that ordinarily (there were exceptions) these requirements would not constitute an effective restraint on the ability of the Federal Reserve Banks to augment the amount of Federal Reserve notes in circulation. The Federal Reserve Banks, unlike commercial banks, would not be motivated to expand their credit to the limit of their reserves. Commercial banks that were members of the Federal Reserve System were required to keep deposits in the Federal Reserve Banks which could be converted into Federal Reserve notes. Here then is how the way was opened to an elastic currency: member banks could borrow from the Federal Reserve Banks and could use the proceeds as their reserve deposits, or they could withdraw them in Federal Reserve notes at any time. Federal Reserve Banks were expected to be able and willing to create the amount of currency needed to satisfy the demands of the public and the banks. The fundamental new element, as compared with the old arrangement, was that now the banks had a place to get currency, and the Federal Reserve Banks would be the fount from which a refreshing currency flow would pour as needed.

The second problem of inelasticity referred to above pertains to the total money stock or the means of payment, consisting of bank deposits plus currency in the hands of the public. The size of the money stock changes as a result of the expansion (or contraction) of the banking system as it acquires assets from the public by lending or buying securities (or by reducing such assets), given of course the reserve ratio(s) and deposit–currency ratio. Thus the money stock depends on the amount of bank credit. The ability of commercial banks to extend credit is based primarily on the amount of reserves they hold. The new element under the Federal Reserve System, as compared with the old arrangement, was that the Federal Reserve Banks, as a central banking system, could provide reserves to the banks, gradually over time or suddenly in an emergency as a "lender of last resort." In addition to currency, the Federal Reserve would create the means for elasticity of the total money stock. As originally designed, the Federal Reserve Banks would do this by lending to the member banks through the process of rediscounting commercial paper presented to them for this purpose by the banks.

To sum up, the Federal Reserve Act gave the United States a fresh monetary start by creating a brand new mechanism, a central banking system, intended to remedy the weaknesses of the existing system. The new institutional arrangements were designed principally to give the country the total money stock and hand-to-hand currency it required, and to do so in a timely manner. Beyond that, the central bank would supervise the commercial banks and improve the efficiency and operating procedures of the banks and the Treasury. The underlying ideas on which the writers, bankers, businessmen, and legislators relied in constructing this new set of arrangements are of particular interest in understanding the monetary development of the United

States. It is to these ideas that we turn next, and, in reviewing the theories, take note also of some of the leading thinkers responsible for advancing them.

The Theoretical Foundation

> If any one has ever really imagined that the price level depends solely on the quantity of money, he should certainly be corrected. But the really important matter is that students of economics should appreciate the existence of a *law* of direct proportion between quantity of money and price level—a law as real, as important, and as fundamental in the economic theory of money as Boyle's law of direct proportion between density and pressure is real, is important, and is fundamental in the physical theory of gases.
>
> —Irving Fisher[22]

By *theoretical foundation* I mean a few fundamental concepts which were accepted by those considered to be the informed interpreters of the financial system in the 1900–1914 period. Such theories served to guide policy. Three concepts or doctrines are of concern: quantity theory of money; real bills doctrine; and gold standard.

The quantity theory of money was a cornerstone of orthodox economic thought early in the twentieth century. It was one of the most venerable economic doctrines, with roots going back to David Hume's classic exposition in "Of Money" (1752) and even earlier. With no rival theory in the field against it, "until the 1930s, the quantity theory of money may be said to have been everybody's theory of money."[23] The quantity theory was best known for explaining long-run changes in the general price level: changes in the quantity of money were the primary cause. While the quantity theorists emphasized changes in the money stock, they recognized that velocity of circulation of money could also vary. They believed that velocity was independent of the quantity of money; while velocity could change autonomously, changes in money were of overwhelming importance in explaining long-run price level changes. The high ground of the quantity theorists was in explaining long-run price level changes, but they addressed themselves to short-run fluctuations also, and in the latter context acknowledged instability of the velocity of spending as a significant factor.

Before turning to the contribution of Irving Fisher on this topic, it is pertinent to tie the quantity theory to the attitudes and policies that have been discussed up to this point. In the late nineteenth century the proponents of silver wanted more money so as to raise prices and output. Although silver was not adopted as a standard money, the increase in gold production, and thus in gold money, served to raise the money supply and so fueled the economic expansion that made the gold standard so acceptable. But the good times were prone to turn into the dust and ashes of recession or depression, even crisis and panic. Money might suddenly become scarce and people might wish to hang on to it or hoard it. The quantity theory provided a north star for policymakers with respect to the journey over long periods of time, but the economy did not stay on course. Under the gold standard the money supply depended on the size of the gold stock together with fractional reserve banking. In the short-run the system could spin out of control. The quantity theory was a basic underlying concept, something that was part of the standard intellectual kit of tools, like the law of gravity, but it would take the application of human ingenuity to keep the economy from suffering dizzy spells. By 1914 it was hoped that the monetary policymakers had imbued the Federal Reserve System with the required ingenuity as well as the technical means to cure the economy's occasional vertigo.

Joseph A. Schumpeter's evaluation of Irving Fisher as "the greatest of America's scientific economists up to our own day"[24] does not seem extravagant. Certainly few would deny that he was among the top two or three American economists of the early twentieth century in terms of his lasting influence. He was unusual in the range of his career, which encompassed, in addition to teaching, not only prolific scholarly work in economics, mathematics, and statistics, but also business activities, a lucrative invention (visible card index file), and writing, as well as campaigning for improved health practices and world peace—a "public figure" actively promoting the public welfare as he understood it. Because he often attributed problems of the economy to monetary factors, Fisher advocated public intervention or management in monetary affairs. In particular he was a tireless proponent of ways to stabilize the purchasing power of money, that is, to maintain a stable price level.

In *The Purchasing Power of Money* (1911), Fisher lucidly and fully explained the forces that determine the price level. His framework of analysis was the equation of exchange, a formulation used earlier by another American, Simon Newcomb, to whom Fisher dedicated the book. The price level depends on five factors related in the following way:

$$MV + M'V' = PQ$$

M = Quantity of money (that is, currency) in circulation

V = Velocity of circulation of M

M' = Quantity of deposits outstanding

V' = Velocity of circulation of M'

Q = Volume of transactions

P = Price level

The traditional quantity theory of money had come under attack, some-thing that Fisher attributed to conflicting financial and political interests. His own view was that the quantity theory was sound, sound in the sense of an exact law. He took the traditional theory and, by examining and developing it fully, provided valuable insights into the operation of the eco-nomic system. Because Fisher argued for the quantity theory as a scientific law, his position has frequently been viewed as rigid, as if he meant that there was an ironclad law which kept the price level and the money stock in lockstep. His discussion of transition periods makes clear that this is a gross oversimplification of his position. Yet in setting out to demonstrate the validity of the quantity theory as a logical proposition with important application to economic life, Fisher appeared to understate the significance of changes in the velocity of spending and in the volume of goods and services transactions. In the words of a prominent French economist and admirer of Fisher, Maurice Allais, Fisher was unable "to free himself from the trammels of the *ceteris paribus* assumption, which Bishop Berkeley had introduced in the eighteenth century,"[25] that is, Fisher's scientific method permitted him to draw logically correct conclusions by suspending disturbing influences under the rubric of "other things being equal."

Fisher's position is that the quantity theory is causally true in the sense that a normal effect of more money is a proportional rise in the price level. He is emphatic that this proportional effect is the *ultimate* effect that occurs following transition periods. The ultimate effect applies *after* a new equilib-rium has been reached. Now, the term *transition period* might suggest a short-lived interval between periods of long-run stability or equilibrium. Normally a 767 jetliner is either in equilibrium on the ground or flying at (say) 25,000 feet; the take-off and landing transition periods are vital, but they are quite brief. This is the usual idea of a transition, a relatively short period of change to a new position. But to Fisher, "periods of transition are the rule and those of equilibrium the exception."[26] He regarded equilibrium in real life as distinguished from what he called an imaginary period, as so elusive as to question whether "such a condition as equilibrium may be said ever to be established."[27] In other words the economy is virtually always in a dynamic condition, in a state of transition.

In explaining transition periods, Fisher presents his theory of the busi-ness cycle. During the expansion phase the money stock and prices rise, with the rate of interest rising more slowly. As prices continue to rise, and there-fore the purchasing power of money continues to fall, the velocity of spend-ing accelerates. "We all hasten to get rid of any commodity which, like ripe fruit, is spoiling on our hands." But the expansion is bound to end. Banks cannot continue to expand loans indefinitely, interest rates begin to rise faster than prices, then faster still, until the higher interest rates overtake prices and "the whole situation is changed."[28] The higher interest rates mean lower prices of securities, such as bonds used as collateral for loans. Firms find it more expensive and more difficult to renew their loans, causing some business failures. Soon banks come under suspicion of holding loans that have gone sour, they become tightfisted and curtail loans to conserve their reserves, and the rate of interest skyrockets. In such circumstances, interest rates for call loans might range from 50 percent to 100 percent.[29] The banks face runs which deplete their reserves. The collapse of bank credit due to loss of confidence is familiar, says Fisher, but what is not well recognized and needs to be understood is that the loss of confidence is the result of the catching-up of the interest rate. The complete credit cycle of expansion, upper turning point, contraction, lower turning point—Fisher used a pendulum for a simile—was a matter of about ten years.

What happens to M and V after the economy has crested? In the gloom of poor business conditions, lenders hesitate to lend and borrowers hesitate to borrow. The money supply contracts, with interest rates now lagging prices downward. Eventually interest rates fall enough so that, together with other slowly emerging encouraging conditions, the stage is set for a revival. But, and Fisher is very explicit, during the depression—a period of months or even years—V is abnormally low.

The next theory to be considered, the real bills doctrine, is not easy to pin down, but was a pivotal idea behind the establishment of the Federal Reserve System. While the concept goes back to the eighteenth century in Great Britain, and was a highly contentious issue in nineteenth century British banking theory, our concern is with its emergence and influence in the United States. It is hard to get it clearly into focus because it was not stated with precision and because its content was altered during the American banking reform discussion. Yet despite its ambiguities and difficulties of practical application, the fraternity of bankers and financial experts generally accepted the real bills doctrine during the two or three decades leading up to the passage of the Federal Reserve Act. Banking reform revolved around this theory.

In view of the widespread front-burner worry concerning the problem of the note issue, it is not surprising that the real bills doctrine gained credence first in relation thereto. Clearly national bank notes could not readily be expanded under the prevailing bond security requirements, so how could hand-to-hand currency be quickly yet safely provided? It was proposed to develop a system of "asset currency," that is, currency issued by commerical banks based upon or backed by the general assets of the banks. The experience of Canada, where bank notes were based on bank assets and where bank failures were not a problem, was cited as a model. There were, however, basic differences in the banking structures of the two countries which made it unlikely that the Canadian practice could be imported by the United States with satisfactory results. In particular, Canada had a system of relatively few banks doing nationwide business and consequently holding diversified assets, whereas the atomistic United States banking structure consisted of many thousands of banks, each typically dealing mainly in its locality with one economic sector. United States banks were inherently more vulnerable as a result of difficulty in particular industries or regions. The logic behind the proposed change to an asset currency was that bank assets (mainly loans) would expand and contract with the economy; if trade increased, the ability of the banks to create currency would increase also, and thus currency elasticity would be built into the system. With the passage of time and the progress of the debate, two important developments occurred. One was that the narrow context of note issues gave way to bank credit; that is, the doctrine was expanded to apply to the *total* money supply. The other development, deserving of close attention, was the narrowing of the asset currency approach, which had been applied to bank assets in general, to one particular type of asset, namely short-term commercial paper.

By the time it was incorporated into the Federal Reserve Act, the real bills doctrine had come to mean that "banks should invest primarily in short-term commercial bills (bills which represent actual production), and . . . that such a practice will allow the needs of trade to regulate the supply of credit without causing inflation or deflation."[30] Such a theory has great appeal, for it purports to show how changes in the money stock can be kept in proportion with changes in real output; that is, M and Q will automatically be kept in step so that just the right amount of money will exist to purchase the output at prevailing prices. The danger of inflation due to excess creation of money is pronounced over—the dragon has been slain. To achieve this, the banks must limit their lending to short-term commercial paper used to finance real transactions. This doctrine held great charm for the banking community, for under it bankers were absolved from blame for the vicissitudes of inflation or deflation. They could present themselves as providing nourishment to the business community by responding to the needs of trade; as long as they made legitimate loans, avoiding loans for speculative purposes or for more than a short time, they had clean hands. The banks and the community would live in mutually beneficial symbiotic relationship. The popularity of the real bills doctrine was great; to many reformers it provided the remedy the American banking system needed.

J. Laurence Laughlin of the University of Chicago was a leading advocate of and, through the National Citizens' League, a business-supported group, propagandist for the real bills doctrine. One of his students, H. Parker Willis, a dedicated real bills man, was involved in drafting the Federal Reserve Act as an expert for a committee of the House of Representatives. Later he served as secretary of the Federal Reserve Board, and afterwards became a professor of banking at Columbia University. The two leading congressional figures responsible for the Federal Reserve Act, Senator Nelson W. Aldrich and Representative Carter Glass, obviously were influenced by the real bills theory.

Having recognized the force of the real bills doctrine, it is essential to note that some of the banking reformers who advocated the key idea of the discounting of real bills by a new central banking system nevertheless rejected the concept of self-regulation. In other words, an important alternative approach parted company with the real bills doctrine on a vital point: since bank credit was not self-regulating, policymakers would have to use their judgment to control it. Instead of being an automatic mechanism, the system needed to be managed. As we shall observe later, this view eventually triumphed after the Federal Reserve System became a going concern. At least two influential academicians pointed out forcefully that the real bills doctrine would not automatically prevent overexpansion of credit, calling the idea "hopelessly fallacious" and "delusive." One was a prominent Harvard economist, O.M.W. Sprague; the second, A. Piatt Andrew, also from the Harvard faculty, became adviser to Senator Aldrich and served as publicist for Aldrich's bill. A third figure who shared this perception, a New York banker named Paul M. Warburg, requires more extended treatment.

The fact that Warburg gained his early banking experience in Europe (he moved from Hamburg to New York in 1902 to join the investment banking house of Kuhn, Loeb) enabled him to view the American banking scene with a fresh viewpoint. Warburg was able to observe the American world of banking "from the outside" although he had become part of it. There is something of a parallel here with Thorstein Veblen, a native American whose immigrant cultural background equipped him to see American society acutely because he felt himself to be an outsider. Soon after coming to this country, Warburg wrote a memorandum on "the cardinal defects of our system." He suggested reforms based on European models, but saw as a great obstacle to the adoption of a European-style central banking system the absence in the United States of modern commercial paper and bankers' acceptances. A senior partner in his firm read the memorandum and showed it in confidence to two friends. The tenor of the time is well conveyed by Warburg's own words describing the response of one of the friends.

> One of these was Mr. James A. Stillman, President of the National City Bank of New York. It was significant, however, of the atmosphere in which we were then living that Mr. Schiff warned me to be careful not to have the memorandum go any further, lest, having just arrived from Europe, I might impair my standing in the banking community by creating the impres-

sion that I was urging a system which, in the final analysis, would have to be built around a central banking organization. I gladly accepted Mr. Schiff's suggestion, and a few days afterwards I found Mr. Stillman standing over my desk. He looked at me silently, as was his wont, through his half-closed, heavy dark eyes.

"How is the great international financier?" he asked with friendly sarcasm. He then added, "Warburg, don't you think the City Bank has done pretty well?"

I replied, "Yes, Mr. Stillman, extraordinarily well."

He then said, "Why not leave things alone?"

It was not without hesitation that I replied, "Your bank is so big and so powerful, Mr. Stillman, that, when the next panic comes, you will wish your responsibilities were smaller."

At this, Mr. Stillman told me that I was entirely wrong, that I had the mistaken notion that Europe's banking methods were the most advanced, while, as a matter of fact, American methods represented an improvement upon, and an evolution of, the European system, America having already discarded its central bank. He had no doubt that progress would have to be sought, not by copying European methods, but by elaborating our own.

Four years later, in the midst of the panic, I found Mr. Stillman once more standing over my desk; and when I looked up, he asked, "Warburg, where is your paper?"

I said to him, "Too late now, Mr. Stillman. What has to be done cannot be done in a hurry. If reform is to be secured, it will take years of educational work to bring it about."[31]

As Warburg grew in influence in banking circles he contributed much to the "educational work." The *New York Times Annual Financial Review* in 1907 published an article of his analyzing the banking situation and suggesting how panics, like the one to strike later that same year, might be obviated. In November, while the panic was in progress, he published a paper entitled, "A Plan for a Modified Central Bank." In 1910, when the National Monetary Commission was just beginning its work, Warburg proposed a single central bank called the United Reserve Bank. The plan contained all of the essential theoretical concepts for the new banking system, and the Aldrich bill that was later submitted to Congress followed his proposals. While the discounting of real bills was central to his design, Warburg warned against reliance on self-regulation and explained how the central bank could use the discount rate to regulate credit. Like Sprague and Andrew, Warburg recognized that short-term commercial bills were kept liquid in a credit crunch environment by the action of the central bank in taking them; they could become immobile if the market for them dried up. For his distinctive contribution Warburg later came to be regarded as the father or chief architect of the Federal Reserve System and served on the first Federal Reserve Board.

The last of our trio of doctrines passing in review is the gold standard. A gold standard country was required to get on the gold standard bus as a passenger, not as a driver. Gold was in the driver's seat, and whether it carried the country's money stock up hill, down dale, or across flat country, the monetary authorities were supposed to keep their hands off the steering wheel. It was a mystery ride determined by the impersonal forces of gold production, inflow, and outflow; whatever route the gold standard took was ipso facto the right route. Human drivers were thought to be prone to driving into ditches through mistakes in judgment, or to take a wrong route due to seductive special interest groups or electoral pressures. Orthodox thought relied instead on a comforting trinity of concepts for the guidance of Man and Society: natural harmony, laissez faire, and the gold standard. The gold standard mentality was so ingrained before World War I that the banking reformers simply accepted it as part of their world.

Given the importance of the size of the money stock to the quantity theory of money, by what device would it best be regulated? Two candidates, the real bills doctrine and the gold standard, had been accepted into the sanctum of official policy. On the one hand stood the real bills doctrine, promising automatically to adjust the money supply to the needs of the economy. On the other hand stood the even more august gold standard, promising the quantity of money that the economy needed. Thus two servants promised the same master the same prize. Unfortunately the two means of regulating money could and almost inevitably would conflict. Perhaps when credit was expanding through the operation of the real bills doctrine, the operation of the gold standard mechanism would require a slowing down or reversal of bank lending. The discount rate and interest rates generally would have to be raised, thereby discouraging bank credit extension. One or the other principle would be forced to give ground. As Warburg, Sprague, and Andrew had warned, the real bills theory did not effectively limit the money stock as the devotees of the self-regulating version believed. In the end, especially in view of the almost mystical attachment to it, the gold standard would seem the likely survivor. There being no statutory law against believing in two incompatible ideas, the Federal Reserve System came into the world under both the real bills and the gold standard banners.

2
World War I and Postwar Adjustment, 1914–1921

Although created for the purpose of protecting the banking system from further convulsions, a goal unquestionably in the national interest, the fledgling Federal Reserve System nevertheless had an uncertain future. No welcome wagons were provided by local bank clearinghouses when the Federal Reserve Banks opened their new offices. On the contrary, many bankers were skeptical of the system and some were clearly hostile, describing it as unworkable or socialistic. It is true that national banks were required to come on board as member banks, but they could jump ship by abandoning their federal charters in favor of state charters. If few banks joined, the system would lack financial strength and influence. It was up to the officials of the Federal Reserve System to develop its latent powers and demonstrate its effectiveness if they could.

Control over the system was divided between the Federal Reserve Board in Washington and the boards of directors and officers of the twelve regional Federal Reserve Banks. It would take interpretation of various provisions of the act through official pushing and pulling, as well as further legislation, to determine over the years just how these powers would in fact be shared. Of the seven members of the Federal Reserve Board, two were ex officio members, the secretary of the treasury and the comptroller of the currency, so although the board was separate from the Treasury, the Treasury was "on the inside" of the board and might, it appeared to some, "capture" the board and control the system. The five other board members were appointed by the president with the advice and consent of the Senate. Each reserve bank was supervised by nine directors, six elected by member banks and three chosen by the board, an arrangement intended to provide a balance of political (public) and banking interests.

As to the system's purposes, we are familiar with the dominant ideas of furnishing an elastic currency and affording a means of discounting commercial paper. In addition the act instructs the Federal Reserve Banks "to accommodate commerce and business." Of course these objectives were meant to be supportive of the supreme objective of bringing an end to financial crises. It soon became apparent, however, that the focus on preventing financial crises raised questions concerning policy implementation. It was assumed at the start that the system should respond passively and automatically to the credit demands of business through the rediscounting process, but this attitude failed to address practical questions of the extent of central bank lending and the discount rate to be applied at any time. As they learned the craft of central banking and gained confidence in their techniques, the officials of the system "gradually broadened the scope of the system's objectives and substituted a philosophy of positive regulation for that of passive accommodation."[1] The broader, more ambitious objectives of general economic stability and stable prices came into prominence from within the system. Perhaps most important, the evolution of the Federal Reserve System involved more than a new institution finding its way in an existing set of conditions: the future development of the system would be conditioned by powerful new forces in the economic and social environment that were totally unforeseen at the birth of the Federal Reserve System.

The Fed Enters the Financial Arena

> In order to be accorded its proper place, the Reserve System must be looked upon as a national monument, like the old cathedrals of Europe, which were the work of many generations and of many masters, and are treasured as symbols of national achievement.
> —Paul M. Warburg[2]

After the initial work of organization, the new central bank had to find its proper niche in the financial environment, in particular to develop suitable working relationships with the commercial banks and the Treasury. But before the system could integrate itself into the financial structure of the nation, the world began to change dramatically as the guns of August 1914 began to roar, marking the start of World War I (or the Great War, as it was called at the time). Although the United States was neutral at the outset of hostilities and planned to remain so, an atmosphere of uncertainty prevailed (the New York Stock Exchange was closed from August 1 to December 11) when the first Federal Reserve Board was sworn in on August 10, 1914. About three months later, on November 16, 1914, the Federal Reserve Banks opened for business, and for the next two and a half years, until the United States declared war in the spring of 1917, the system felt its way, concerned mainly with working out operating procedures.

What major monetary developments occurred during the period from the outbreak of the war in August 1914 to the time the United States entered the conflict in April 1917, and how was the Federal Reserve System involved? Perhaps most important, the rock on which the international monetary system was thought to be built, the gold standard, was shattered as the belligerent countries left the gold standard. The Allies shipped massive amounts of gold to the United States in payment for supplies; during this period of American neutrality the U.S. gold stock rose by about $1.3 billion, an increase of 82 percent over the prewar level. The gold inflow had the effect of increasing high-powered money, which in turn provided the basis for a rapid growth in the money stock.[3] The money stock increased by about 43 percent, and wholesale prices rose by about 77 percent. While the effects of the gold inflow on the money stock and economy of the United States were expansionary, the countries losing gold did not permit the deflationary effects called for under gold standard rules. In fact, prices rose considerably more rapidly in Great Britain and France, from which gold flowed, than in the United States. Wartime conditions required extraordinary measures: the Allied governments commandeered their nations' liquid assets of foreign balances, foreign securities, and gold to pay for urgently needed supplies. In ending the convertibility of their currencies into gold they intended only a temporary halt; and indeed, following the war the gold standard was briefly reestablished. Yet, although it would not become clear until later, from the standpoint of Federal Reserve policy, "the gold standard never again played the role that the framers of the act took for granted."[4]

If the Federal Reserve authorities had wished to neutralize the monetary effects of the flood of gold coming into the country, they could not have done so with the means at their disposal. If the Federal Reserve had had securities to sell on the open market it could have soaked up bank reserves, but at this early stage of its existence it did not hold a portfolio of bonds or other liquid assets to be used for this purpose. Under the circumstances it was a one-way central bank: it could pump out bank reserves by rediscounting paper or buying securities, but it could not reverse engines and draw reserves out of the system. The Federal Reserve Banks created a modest amount of credit at this time, thus adding to high-powered money. By acquiring a portfolio of assets they obtained a flow of income. Although not intended as profit-making institutions in the ordinary sense, the reserve banks saw no reason why they should not make a profit while carrying out their functions, thereby enhancing their independent status. On its opening day the Federal Reserve Bank of New York set its discount rate at 6 percent but quickly reduced it to 4 percent early in 1915, then to 3 percent in late 1916 and for most of 1917. When such "discount prices" failed to generate much rediscounting by the commercial banks, the Federal Reserve Banks went into the market and purchased bills and acceptances, as well as U.S. and municipal securities.

Some additional points are relevant to the period of U.S. neutrality. Initially member bank deposits in the Federal Reserve Banks came from the deposit of cash, that is, "lawful money" consisting of gold or other currency convertible into gold at the Treasury. At this early period the Federal Reserve System viewed the reserve requirements of the member banks as a means of facilitating the convertibility of bank deposits into currency, and not yet as a fulcrum for controlling the money stock.[5] Finally, the war began while economic activity was declining in the United States. The contraction ended in December 1914 and a vigorous expansion, propelled by rapidly mounting demand from Europe, lasted for three and a half years to a peak in August 1918.

Financing U.S. Participation in the War, 1917–1918

> We must, if possible, persuade . . . (Secretary of the Treasury McAdoo) to permit the Reserve Banks to become the real, active and effective fiscal agents for the Government. If he does that, our place in the country's banking system will be established for all time. If he does not, we will rock along for a good while, leaving people in some doubt as to whether we are fish, flesh, or good red herring.
> —Benjamin Strong[6]

Following the declaration of war by the United States against Germany on April 6, 1917, the Federal Reserve System devoted itself to the financial requirements of the government. The methods used to carry out this supportive role until the Armistice ended the war on November 11, 1918, will now be discussed.

The entry of the United States into the war added to the demand for war production that had been in progress for several years, thereby intensifying pressure on the American economy to employ its resources fully and to direct a growing proportion of them into meeting wartime needs. What changed was the means of providing the money to pay for the growing output. The parts played by gold and by the Federal Reserve Banks were quite different from those of the years from 1914 to early 1917.

The gold inflow into the United States ended with U.S. belligerency; the size of the monetary gold stock was virtually unchanged from April 1917 to November 1918. Trade deficits of the Allies with the United States were covered by loans extended by the U.S. Treasury; the embattled European countries no longer needed to obtain scarce dollar exchange by exporting gold or by entering the private capital markets to float loans and sell securities. When U.S. trade with the rest of the world tended to cause a gold outflow, the president on September 7, 1917, banned gold exports that were not approved by the Treasury as well as the Federal Reserve Board, and placed controls over foreign exchange. Thus the monetary role of gold during the period of American participation in the war was negligible.

The great wartime financial problem was how to raise the huge amounts of money required for the cost of this country's war effort plus loans to other nations. The national debt grew from about $1 billion to approximately $25 billion over a three-year period ending in mid-1919. Since tax receipts paid for about 30 percent of war costs, and straightforward printing of Treasury money was eschewed, roughly 70 percent came from borrowing by the Treasury. To assist the Treasury in raising funds, the Federal Reserve System performed two related functions: one was that of fiscal agent, and the other was to provide credit. Each deserves some explanation.

Section 15 of the Federal Reserve Act authorized, but did not require, the deposit of Treasury funds in Federal Reserve Banks, "which banks, when required by the Secretary of the Treasury, shall act as fiscal agents of the United States." Very little use of the reserve banks was made by the secretary before U.S. involvement in the war, perhaps due to lack of confidence in them, reluctance to forgo interest on deposits in commercial banks, and protection of appointive jobs in the Independent Treasury System then still in operation. Bureaucracies are hardly notorious for eagerness to hand over segments of their operations to other, potentially rival, organizations. From the standpoint of the Federal Reserve System, becoming the government's banker would add prestige, open the opportunity to perform important technical functions, and, by the transfer of Treasury deposits, add to the gold reserves of the Federal Reserve Banks. It may have been the persuasiveness of Federal Reserve officials, or Treasury Secretary McAdoo might have decided that he could use a helping hand, or both, for the reserve banks were made fiscal agents of the government. By collecting and paying out funds skillfully so as to keep the money market calm, and by managing the bulk of the securities that comprised the national debt, the Federal Reserve Banks performed a major service and earned coveted status and recognition. There was no question of the Federal Reserve System being independent of the Treasury in this area. Treasury officials had full authority to direct the reserve banks on fiscal agency affairs without consulting the Federal Reserve Board. After the war the Independent Treasury System, having become superfluous, was dissolved in 1920; the Federal Reserve Banks had become the principal fiscal agents of the government.

The strategy of financing the war was to do so out of savings. To the extent that society saved out of current income, and the savings were siphoned to the government, national output could be directed to fulfilling essential national needs with a minimum of inflation. Saving was of two types: (1) taxation (forced saving); (2) voluntary saving, by far the larger share, which required persuading people to buy the Treasury's newly issued securities. It was necessary for bank credit to provide additional funds temporarily because the collection of taxes and the rate of voluntary saving lagged behind the surge of government spending. Ideally there would not be any permanent expansion of credit by the banking system.

When the Treasury, in the ongoing process of wartime finance, needed to get more money, it sold short-term obligations, mainly certificates of indebtedness, a large portion of which the banks bought by creating new deposits. Then when the Treasury received taxes and sold bonds to the public, it used the proceeds to retire the short-term debt and the associated bank credit. During the war four campaigns known as Liberty Loans were carried out and a postwar Victory Loan was floated in 1919. Great efforts were made to sell the bonds to the general public by appeals to patriotism. People were urged to buy bonds in amounts greater than they could pay for with their current funds by borrowing from the banks on the basis of the bonds as collateral. This of course meant credit extension and money creation by the banks. Treasury and Federal Reserve officials viewed such lending as superior to the sale of the bonds to the banks themselves, on the grounds that the people who owed the banks would be impelled to save in the future to pay off their debts. In the end, despite the efforts to avoid it, a very significant part of the increased national debt was financed by bank credit. At the end of June 1919 the commercial banks held about $5 billion of Treasury securities, or 20 percent of the total, and in addition held some $3 billion of loans on such securities.[7] Federal Reserve Banks and certain federal agencies held much smaller amounts. Still, some 75 percent of the total U.S. government debt was held by nonbank investors.

While fiscal agency and credit creation are conceptually separate functions, in fact they were closely linked. It was necessary that the bond drives be successful; the Federal Reserve System had to provide the economy with enough money to absorb the bonds; the banks had to have sufficient reserves to support the additional bank deposits; and the demand for more currency in circulation had to be met.

Total reserve bank credit outstanding rose from about $280 million on the eve of U.S. entry into the war to $2.5 billion by the end of 1918, most of the increase consisting of bills discounted. The heart of the Federal Reserve wartime credit policy was to lend at "preferential" discount rates to commercial banks with Treasury securities as collateral. Such rates were lower than for commercial paper and also were a fraction of a percentage point lower than the yield on the Treasury securities, giving the banks a profit. In other words, the Federal Reserve System as fiscal agent could raise all the funds the Treasury needed, because in its credit creating capacity it extended loans to the commercial banks to ensure the success of Treasury borrowing. The banks could borrow from the Fed to finance their own purchases of certificates of indebtedness, and they could also borrow from the Fed by rediscounting their customers' paper taken for loans to finance bond purchases. In the latter case, the banks charged their customers the same interest rate as that paid on the Liberty Bonds, but could borrow from the Fed at the lower preferential rate.

When the gold inflow ended in the spring of 1917, the Federal Reserve took over as the source of monetary expansion. Between April 1917 and November 1918 the money stock rose by 19 percent; the wholesale price index rose by 17 percent to 107 percent over the 1914 level. The rate of inflation was slower during the period of U.S. involvement in the war than in the prior period reaching back to the beginning of 1916. Friedman and Schwartz point out that whereas the money stock rose proportionately less than high-powered money during the wartime period, it rose proportionately more in the immediately preceding and succeeding periods. In wartime the public held more currency relative to bank deposits than previously, so whereas the expansion of Federal Reserve credit added to high-powered money, the drain of currency acted as a partial offset to its expansionary effect.[8]

The credit creating method of the Federal Reserve System that has been described is a far cry from the real bills doctrine. Banks borrowed from the Federal Reserve on the basis of government securities at the preferential discount rate rather than on commercial paper at the ordinary discount rate; the preferential rate was the effective rate. As early as 1916 the Federal Reserve Act was amended to allow advances to member banks on their own fifteen-day notes, with either eligible commerical paper *or* government securities as security. Under these circumstances, the notion that the central bank would automatically expand the money stock in step with the legitimate needs of trade was vitiated.

It was in fact impossible for the Federal Reserve to regulate total lending by the banking system. By its policy of making sure that the banks had the needed reserves to lend to the Treasury directly and to the public to buy Liberty Bonds, it could not keep the banks from lending to other types of borrowers as well. Any time they wished, the banks could draw on their portfolios of government securities or loans made against such securities, tap the discount window of the regional Federal Reserve Bank, and so replenish their reserve balances. The result is quite instructive: commercial bank total loans and investments rose by twice the amount of their holdings of Treasury securities plus loans to finance Treasury securities. Whereas the Federal Reserve System intended that the war should be paid for out of savings as far as possible, and then found it necessary to extend credit to guarantee the successful flotation of all Treasury securities so that the financial needs of the government would be met, it found itself with the monetary reins slipping from its hands and the horse starting to run away. To try to keep the monetary horse from bolting altogether, the Fed resorted to some new tricks that were not in the book. The Federal Reserve Board and the Federal Reserve Banks, hoping that the patriotic motive could check the profit motive, urged the bankers to cut down on lending for purposes considered nonessential for national needs. To avoid overtaxing the independent judgment of the lenders, a Capital Issues Committee was set up to screen private as well as state and local government securities issues, which may have had some effect in slowing the growth of credit. Federal Reserve Bank officers worked hard in supporting the efforts of public service organizations to get people to buy Treasury bonds. There was even brief and limited use made of a selective credit control, a margin requirement on stock exchange loans. As military victory came to be anticipated in the late summer and fall of 1918, stock speculation became a matter of concern. In New York City a subcommittee ("Money Committee") of the Liberty Loan Committee was set up and for a short time regulated the height of margin requirements through agreements with New York City banks and requested the members of the Stock Exchange to limit their borrowing.

Post–World War I Adjustment, 1918–1921

> The business cycle from 1919 to 1921 was the first real trial of the new system of monetary control introduced by the Federal Reserve Act. . . . Its poor performance in that trial is understandable. . . . There was a natural, if regrettable, tendency to wait too long before stepping on the brake, as it were, then to step on the brake too hard, then, when that did not bring monetary expansion to a halt very shortly, to step on the brake yet again.
> —Milton Friedman and Anna J. Schwartz[9]

When the war ended, would the economy collapse or maintain its momentum during the transition to "normal" peacetime conditions? For some months the answer was unclear as the economy hesitated before resuming vigorous growth. With the termination of orders for war materiel, economic activity and prices began a gradual decline in the fall of 1918 that lasted until a renewed expansion began in the spring of 1919. A booming market for exports financed by government loans to wartime allies, together with a strong surge of domestic demand for civilian goods, drove up prices and incomes. From a low point in March 1919 to a peak in January 1920, the economy experienced an inflationary boom characterized by speculation in commodities (not in stocks), inventory accumulation, and spending on luxuries. From November 1918 to a peak in March 1920 the money stock (currency plus demand deposits) rose by 21 percent and wholesale prices by 15 percent—22 percent at their peak in May 1920. Then came the morning after as the economy plunged from the first quarter of 1920 into a deep depression that hit bottom in the third quarter of 1921. We shall examine in turn the monetary policies employed in the boom and the following bust.

As the economy accelerated during 1919, the Federal Reserve Banks kept their discount rates low until late in the year. The New York Fed maintained a 4 percent rate until November, when it was raised to 4.75 percent before being jacked up to 6 percent in January 1920. Reserve bank credit outstanding increased from $2.4 billion at the time of the Armistice to the $3.4 billion level early in 1920 and held quite steady until beginning a descent late in the year. The bulk of the increase was in the form of bills discounted. This central bank credit expansion much more than offset a $300 million external drain of gold between June 1919, when the embargo on gold exports was removed, until April 1920. High-powered money increased from approximately $6.5 billion when the war ended to $7 billion by the beginning of 1920. Clearly the Federal Reserve System failed to restrain the surging postwar inflation.

The Federal Reserve Board and officials of Federal Reserve Banks were quite concerned about the speculative boom. They discussed tightening credit, but in practice limited themselves merely to trying to persuade the banks to refuse to lend for nonessential purposes. They could instead have controlled the expansion of the money supply by selling securities that had been purchased in prior years and by raising discount rates. Monetary expansion was permitted even though it ran counter to the requirements of the gold standard during the period of gold outflow beginning in June 1919.

Why did the Federal Reserve System not adopt an effective program of credit restraint? Its first duty, it decided after some soul-searching, was to continue to defer to the Treasury. The end of the war did not end the Treasury's need for more borrowed money. In the spring of 1919 the final big war loan, the Victory Loan, was floated at an interest rate only slightly higher than for prior loans. Following the completion of the Victory Loan drive in May, the Fed kept interest rates low until November to assist the Treasury in funding its floating debt and also, apparently, to carry out a commitment to the commercial banks to keep the interest rate from rising on Victory Loan bonds for six months so as to prevent a decline in the price of the bonds held by the banks or on which they had made loans. We may recall that, in the spirit of the real bills doctrine, the Federal Reserve Act called for a policy of "accommodating commerce and business," but in accommodating the Treasury the Federal Reserve System was also accommodating the banks and their customers for reasons having nothing to do with real bills.

The failure of the Federal Reserve System to raise discount rates and restrict the expansion during the first half of 1919 is looked upon as the System's first big mistake. The Federal Reserve Board has been accused of weakness at that time, of caving in to Treasury pressure. That the Federal Reserve Board had a difficult choice is beyond question. It had acted properly in teaming up with the Treasury *during* the war; how soon *after* the war should it have severed the partnership? By statute the chairman of the Federal Reserve Board was also the secretary of the Treasury, and so compelled to wear two hats, but by natural law he had only one mind to make up under them. In 1919 the secretary, Carter Glass, along with another influential Treasury official, Assistant Secretary Russell C. Leffingwell, were distinctly hostile to any tightening of the money market that might create difficulties for Treasury financing. The Federal Reserve System was wedged tightly between a rock and a hard place: cooperation with the Treasury, seen as a duty by the board at the time, has been considered a cop-out by critics of the board. The unfortunate governor of the board, W.P.G. Harding, later pointed out that if the Federal Reserve had failed to cooperate with the Treasury, it might have been stripped of its power by executive order of the president. A wartime law then still in effect, the Overman Act, empowered the president to transfer any of the functions of the Federal Reserve Board to the secretary of the treasury.

Individual Federal Reserve Banks tried to get approval for higher discount rates at various times during 1919, but the board refused them. The board was torn between the two objectives of resistance to inflation on the one hand, and keeping the cost of Treasury borrowing low and preventing a fall in the price of Treasury securities on the other. As a new institution, the Federal Reserve was seeking to find its proper role while still under the dominating influence of the well-established and powerful Treasury. The Treasury's policies were to a large extent politically determined. A strong case has been made that the Federal Reserve Board should have been more persuasive and more determined in pressing the anti-inflation cause with the Treasury. If the Fed had acted to moderate the boom of 1919 there would have been less of a contractionary recoil in 1920–1921. In addition, the reserve position of the system would not have deteriorated so markedly.

In January 1922 the ten-member Joint Commission of Agricultural Inquiry of Congress, while recognizing the difficult position of the system concerning Treasury financing, and exonerating it from a charge of discrimination against agriculture when the economy was subsequently deflated, took the view that the system should have raised the discount rate and restricted credit in the early part of 1919 despite the Treasury's problems. In effect, the commission's report to Congress blamed the Federal Reserve for failing to close the barn door before the horses of speculation and extravagance could get loose. Considering the much more powerful position of the Treasury, it seems inappropriate to concentrate on the Federal Reserve while ignoring the Treasury in policy determination. Indeed the case has been made that "the real blame lies not with the Federal Reserve System (certainly not with the reserve banks) but with the Treasury and its insistence on low discount rates to aid government funding operations."[10]

Economic activity began to head down early in 1920, slowly at first but rapidly after mid-year, until bottoming out in the third quarter of 1921. The economy behaved like a roller coaster, with steeply falling prices, production, and employment. It subsequently rose again sharply, but the collapse, while short, was one of the steepest in our history. The money stock which peaked at $23.9 billion in March 1920 fell by 14 percent in the next eighteen months to $20.5 billion in September 1921.

Just as the economy reached a cyclical peak in January 1920, the discount rate at the Federal Reserve Bank of New York was made to take a big step up from 4.75 to 6 percent. At this time the Treasury abruptly switched its position to favor the increase. The economy was poised on the brink of collapse, its perilous position clear enough with hindsight but not at all obvious at the time; it was not until early autumn that the severity of the contraction came to be appreciated. What seems particularly perverse, however, was a further rise in the discount rate to 7 percent on June 1, a rate maintained for nearly a year as the economy plunged into deep depression. Then from May 1921 to June 1922 the discount rate was lowered gradually to 4 percent. If it was a mistake to have kept discount rates low in 1919, it seems inexcusable to have impaled the economy on high interest rates in 1920 and well into 1921.

Again, as in 1919, the Federal Reserve did not consider itself a free agent, this time because of the reserve requirements it had to meet. The Federal Reserve Act required a gold reserve of 40 percent against Federal Reserve notes and a gold (or lawful money) reserve of 35 percent against deposits. It was because of this requirement that the Treasury in January 1920, fearing forced departure from the gold standard, came out fervently in favor of higher interest rates. By early 1920 the ratio of the system's reserves to its deposit and note liabilities had fallen close to 40 percent. Not until the ratio had gone back up to 56 percent in May 1921 was the discount rate high-jump bar lowered a notch from 7 to 6.5 percent.

In one important respect the monetary system performed better than it had historically during a severe contraction. There was no panic—no rush by the public to convert bank deposits into currency or attempt by the banks to build up their reserves relative to deposits, although bank failures rose sharply from about 60 in 1919 to some 500 in 1921. When the war ended, the country had about 27,000 commercial banks, up some 2,000 over 1914, and the total grew to almost 30,000 by 1921.

The Federal Reserve was not really locked into a rigidly restrictive posture, for the Federal Reserve Act allowed the gold reserve requirement to be suspended by the board provided only that a very low graduated tax be applied to the deficiency. By adhering to the gold reserve ratio the Federal

Reserve sacrificed the opportunity to stabilize the economy. However, in judging the performance of the Fed it is only fair to keep in mind that orthodox thinking of the time was still under the spell of the gold standard. We should hardly be surprised that those who were appointed keepers of the ark gave more than lip service to the ideals of the creed with which they had been imbued.

Fierce criticism was directed at the Federal Reserve System as a result of the depression, particularly because of the drastic fall in agricultural prices. So great did the onslaught become that a resolution was introduced in the Senate at the request of the Federal Reserve Board itself for an investigation into the board's actions. Thus the Joint Commission of Agricultural Inquiry referred to earlier came to conduct its inquiry into monetary affairs. In less than a decade after it was created by Congress, the Federal Reserve System was investigated and found wanting by its creator. It was not considered fatally flawed, however, and the system was allowed to resume its development without modification, although Governor Harding paid the price of not being reappointed when his term expired in 1922. Any psychic pain that he suffered may have been assuaged by his appointment as governor of the Federal Reserve Bank of Boston at more than twice his old salary at the board.

The postwar experience of the Fed has been put in a nutshell: "The Federal Reserve, facing its first major test, could not be said to have passed with flying or any other colors. By common agreement it assisted the boom and worsened the bust. This has always been considered an especially interesting error."[11] Yet the establishment of the new central bank, despite its faults, may on balance be viewed as a constructive step.

> The Federal Reserve did not prevent a strong inflation developing during the First World War; but neither did the Bank of England. By too strong a deflationary policy, it may have intensified the post-war depression; the Bank of England acted similarly. We cannot doubt that the troubles would have been far more severe if the United States had had to face the vast strains of war without a central banking organization.[12]

3
The Prosperous Twenties,
1922–1929

The pleasant state of the economy in the 1920's created for the first time the vision of a state of affairs never before achieved in any part of the world—a condition where there would be well-paying jobs for all, where poverty would be abolished, where high productivity and enterprise would create a level of comfort and well-being which would extend throughout the mass of the population.

—Paul B. Trescott[1]

The economy rebounded quickly from the 1920–1921 depression and entered a period of quite vigorous growth without general price inflation that lasted to the end of the decade. At the beginning of this period the Federal Reserve System became more fully aware of the monetary significance of its open market operations, and it developed a new rationale for the use of its control mechanisms. Equipped with better understanding of their powers and with fresh ideas as to their use, the central bankers applied their techniques in the optimistic environment of the Roaring Twenties and met with success. Monetary policy seemed able to guide the economy along a stable path. Compared with the bitter boom-and-bust experience of 1919–1921, and with the much longer and deeper miseries of the Great Depression to come, the twenties were halcyon days. Unfortunately, as the decade drew to its close the Fed was faced with the dilemma of either subduing stock speculation and thereby putting a clamp on credit in general, or trying to escort the economy along the path of steady progress, hoping that the flames of Wall Street would not envelop Main Street. Unable to meet the challenge, it vacillated, failed to prevent economic collapse, and soon thereafter found that much of the influence and kudos acquired during the twenties were gone.

A Major New Tool for the Fed's Kit

There can be no doubt, however, that most of the progress came from the discovery and development of a new policy implement: open-market operations in United States Government securities. Here at

last was an instrument almost perfectly adapted to the new philosophy of positive control. The Reserve Banks on their own initiative
could now inject money into the market or withdraw money from
the market at such times and in such amounts as they wished.[2]

In 1922 the Federal Reserve Banks began to carry out open-market operations for credit policy purposes. Previously they had been undertaken for the
more mundane purposes of gaining income and providing collateral for Federal Reserve bank notes that were issued as replacements for national bank
notes. In response to a sharp drop in their earnings as the volume of bank
discounts declined in 1921, the reserve banks, acting individually, bought
U.S. government securities. As they did, they competed with each other, on
occasion causing unwelcome fluctuations in the government securities market. Much more important, it was realized that open-market purchases of
securities by the reserve banks pumped reserve balances into the commerical
banks and could be used as a major credit policy instrument. It was observed
during 1922 and 1923 that when purchases (sales) were made on the open
market, the volume of discounting fell (rose). In other words, the Federal
Reserve Banks were causing changes in credit conditions as a side effect of
their investment policies. This tendency of Federal Reserve holdings of
securities and discounts to move in opposite directions in response to open
market operations was dubbed the scissors effect. It dawned on the authorities that Section 14 of the Federal Reserve Act invested them with a major
policy instrument; they actually held much greater power to control credit
than they had thought!

> Federal Reserve officials soon discovered, however, much to their amaze-
> ment at first, that open-market purchases and sales brought about marked
> changes in money market conditions even though total earning assets of the
> Reserve Banks remained unchanged. When the Federal Reserve sold secu-
> rities and extracted money from bank reserves, more banks were forced to
> borrow from the Reserve Banks, and those already borrowing were forced
> more deeply into debt. Since banks had to pay interest on their borrowings
> and did not like to remain continuously in debt, they tended to lend less
> liberally, which raised interest rates in the market. On the other hand, when
> the Federal Reserve injected money into bank reserves to pay for its pur-
> chases of government securities, banks were enabled to repay some of their
> debts to the Reserve Banks and because of this were willing to lend more
> freely.[3]

When the significance of open-market operations came to be appreciated, arrangements were made to carry them out in a coordinated manner
by the several reserve banks. By law the Federal Reserve Banks could engage
in open-market operations under rules set by the Federal Reserve Board. In

May 1922 a Committee on Centralized Execution of Purchases and Sales of Government Securities, consisting of four Federal Reserve Bank governors, was established by the Conference of Governors of the Federal Reserve Banks.[4] Later that year it was expanded to five governors and authorized to make nonbinding recommendations to the reserve banks concerning open-market purchases and sales. The need for system-wide uniformity led to the creation in 1923 of the Federal Open Market Investment Committee by the Federal Reserve Board. This body replaced the earlier committee with the same membership, but it differed in being under the supervision of the Federal Reserve Board, and was assigned the task of recommending plans for open-market operations consistent with principles laid down by the board. In terms of the structure of the system, this development, by tending to concentrate open-market operations in the board, marks a decline in the policy-making powers of the reserve banks. Later in 1923 the board and the Federal Reserve Banks set up an open-market investment account, to be shared by the reserve banks on a pro rata basis, which could be increased or decreased by the committee with board approval. Yet the board did not have full control— individual reserve banks could still undertake open-market operations for their own accounts, and could opt out of proposed committee transactions. Although administratively awkward, this arrangement was used until further changes were adopted in the 1930s.

Another structural development occurred in June 1922 when the membership of the Federal Reserve Board was increased from seven to eight. Congress amended the Federal Reserve Act in this manner in response to pressures from farmers suffering from disastrously low prices for agricultural products. The additional board member to be appointed would represent the interests of agriculture.

Setting the Course

> No other peacetime period in the history of the System has witnessed a faster development of both Federal Reserve thinking and policies than that starting around the end of 1921 and culminating in 1924. At the beginning of this period, Federal Reserve officials were confused and uncertain as to both ends and means. They were questioning old objectives and policy guides but had not yet developed new ones; they neither understood the instruments at their disposal nor were skilled in their use. By 1924 they had made almost incredible progress.[5]

The *Tenth Annual Report* (for 1923) of the Federal Reserve Board is celebrated for its high quality, particularly for its analytical discussion of credit policy.[6] Now free from Treasury constraints, the Federal Reserve System set about defining its role as an independent central bank. The report is concerned with the problem of what is necessary to maintain economic activity at a satisfactory level, and focuses on equilibrium between aggregate production and consumption. It points out that if credit is permitted to be used speculatively to accumulate excessive stocks of commodities, an imbalance will result that will lead to a recession. To avoid the danger of excessive credit creation, it is necessary to restrict Federal Reserve Bank credit to productive uses. The cyclical fluctuation of 1919–1921 led to the development of an inventory theory of business cycles that became merged with the familiar productive uses concept of the real bills theory. At this time the board was concerned about speculation in commodities rather than in securities; later, in the 1928 and 1929 annual reports, the alarm was raised over stock market speculation.

The experience of 1919–1921 was a vivid object lesson apropos of the danger of single-minded adherence to the real bills doctrine. Overinvestment in inventories during the immediate postwar boom was to a large extent financed by bank credit extended on the basis of real bills. The problem was that the bills drawn by businesses wishing to stockpile were no different in appearance from the "legitimate" ones. The fallacy of the real bills doctrine was exposed: extending credit on the basis of qualitative standards alone in accordance with the real bills doctrine was no guarantee against inflation from excessive credit creation. The *Tenth Annual Report* is explicit, even emphatic, in stating that the board was well aware of the importance of the quantity of credit as well as its quality or type. Eligibility requirements alone were not a sufficient basis for credit extension. In the *Tenth Annual Report* the board reiterated the view that credit should be restricted to productive uses, but it did not assert, as the real bills doctrine did, that real bills necessarily imply credit for productive purposes. There is something of a Cheshire cat effect here: the real bills doctrine as a policy guide had vanished, but the grin of relying on productive uses as a credit criterion remained. The idea that productive credit is self-regulating and safe from overexpansion is immaculate, but it had become clear that the real bills doctrine could not be relied on as a litmus test of productive uses, and therefore it failed to provide a policy guide. The position of the Federal Reserve Board was that the system should extend the right amount of productive credit while recognizing that adherence to the real bills doctrine did not automatically result in the right amount. As pointed out in chapter 1, the real bills doctrine was a widely held concept at the time the Federal Reserve Act was passed, and it provided a rationale for the credit-creating mechanism of rediscounting at the regional reserve banks at the time they were established. In terms of actual policy-making, however, the real bills doctrine was of very limited importance. As a result of the brief but painful lessons of 1919–1921, the real bills doctrine was reexamined and, while vestiges of it remained, by 1923 it was not an important policy guide for the system.

The other prewar pillar of monetary policy, the gold standard, was also cracked and broken at this time, but it was thought capable of being restored to its former eminence. The *Tenth Annual Report* rejected the gold reserve ratio as its policy guide on the grounds that the international gold standard was not in operating order; controls and exchange regulations in many foreign countries kept it from serving as an automatic, self-correcting mechanism. The Federal Reserve Board was loyal to the gold standard ideal, however, and would do its part to help reinstate the international gold standard as an operational system. It was thought that when that had been accomplished, the Federal Reserve System would comply with the rules of the game, and then the gold reserve ratio would resume its place as policy guide. But that would take some time, and in the meantime it was necessary to devise a substitute policy guide. Still smarting from the severe economic fluctuations of 1919–1921, the Federal Reserve System now attempted "for perhaps the first time in monetary history, to use central-bank powers to promote internal economic stability as well as to preserve balance in international payments and to prevent and moderate strictly financial crises."[7] Here then is an important mutation of central banking policy. The central bank, unable to function (as intended) automatically as a mechanism for transmitting forces coming from the movement of gold, or from the productive needs of business, now began to exercise control over credit in the cause of stable economic conditions. The Federal Reserve System was finding a new niche for itself, and in the process fostered a new "economic world view" of great significance; the old laissez-faire doctrine gave ground to a new faith in the ability of government to provide stability to the economy. In the absence of a clear rule to follow (gold reserve ratio), the Fed decided to rely on its informed judgment. It would monitor economic activity as measured by current data on employment, production, inventories, and so on, and use its credit control instruments of open-market operations and discount policy to try to maintain the desired equilibrium between total production and consumption.

In the view of John Maynard Keynes, the time had come to adopt managed money permanently rather than return to the gold standard. In *A Tract on Monetary Reform* (1923), written in response to the severe inflations that followed World War I, he sought the best means of achieving a stable price level. He advocated vesting discretionary control over currency and credit in the central bank authorities in various countries, a policy with recently established beachheads in Britain and the United States.

> Those who advocate the return to a gold standard do not always appreciate along what different lines our actual practice has been drifting. If we restore

the gold standard, are we to return also to the pre-war conceptions of bank rate, allowing the tides of gold to play what tricks they like with the internal price level, and abandoning the attempt to moderate the disastrous influence of the credit cycle on the stability of prices and employment? Or are we to continue and develop the experimental innovations of our present policy, ignoring the "bank ratio" and, if necessary, allowing unmoved a piling up of gold reserves far beyond our requirements or their depletion far below them?

In truth, the gold standard is already a barbarous relic. All of us, from the Governor of the Bank of England downwards, are now primarily interested in preserving the stability of business, prices, and employment, and are not likely, when the choice is forced on us, deliberately to sacrifice these to . . . outworn dogma. . . . Advocates of the ancient standard do not observe how remote it now is from the spirit and the requirements of the age. A regulated nonmetallic standard has slipped in unnoticed. *It exists.* Whilst the economists dozed, the academic dream of a hundred years, doffing its cap and gown, clad in paper rags, has crept into the real world.[8]

The Fed Wins Its Spurs

> Although the System was originally conceived chiefly as a means of preventing banking panics and of providing an elastic currency, it came in the post-war period to be looked to . . . as an instrumentality for accomplishing business and price stability. The ability of the Federal Reserve System to determine or influence interest rates, to buy and sell government securities in the open market, and to deal in gold was frequently set forth as an influence which should go far toward mitigating or abolishing cycles of business boom and depression.
>
> —Edwin G. Nourse[9]

After its strong recovery from the depression of 1921, the economy maintained a high and growing level of income until 1929, with the exception of two periods of gentle decline, hardly noticed by the general public, each lasting a little over a year. The first of the downturns ran from the spring of 1923 to the summer of 1924, and the second covered the period from the fall of 1926 to the fall of 1927. The Federal Reserve System used its monetary control powers to stabilize the economy, applying the brakes when expansion became overly vigorous and stepping on the accelerator when the economy lost momentum. The results were impressive: the two downturns were mild and fairly promptly reversed; the expansions did not become inflationary booms; the economy was prosperous, yet the gauge indicating the general level of prices showed only slight fluctuation. The experience gained by the central bankers from their on-the-job training seemed to be paying off in relatively stable economic growth. As a result, monetary policy gained status as a mechanism able to keep the economy from veering off course; its practitioners experienced increasing self-confidence and were accorded new respect. The buoyant optimism of the twenties that accompanied the tangible changes—rapid growth of mass production industries, notably automobiles and household appliances; urban construction; the move to the suburbs—resulted in public confidence that as a nation we now knew how to keep the economic engine humming.

Let's take a brief closer look at what the Fed did that paid off so handsomely on the central bankers' bottom line of economic stability.

1. When the 1921–1923 recovery threatened to become too rapid early in 1923, government securities were sold and the discount rate was raised. The resulting drop in Federal Reserve credit neutralized or "sterilized" most of the gold that flowed in during 1923–1924, and the growth of the money stock was checked. The economy stopped growing and entered a period of mild recession.

2. The recession of 1923–1924 was counteracted by substantial purchases of government securities and a series of discount rate cuts. The economy promptly recovered. A supplementary motive was to assist the return of European nations to the gold standard; greater availability of dollars tended to strengthen European currencies and so curb the inflow of gold to the United States.

3. During the expansion from mid–1924 to the fall of 1926 there was a real estate boom; the stock market set out into the foothills of the peaks to be reached in 1928 and 1929. The Fed applied its credit brakes gently in 1926, and the economy slowed.

4. The slight recession of 1926–1927 was met by expansionary credit policies as in 1923–1924, and again the economy recovered. At this juncture international considerations became very important. As discussed below, the decision to ease credit in 1927 became a focal point of sharp criticism.

The six years of gentle undulation of the economy from 1922 through 1927 mark one of the most placid and satisfying periods of monetary policy in the life of the Federal Reserve System. Before taking up the divisive and frustrating final two years of the decade, there are some other features of the twenties to consider.

Pride of place belonged to the objective of economic stability, but the Federal Reserve had other goals as well. It was of course intended that the international gold standard be restored, so the monetary authorities sought to use their powers to promote its restoration and to maintain balance in America's international payments. But whereas the Federal Reserve System very clearly stated that it gave great weight to gold standard restoration, it neglected to explain how this was to be achieved. The Fed wanted both internal economic stability and the gold standard link to the external (world) economy; it was quite willing to expatiate on how to achieve the first, but its lips were sealed concerning the second objective. There is a self-protective aspect inherent in this behavior in that the two goals might require conflicting policies and pose a difficult choice that would be exposed for all to see. It has been plausibly argued that despite the dual objectives the system based its policies primarily on domestic considerations. Whenever the foreign-oriented objectives could also be served by the same policies, they would be brought in to make an even stronger case. If external objectives required different policies they were put on hold. Another aspect of this issue involves the locus of decision-making power within the system. The international policies were largely the province of the Federal Reserve Bank of New York under Governor Benjamin Strong, of whom more will shortly be said, rather than under the control of the Federal Reserve Board in Washington.

The decision to ease credit conditions in 1927 provides a classic illustration of a strategic and controversial monetary policy decision. The actions taken were not dramatic, but they came to be viewed as feeding the fires of speculation in the stock market and, to many, contributing to the depression that followed.

In July 1927 Governor Strong arranged a conference, or in today's journalese a "financial summit," in New York with Governor Montagu Norman of the Bank of England, Governor Hjalmar Horace Greely Schacht of the Reichsbank, and Deputy Governor Charles Rist of the Bank of France. It was an effort by Strong to bring about cooperation among the world's preeminent central bankers. J.K. Galbraith has noted the gingerly manner in which these financial Titans gathered:

> On July 1, 1927, the *Mauretania* arrived in New York with two notable passengers, Montagu Norman, Governor of the Bank of England, and Hjalmar Schacht, the head of the Reichsbank. . . . The secrecy covering the visit was extreme. . . . The names of neither of the great bankers appeared on the passenger list. Neither, on arriving, met with the press, although, according to the *New York Times,* Dr. Schacht, on emerging from the dining room on the way in from quarantine, "paused long enough to announce that he had nothing to say." Sir Montagu hurried upstairs, waving his hand, and was altogether less cooperative.[10]

Benjamin M. Anderson's account of the meeting almost suggests a conspiracy:

> The conference was, indeed, meant to be very secret. Gates W. McGarrah, chairman of the Board of Directors and Federal Reserve agent of the Federal Reserve Bank of New York, had asserted his right to be present at the conference; but Governor Strong refused, and McGarrah, instead of fight-

ing, left the city. The whereabouts of the members of the conference was kept secret from the banking community of New York.[11]

The governors of the Federal Reserve Banks who were on the Open Market Investment Committee were invited to the formal sessions of the international group by Strong, but he went behind the backs of almost all of the members of the Federal Reserve Board, inviting only Governor Crissinger of that body.

After the exchange of views in New York, the significant subsequent development was an easier money policy by the Federal Reserve System during the second half of 1927; the discount rates were reduced at the reserve banks and large securities purchases were made on the open market. When Strong went to Washington he gained the approval of the Federal Reserve Board for his easier money policy proposals. According to Anderson, "Norman and Strong forced through their programs of cheap money in the United States" because the Federal Reserve Board was "rather supine" except for Adolph Miller, who was overmatched by Strong and Norman.[12] The board justified its action as an aid to economic recovery and as assistance to foreign countries, both to finance their purchases of U.S. crops and to help their foreign exchange positions. After the board sanctioned the policy, the various Federal Reserve Banks lowered their discount rates according to Hoyle, except for the Federal Reserve Bank of Chicago, which refused to budge. The Federal Reserve Board held a special meeting and voted four to three to end dissension in the ranks by forcing the Chicago Fed to cut its rate. By successfully asserting its authority to control discount rates (although in a formal sense the reserve banks set them), the board extended its power over the monetary control mechanism. Three years earlier, it will be recalled, the board assumed the primary role in determining open-market operations.

While it is true that the easier money policy was justified on the dual grounds of encouraging domestic economic recovery and supporting the international gold standard, there is little doubt that under the circumstances the gold standard criterion was foremost at the time. Great Britain had returned to the gold standard in April 1925 at its prewar value of sterling and was struggling to maintain an adequate gold stock. France was preparing to return to the gold standard. The United States had experienced a gold inflow earlier in the 1920s and had been absorbing gold rapidly from abroad during 1927. A cheaper money policy in the United States would tend to return gold to Europe, or at least keep Europe from losing more gold, and therefore would make an important contribution toward restoring the gold standard mechanism. In doing this, the United States was not acting in compliance with the rules of the gold standard, but was acting to reestablish the gold standard. The chief mover in all this was Benjamin Strong, who took very seriously the responsibility that he felt for reestablishing the gold standard. Strong was the Jim Thorpe of central banking: he grabbed the ball and headed for the gold standard goal with deft footwork and determination.

If the easy money policy was good for the gold standard, helpful to domestic economic recovery generally, and in the view of many would stimulate demand for American farm products, why did Adolph Miller and Benjamin Anderson lead an attack on it? It was recognized that cheap money could stimulate credit expansion that was already fueling stock market speculation. Despite the sluggish behavior of the economy, the stock market advanced steadily throughout 1927. Member commercial banks expanded their security loans and added to their security investments, while commercial loans were essentially flat. We thus return to the view that credit expansion is dangerous if it is used for speculation rather than production. If money creation is not for productive purposes, then monetary policy fails the qualitative test that was the part of the real bills doctrine worth preserving.

There is an interesting sequence of observations by prominent writers on the importance of the Fed's easy money policy for the subsequent stock market speculative boom and collapse. In *The Great Crash* (1955), Galbraith took the view that to blame the Federal Reserve "assumes that people will always speculate if only they can get the money," which is not true. In *A Monetary History of the United States 1867–1960* (1963), Friedman and Schwartz retort that the Federal Reserve could have broken the bull market by clamping down on money creation. In *Money* (1975), Galbraith accepts the point that the Fed can be held responsible for failing to stop the stock market boom even if it didn't cause it, but he also stresses the point that if credit had been made generally tighter, then the economy would very likely have suffered from the curbing of loans for commerce, industry, agriculture, and housing. To get the stock market on a satisfactory monetary diet might have required starvation of the economy as a whole.[13]

How did the monetary aggregates behave during the twenties? For the four years from December 1921 to December 1925 the money stock rose by 26 percent as a result of surges during the upswings of 1921–1923 and 1924–1926. Over the next four years, December 1925 to December 1929, the money stock hovered at about the same level, with only a 1.5 percent increase for the period. The monetary base from 1923 onward was held quite steady as a result of Federal Reserve management, despite a rise in the gold stock from $3 billion in mid-1921 to $4.2 billion in 1924 and a drop from $4.3 billion in mid-1927 to $3.8 billion in mid-1928. Gold movements in and out of the country were prevented by approximately offsetting increases and decreases in Federal Reserve credit from causing much change in the monetary base. By deliberately isolating the monetary base (and by extension the money stock, price level, production, and so forth) from the effects of the gold flows by using open-market operations and discount policy (a practice known as the sterilization of gold), the Federal Reserve System was able to protect the domestic economy from undesired external trends and shocks. Initially the gold sterilization policy was viewed as appropriate to the special conditions of the postwar period when the international gold standard was in the process of rehabilitation. But as countries returned to gold, in particular after Great Britain returned to the fold in 1925, this justification atrophied. The objective of maintaining stable internal economic conditions for the nation through monetary policy was an idea whose time had clearly come. Economic stabilization was indeed the desideratum, but unfortunately it came directly into conflict with maintenance of the gold standard. The essence of the international gold standard is the willingness of nations to permit the monetary, price, and income changes that follow from inflows and outflows of gold. To sterilize gold flows was to prevent the automatic process of the gold standard system from operating. In other words, sterilization subverted the gold standard. If some countries sterilized but not others, the burden of adjustment would fall entirely on the latter. If the United States, for example, sterilized gold inflows, then the gold-losing countries would have to bear the brunt of the adjustment by a deflationary spiral. The conflict between national economic stabilization and adherence to the gold standard posed a fundamental problem, and the failure to face up to this problem, much less resolve it satisfactorily, is probably the most important monetary issue to emerge in the interwar era.

Important changes occurred in the American commercial banking sector during the twenties. The composition of bank loans shifted toward security and real estate loans and away from commercial loans, which had traditionally been predominant. Business firms found themselves better able than in the past to obtain funds for expansion through the sale of securities and by ploughing back the ample profits brought by prosperity. The new practice of buying on the installment plan, typical of financing automobiles and other big-ticket consumer goods, was carried out through finance companies that borrowed from the banks.

A major development of commercial bank operation was the increased role of investments relative to loans. The banks bought securities issued by federal, state, and local governments, but they did not stop with such "safe" investments; they acquired the securities of domestic corporations and foreign debtors. Banks in large cities created companies known as affiliates for dealing in securities, both stocks and bonds, new issues of which they underwrote and distributed, and in which they would speculate by purchases for their own account. National banks, under the provisions of the Federal Reserve Act, were permitted to carry out trust functions. Securities handled by bank affiliates might easily come to rest in trust accounts administered by the parent bank.

The large commercial banking institutions were at the center of distribution of vast amounts of foreign securities, many of dubious worth. Here was an innovation whose time had suddenly come and would even more suddenly go. Selling securities was a highly lucrative activity, so much so that competition among investment bankers and the investment affiliates of major banks took the form of searching out potential issuers of stocks or bonds. The intensity of the bankers in this scramble for "deals" suggests the spirit of the Oklahoma land rush but in pursuit of intangible rather than real wealth.

> One sort of security which it was very easy to sell was the bonds of foreign states, and here the strenuousness of the competition approached the ridiculous. Young men representing big New York banks camped in Balkan and South American capitals in the frantic hope of inducing the local financial dignitaries to issue bonds. Sometimes these young men were not only ignorant of the language of the country but of its customs and traditions, and even of its political and financial record; and there might be three or four of them maneuvering for a single bond issue, each eager to get ahead of the others by whatever means could be contrived. Small wonder, under the circumstances, that some of this headlong financing did not redound to the credit of the banks which made the loans and sold the bonds, or that it led in due course to the shrinkage of assets of hundreds of American banks and to the impoverishment of thousands of embittered investors.[14]

In the euphoric atmosphere of the time, the regulation of bank activities was relaxed in various ways, a process later much regretted.

Historically, as the country grew, the number of commercial banks increased until peaking at almost 30,000 in 1921. Throughout the twenties, however, despite the expansion of the economy, the number of banks declined year after year to about 24,000 at the end of 1929. This reversal of form involving the disappearance, by failure or merger, of almost 6,000 banks was not nearly as important as the sheer numbers might suggest; it was not the result of financial panic or a breakdown in either the real economy or the banking structure. The vast majority of banks that ceased to exist were very small fish in very small ponds; they had capital of $25,000 or less and were located in prairie towns. They were pushed into oblivion by forces beyond their control: agriculture suffered chronic overproduction; developments in transportation favored the larger urban centers at the expense of the small towns with their small local banks. In short, environmental changes deprived numerous small banks of their reason for existence; they could not survive, for their place in the scheme of things had gone.

The Fork in the Road

> The dispute between the Board and the New York Bank largely paralyzed monetary policy during almost the whole of the important year

1929. In addition, it was probably the crucial engagement in the struggle for power within the system.

—Milton Friedman and Anna Schwartz[15]

As the year 1928 opened, President Coolidge, after conferring with Treasury officials, announced that "he was satisfied that there was nothing alarming about the speculative activity in the stock market."[16] Evidently he thought it desirable to be reassuring. His decision not to run for a second term might suggest that he had second thoughts or a premonition that all was not well, but when he left office in March 1929 he still maintained that prosperity was secure. In June 1929 Bernard Baruch, a well-known financier and perennial adviser to presidents, observed that "the economic condition of the world seems on the verge of a great forward movement." In October 1929 Irving Fisher, never confined to an ivory tower, viewed stock prices as having "reached what looks like a permanently high plateau."[17] These public figures were among the most prominent of many who spoke "bullishly" of the future on the eve of the stock market crash. It would be understandable if later they wished they had followed the advice attributed to movie mogul Samuel Goldwyn: "Never prophesy, especially about the future." Paul M. Warburg was among the relatively few who understood the precarious reality of the situation and said so publicly. In March 1929 he observed that the power to control events had "passed into the hands of stock-exchange operators, who have now for many months governed the flow of money." and added that "speculative overexpansion invariably ends in overcontraction and distress."[18] The chief architect of the Federal Reserve System and member of the Federal Reserve Board from 1914 to 1918 found it necessary to fault the system for failing to exercise the necessary leadership.

It was not that the Federal Reserve System was unaware of the danger or unwilling to act; it tried but failed to cope with the problem. In addition to the goals of maintaining stability in the national economy and restoring the international gold standard, a third policy criterion of the Federal Reserve System was the control of speculation. Whereas in 1920–1921 the problem was speculation in commodities, attention in the late twenties was of course on securities; in 1928–1929 stock market speculation became the system's dominant concern. The day after Coolidge said there was nothing to be alarmed about, the Federal Reserve Board was advised by its research director, E.A. Goldenweiser, that the situation was grave. In mid-January 1928 the Open Market Investment Committee even changed its meeting place from New York to Washington, lest its presence in the financial center be too unsettling to the financial markets. Common stock prices had risen throughout 1927 and continued to rise, fed by large flows of money into brokers' loans, the chief source of financing of stock purchases on margin. The monthly index of common stock prices (1926 = 100) stood at 134 in

January 1928, on its way to 171 by December and a peak of 225 in September 1929. The Dow–Jones industrials average went from 200 in January 1928 to 300 by December and peaked at 381 in September 1929.

The system adopted a restrictive policy early in 1928, selling securities and raising the discount rate in three steps to 5 percent by July. A policy of steady restraint was continued until the fall of 1929 with the intention of bringing speculation on the stock market under control without bringing on a recession or depression. The monetary aggregates held quite steady: the money stock and the monetary base fluctuated only slightly. The wholesale price level declined somewhat from late 1928 through 1929, resulting in "the first cyclical expansion since 1891–93 during which wholesale prices failed to rise."[19] The stock market rise was fueled by money flooding in to brokers who financed the purchase of stock by speculators large and small as the puritan ethic lost ground to the get-rich-quick mania. The banks of course were lenders to brokers on call loans which had increased substantially since 1921, but during 1928–1929 the amount of money loaned *by banks* did not provide additional funds to finance the stock market boom. The money, while often channeled through the banks, came from sources outside the banks, from corporations and individuals, and from outside the country, as Wall Street acted as a powerful money magnet. With interest rates on brokers' loans running as high as 12 percent with a high degree of safety, since the loans were collateralized by securities and could be called by the lender, and with the nominal interest equal to real interest as prices of goods and services were stable, the attraction is understandable. Between January 1, 1928, and October 4, 1929, the total amount of brokers' loans nearly doubled; loans by banks decreased, while loans by "others" increased by 263 percent and provided over 75 percent of total brokers' loans at their highest level.

The problem of how to arrest security speculation led to a dispute between the Federal Reserve Board and the Federal Reserve Bank of New York. The board took the position that to curtail speculation by open-market and discount policies ran the risk of severely cutting off funds for productive purposes. Therefore the board favored a selective credit control policy referred to as "direct pressure," under which member banks making loans on securities would lose their rediscounting privileges. The reserve banks rejected this approach and advocated reliance chiefly on higher discount rates. The Federal Reserve Bank of New York tried repeatedly to raise the discount rate above the 5 percent level adopted in May 1928 but did not gain board approval until August 1929, when the rate went to 6 percent (still below the 7 percent of 1920–1921) for about three months before descending again. Although this conflict within the system had appeared on earlier occasions, it now became something of a cause célèbre. Benjamin Strong at the Federal Reserve Bank of New York resisted the dominance of the board, but after the untimely death of this very influential figure in October 1928, the power within the system passed almost completely to the board, the culmination of a trend noted earlier with respect to open-market operations and discount rates. A statement by the board in February 1929 called attention to the large amount of credit going into security loans and pressed a policy of moral suasion on the member banks by advising that they should not expect rediscount facilities at the Federal Reserve Banks if they were borrowing to make or maintain speculative loans. Of course, this policy could not intercept the torrent of funds from "outside" sources going into the stock market.

The Federal Reserve Board tried to find a judicious combination of policies which would check stock market speculation before it got completely out of hand and yet provide enough credit to keep output and employment at high levels. It failed to achieve either goal. A clear slowdown in economic activity began some months before the stock market began to slip early in October 1929. Some critics of the Federal Reserve System consider the discount rate reduction of August 1927 as the event which signaled loss of control over stock market speculation. The case is also made that if the Fed had acted more forcefully in 1928 to control credit, it could even then have prevented the stock market debacle. It is important to remember, however, that the system had other important domestic and international objectives. A restrictive policy in 1927 was not consistent with those objectives, and a considerably more restrictive policy in 1928 and 1929 could hardly have failed to result in economic contraction. The lesson drawn a few years later was that the stock market speculation could not adequately be controlled with general credit control powers alone. As a result, the Federal Reserve Board acquired new selective control authority, a development described in chapter 4.

The Strong Man of the Fed

> Not the least of our debts to Ben Strong is for his example of monetary statemanship. Rare indeed are leaders of his ability, enterprise, personal force, courage, integrity, and utter devotion to the public interest.
>
> —Lester V. Chandler[20]

Benjamin Strong came to central banking from a trust company background in New York City. He played a significant part in J.P. Morgan's banking rescue efforts during the Panic of 1907, as a result of which he gained stature in financial circles and became an advocate of reform of the nation's banking structure. He left the presidency of Bankers Trust Company to head the Federal Reserve Bank of New York at its inception in 1914.

In his capacity as a reserve bank governor for fourteen years until his death in October 1928, Benjamin Strong was the dominant figure influencing American monetary and banking policies, and he also played a leading role in international finance. Strong's frequently controversial policies earned high praise and some harsh criticism; that he exercised leadership within the Federal Reserve System and in the banking community generally is unquestioned. He did so despite repeated periods of poor health which required lengthy leaves of absence.

During his tenure as governor of the Federal Reserve Bank of New York, Strong was involved in numerous internal system conflicts. Struggles for power within a bureaucracy are no novelty, of course, but in the case of the Federal Reserve System they were built into the organization by the fact that the Federal Reserve Act was worded in quite general terms in order to secure its passage. The result was that the officials of the system had to settle controversial issues and provide specific meaning to general concepts. One basic question to be resolved was the division of authority between the Federal Reserve Board in Washington and the Federal Reserve Banks. If the powers of the board were broadly interpreted, there would be centralization of authority in the hands of presidential appointees. On the other hand, the board might be construed as possessing only limited powers of a supervisory and regulatory nature, with the reserve banks, controlled by bankers, having the active operational role. Strong became the leader of the officers and directors of the regional banks with the objective of unifying their practices into a cohesive system and preserving their decision-making initiatives, while simultaneously resisting the concentration of control in the Federal Reserve Board. Below the surface there was a continuation of the old conflict between public (political) and banking (Wall Street) interests and attitudes.

As discussed earlier, the Federal Reserve cooperated fully with the Treasury during World War I, chiefly by lending to banks and by serving as fiscal agent. By demonstrating competence and usefulness, the system gained acceptance. Shortly after the war, in 1919, the Treasury and Federal Reserve split over monetary policy as the Fed pressed for higher interest rates before the Treasury was ready for them. At this time Strong, almost alone within the system, struggled to free it from the dominating influence of the Treasury. After the inflationary boom of 1919–1920 turned into the depression of 1920–1921, the Federal Reserve was severely criticized for allowing both to occur. When the congressional Joint Commission of Agricultural Inquiry investigated banking and monetary policy in 1921, Strong defended Federal Reserve policies in three days of testimony in which he presented an impressively cogent explanation of system operations and policies. One point of his testimony is of particular interest in terms of the development of monetary policy. Strong defended the maintenance of high discount rates during much of the deflationary period by pointing out that the reserve banks were ready lenders and had prevented a financial crisis. Since the Federal Reserve System had been established chiefly to prevent a recurrence of panic, and in its absence one would very likely have occurred, this was a cardinal point. In 1920–1921 the Federal Reserve Banks were much concerned about their falling reserve ratios which seemed to require a restrictive monetary posture. Again, the central bankers were still at this time influenced by the prewar view that their proper modus operandi was passive accommodation, not control.

Yet it seems anomalous that the Fed persisted in a restrictive policy at a time when the economy was in the throes of contraction. Such a deflationary monetary policy soon came to be considered inexplicable and perverse as monetary policy developed into a positive instrument for promoting high levels of output and economic growth. The experience of 1920–1921 contributed to changed attitudes shortly thereafter. Only three years later, in 1924, when a mild recession developed, Strong pursued a countercyclical policy of expanding Federal Reserve credit through open-market purchases of securities and reduced discount rates. As the economy moved away from the primary post–World War I depression period into the new era of prosperity beginning in 1922, there was a pronounced change in thinking about monetary policy. The Federal Reserve's policies of 1919–1921 look less culpable from the older perspective then when judged by the later concepts of monetary policy.[21]

Governor Strong questioned the validity of the real bills doctrine or commercial loan theory of banking as a guide to policy. He made the case for quantitative control of the money stock in place of the automatic qualitative rule in a lecture at Harvard in November 1922 which blended banking experience with monetary theory. Since the real bills doctrine has had a pervasive influence in American monetary history, a fairly extended quotation from this illuminating talk seems appropriate.

> Now as to the limitations which the Federal Reserve Act seeks to impose as to the character of paper which a Reserve Bank may discount. When a member bank's reserve balance is impaired, it borrows to make it good, and it is quite impossible to determine to what particular purpose the money so borrowed may have been applied. It is simply the net reserve deficiency caused by a great mass of transactions. The borrowing member bank selects the paper which it brings to the Reserve Bank for discount not with regard to the rate which it bears, but with regard to various elements of convenience—that is, the denomination of the paper, its maturity, whether it is in form to be easily and inexpensively delivered physically to the Reserve Bank or not—and it makes little difference to the borrowing bank what transactions may have caused the impairment of its reserve, because the

paper which it discounts with the Reserve Bank may have no relation whatever to the impairment that has arisen. To specify more exactly—because this is an important point—suppose a member bank's reserve became impaired solely because on a given day it had made a number of loans on the stock exchange; it might then come to us with commercial paper which it had discounted two months before and which had no relation whatever to the transactions of the day; and with the proceeds of the discount make good the impairment. If it was the design of the authors of the Federal Reserve Act to prevent these funds so advanced by Federal Reserve Banks from being loaned on the Stock Exchange or to non-member state banks or in any other type of ineligible loan, there would be only one way to prevent the funds being so used, and that is by preventing the member banks from making any ineligible loans whatsoever, or deny it loans if it had. . . .

The eligible paper we discount is simply the vehicle through which the credit of the Reserve System is conveyed to the members. But the definition of eligibility does not affect the slightest control over the use to which the proceeds are applied.[22]

Strong became an advocate of price level stability as a major objective by 1922, but he argued forcefully against the adoption of a law which would order the Federal Reserve to stabilize prices. He maintained that such legislation would raise hopes which could not be met. By controlling credit, the Federal Reserve System could certainly influence prices, but other forces outside the control of the central bank could also affect prices. Directing the system to stabilize prices assumed that it had greater power than it actually possessed; there were other important objectives as well, so it would be inappropriate to force the central bank to concentrate on one alone.

From 1924 to 1928 Strong was much concerned with reconstructing the international monetary system and bringing about cooperation among the leading central banks. While the famous easy money policy of 1927 was a system policy, it was conceived and initiated by Strong. Benjamin Anderson contended that Strong's policies expanded the money supply too rapidly after 1924 and especially in 1927, and he was quite biting in his evaluation of Strong as a central banker.[23]

By 1928 the desire to restrict credit to combat stock market speculation came into serious conflict with the system's broader objectives. While Strong wanted to dampen stock speculation, he believed that the system should be concerned more with the level of total economic activity than with particular economic sectors. He rejected "direct controls" designed to cut off bank lending for stock purchases. They would not have applied to nonbank lenders and would have directly affected only banks that were borrowers from the Fed. The direct controls under discussion in the late twenties were quite different from the margin requirements introduced in 1934; the latter apply to borrowers as well as lenders and are not limited to loans from banks.

Galbraith has suggested that the Federal Reserve could have asked Congress for power to set margin requirements. As noted in chapter 2, a voluntary arrangement to control stock exchange lending was utilized briefly at the end of World War I, so the idea had surfaced earlier. But however desirable, it was probably too radical a concept to be given serious consideration during peacetime in 1928–1929.

The five original appointive members of the Federal Reserve Board were men of high caliber. Two came from careers in banking, Paul M. Warburg and William P.G. Harding. Warburg, whose contributions to the formation of the Federal Reserve System were described in chapter 1, was certainly a potential leader, but his German origin led to his departure from the board in 1918. Harding, an Alabama commercial banker until his appointment to the board, served very ably as governor for six years but was not reappointed when his term expired. One academic economist, Adolph C. Miller, provided the board with a broad view of the effects of Federal Reserve activity on the economy as a whole. Charles Hamlin, a lawyer and former assistant secretary of the Treasury, and Frederick A. Delano, a former railroad executive, were the other two initial appointees.

In 1922 President Warren Harding replaced Governor Harding with Daniel R. Crissinger, of whom it was said that his only qualification was that he was Warren Harding's personal friend from Marion, Ohio. This blatantly political appointment over the protest of Secretary of the Treasury Andrew Mellon, among others, "broke the heart and courage of the Federal Reserve Board."[24] There were other appointments of men in the twenties whose qualifications for the board were very questionable. Not all evaluations of the board at this time are as sharp as Galbraith's observation that "the Federal Reserve Board in those times was a body of startling incompetence," but they are hardly flattering. Benjamin Strong, on the other hand, is widely seen as the most important American central banker since Nicholas Biddle, who headed the Second Bank of the United States a century earlier.[25] Miller and Hamlin served very ably but did not have leadership ability; with the removal of Governor Harding from the board, there was no challenge to Benjamin Strong's leadership of the system, although he was governor of the Federal Reserve Bank of New York and not a member of the Federal Reserve Board in Washington. In 1927 Crissinger resigned and was succeeded by a much better qualified person, Roy A. Young, as governor of the board.

4

The Great Depression, 1929–1939

The Pre–New Deal Phase

> My mother brought us to Newark in January 1931. The stock market had collapsed fifteen months earlier, but though business was bad, Washington people who understood these things did not seem alarmed. President Hoover refused to use the scare word "recession" when speaking about the slump. It was merely "a depression," he said. Nothing to panic about. Good times were just around the corner.
>
> —Russell Baker[1]

The Great Depression that began in mid-1929 lasted twelve years to mid-1941, for it was not until then that the rearmament program induced enough spending to drive the economy to full employment and output levels. The path from 1929 to 1939 involved a deep descent to 1933, a partial recovery to 1937, a relapse to 1938, and then the final recovery leading into the war years. By 1939 the German attack on Poland that started World War II brought a changed international climate that materially altered the economic situation and outlook; the economy began its conversion to a wartime basis.

Concatenation of Events on the Way Down

> America was totally unprepared philosophically, politically, financially, and administratively to cope with the massive unemployment, loss of incomes, and poverty that came with the great depression.
>
> —Lester V. Chandler[2]

For almost four years—from the cyclical peak in the summer of 1929 to the trough in the winter and early spring of 1933—the U.S. economy plunged into the Great Depression. From the *ex ante* view of people living at the time, not knowing what was coming next, there was no reason to expect a calamity. Economic activity had its ups and downs; like inclement weather, recession was to be expected occasionally, at least until such time in the future when the art of central banking might be so perfected as to abolish the business cycle from the capitalist system. But there was no reason in 1929 or 1930 to expect that the decline in output would become progressively worse until finally real net national product had fallen by more than one-third, unemployment was a quarter of the labor force, and the banking system had collapsed. Policymakers were unprepared for the series of shocks that overwhelmed them; the system could not withstand the strain placed upon it, and attempts to cope with the problem were ineffective. As we trace the sequence of developments, we may vicariously experience the economic equivalent of a trip down the Potomac River by a canoeist who gets into some white water. Expecting a brief passage through moderate rapids, he finds himself out of control as he passes through the Great Falls of the Potomac.

The stock market crashed in October 1929, with panic conditions during the week of October 23–29. At the time, the economy was already declining quite rapidly from the cyclical peak reached in August. As early as March, the number of building contracts awarded was falling fast; automobile production fell drastically after March, and so did industrial production as a whole after June. Clearly the stock market crash did not trigger the onset of the economic slump. It would be wrong, however, to slight its significance. On the one hand it was a response to the reduction in business activity; a decline in output and prices meant lower prospective earnings and therefore the market value of stocks fell, the more so because of the previous rosy expectations. Much more important, by its psychological impact on expectations of businessmen and the general public, and by the reduction of the value of financial assets, it discouraged spending for investment and consumer goods. By constraining spending for output and stimulating the demand for money balances instead, it contributed to the contraction. The economy was stumbling, and the stock market crash gave it a strong shove on its way down.

During the early part of 1930 the economy showed some resilience. Industrial production and employment leveled off—stock prices rose temporarily from their earlier lows—and President Hoover on May Day stated that he thought the worst was over.[3] The sun had come out only briefly; output fell rapidly for the rest of the year, with a particularly steep drop in industrial production. From 1929 to 1930 real income fell by 11 percent. By October 1930, one year after the stock market crash, the economic system was jolted once again as a wave of bank failures swept across the country.

Failures were endemic in our banking system, of course—during 1921–1929 some 5,700 banks had failed, an average of about 635 per year—but in 1930 the number of failures was 1,350, with the bulk of them coming in the fall of the year. In November the dollar value of deposits in suspended banks reached a height far above the highest previous amount since monthly data began to be kept in 1921. Clusters of bank failures in several states spread alarm over a wide area of the country, leading to the withdrawal of currency from banks by depositers on a large scale. The contagion, while greatest among small nonmember banks, spread to member banks and in December brought down the Bank of United States in New York City, the largest commercial bank ever to have failed in our national history up to that time. Its name may have misled people to think it was a "government" bank rather than an ordinary bank. It was a notable failure, not only because of its large size but also because the private clearinghouse banks in New York rejected the efforts of the Federal Reserve Bank of New York to arrange a joint support operation to save it. As the public withdrew currency (reserves) from the banks, the banks reacted by shoring up their own liquidity positions. For the first time since 1907 a liquidity crisis gripped the financial system. The Federal Reserve System had been devised to prevent banking panics, and until now had been thought capable of doing so.

Early in 1931 the banking crisis abated; banks ceased their efforts to become more liquid, giving hope that the aberration was temporary and had spent itself. Data measuring economic activity for the first few months of 1931, like those of 1930, gave reason to think that the slide in economic activity was being arrested and a turnaround imminent. Industrial production in April was actually higher than in January. It was again a false dawn; in March a second banking panic began as the public converted large amounts of deposits into currency, and then in reflex action the banks liquidated assets to meet claims for payment and build up excess reserves. A further blow to the financial structure came as a result of Britain's departure from the gold standard on September 21, 1931. The gold standard, after having been restored gradually during the twenties, was in process of collapse during the early thirties, with 1931 the year of disaster for the system. Financial panic in Europe culminated in a run on sterling, and after Britain was forced to abandon convertibility into gold, the U.S. dollar came under pressure. Europeans, including central bankers, fearing that the United States might follow Britain in abandoning the gold standard, sold dollar assets to obtain gold. Thus the American banking system suffered heavy losses of reserves from both an external drain as gold was withdrawn and an internal drain as currency was withdrawn. Bank failures in 1931 numbered 2,293, involving deposits of $1.7 billion, twice the amount for 1930. The decrease in the money stock was much greater than in 1930.

The second wave of bank failures subsided after January 1932, and for the year 1932 "only" 1,453 banks failed, or 840 fewer than in 1931. The improvement was temporary—much worse was to come in 1933. Several constructive steps were taken by the federal government in 1932 to buttress the financial structure. In January the Reconstruction Finance Corporation

(RFC) was authorized, given some direct federal financing, and empowered to borrow much more on the basis of federal government guarantee. It made loans primarily to banks and other financial institutions, and some to various other borrowers also. By the time the Roosevelt administration came into office in March 1933, it had provided $1.4 billion to financial institutions. By providing liquidity it helped to stem the tide of liquidation. Like a fire department called late to the scene of the fire, it was able to rescue some beleaguered inhabitants, but did not prevent further collapse of the structure. In February 1932 the Glass–Steagall Act was passed, enabling the Federal Reserve System to be more expansive in its monetary policy, a point developed in a later section. In July a system of twleve regional Federal Home Loan Banks was established. With funds from the federal government and from private instititutions that became members of the Home Loan Bank System, the banks could lend on home mortgages to savings and loan associations, insurance companies, and others. The amount of lending that resulted was very small relative to the need. For a short time in the summer of 1932, the indicators of general economic activity again promised better things to come as the rate of slide of personal income and employment slowed, and industrial production registered more than just a blip upward for a couple of months. But for the year as a whole the economy sank much further into the abyss. Real income fell by 18 percent from 1931 to 1932, twice the rate of fall from 1930 to 1931. The value of stocks on the New York Stock Exchange had fallen in the three years since the crash of 1929 from $90 billion to $15 billion. We may note that in June 1932 federal taxes were raised, and in the presidential election of that year both incumbent Hoover and challenger Roosevelt promised a balanced budget. Like recovery, the idea of fiscal stimulus was still around the corner!

One final devastating relapse—marked by the banking panic of 1933—had yet to be endured. The familiar and dreaded sequence unfolded once more as bank failures spread across the land in the final months of 1932, becoming more numerous and involving much larger amounts of deposits as 1933 began. During this third wave of the series of banking crises that began in October 1930, for the first time statewide bank holidays were declared. The term holiday suggests a time for celebration, hardly the case at this time. Bank holidays were the means used, through legislation or executive order, to stop or limit the drainage of funds from the banks. Depositors were restricted, in whole or in part, from getting currency from the banks. The objective was to provide a time out, with the hope that when play resumed the behavior of the players would be normal. Until this time, runs on banks took the form of currency withdrawals; a new development in the early weeks of 1933 was the demand for gold coin and gold certificates rather than Federal Reserve notes or other nongold currency.

Friedman and Schwartz consider the handling of the 1929–1933 experience as inferior to that of 1907–1908. In both cases panic came to a climax with the restriction of payments by banks, but with quite different timing and effects.

> In both cases, the financial climax was the restriction of payments by the banking system. But in the 1907–08 episode, the climax occurred early before the banking structure had been seriously affected and, if our analysis is correct, served to prevent widespread bank failures, to cut short a possible major deflation, and to keep the maximum decline in the stock of money to less than 8 percent. In the 1929–33 episode, the climax occurred after more than three years of dragging deflation, after bank failures had cut the number of banks by more than a quarter and after the stock of money had fallen by nearly a third, and served only to close the stable door after the horse had been stolen. Finally, the climax itself was much more severe. The 1907 restriction involved the refusal of banks to convert deposits into currency at the demand of the depositor; it did not involve, on any large scale, even the temporary closing of banks or the cessation of their financial operations, let alone the permanent failure of any substantial number.[4]

A sort of quasi interregnum existed in the federal government in the sense that the outgoing lame duck administration of Herbert Hoover remained in office but refrained from new initiatives as the country awaited the inauguration of Franklin Roosevelt on March 4, 1933. Bank holidays were widespread at this time; even the Federal Reserve Banks were closed on inauguration day. On March 6 President Roosevelt proclaimed a national bank holiday; all banks were closed, and gold redemption and gold exports were suspended. Banks were permitted to reopen if and when licensed by the appropriate banking regulatory agency during March 13–15. As the baton of national leadership passed from Hoover to Roosevelt, the economy was at its lowest point. The first quarter of 1933 marked the trough of the depression—the contraction had gone on for 43 months from August 1929 to March 1933.

The Money Stock, Interest Rates, and Monetary Policy

The main fact concerning the money stock is that it fell drastically from August 1929 to March 1933, by 28 percent for the M1 definition and by 35 percent for the M2 definition. (M1, the "narrow definition," consists of currency and commercial bank demand deposits; M2 adds commercial bank time deposits). The rate at which money was spent also fell, by about the same magnitudes as for the stock of money. Between 1929 and 1933 velocity fell by 36 percent for the M1 definition of money and by 29 percent for the M2 definition. Money stock and velocity data are shown in Table 4–1.

While the money stock fell continuously from 1929 to 1933, the rate of

Table 4–1
Money Stock and Velocity of Money, 1929, 1933

Money Stock	August 1929	March 1933
M1	$26.5 billion	$19.1 billion
M2	$46.3 billion	$30.0 billion
Velocity[a]	1929	1933
M1	3.42	2.19
M2	1.95	1.38

Adapted from Milton Friedman and Anna Jacobson Schwartz, *A Monetary History of the United States 1867–1960*, a study by the National Bureau of Economic Research. Princeton: Princeton University Press, 1963, pp. 712–713, 774.

[a]Velocity refers to money income divided by the money stock.

decline varied greatly over time. Using the M1 definition, the decline from September 1929, just before the stock market crash, to September 1930, the month before the first banking crisis started, was just over 5 percent. In this early stage of the depression, depositors had not yet come to distrust the banks. Over the next six months the money stock declined only marginally, despite numerous bank failures at the end of 1930. However, for the year beginning with the onset of the second banking crisis in March 1931 and extending through Britain's departure from the gold standard in September to March 1932, the month after the Glass–Steagall Act was adopted, the M1 money stock fell by $3.7 billion, or by almost 15 percent. In the next year to March 1933 the final drop was close to 10 percent. In summary, the pattern was essentially that of a gradual although significant decline for the eighteen months from the fall of 1929 to the spring of 1931; then, over the last two years from March 1931 to March 1933 the reduction was remarkably steep, 23 percent.

The discount rate at the Federal Reserve Bank of New York was reduced from 6 percent to 5 percent on November 1, 1929, in response to the need for liquidity in a faltering economy. On November 15 the rate was cut to 4.5 percent. Four more "half a point" cuts during the first half of 1930 plus another in December reduced the rate to 2 percent, and then by mid-1931 it went down to 1.5 percent. In short, over the first two years of the depression the discount rate was steadily lowered until it was set at only half the previously lowest level of 3 percent. The downward trend was of course consistent with the need for monetary ease. But then, during October 1931, in the wake of the British departure from gold, the discount rate was raised by 2 percentage points within a week to 3.5 percent, a strikingly large increase. It was subsequently lowered in two steps to 2.5 percent by mid–1932 but again raised to 3.5 percent on March 3, 1933, the day before the inauguration of the new president.

In October 1929 interest rates in general began to fall. When the first banking crisis hit in October 1930, the yields on lower-grade corporate bonds parted company from those on government bonds. As lower-grade bonds were jettisoned by holders seeking more liquidity, including banks, their market prices dropped and their yields therefore rose. For almost the next two years the yields on such securities trended upward until they reached the 10 percent–plus area in 1932. Government bonds, above suspicion of default, served well as secondary reserves for banks; their yields continued to drift downward until the fall of 1931. The second wave of bank failures that began in March reinforced the trends already in progress. However, when Britain left the gold standard in September 1931 and the Federal Reserve System reacted with a restrictive stance, interest rates in general shot up, short-term and long-term, government bond yields included. During 1932 interest rates receded considerably from their high levels in the final quarter of 1931. In early 1933 they rose once more during the final banking crisis.

During the first phase of the depression to October 1930 the monetary base declined as the money stock declined. The fall in high-powered money resulted mainly from a reduction in Federal Reserve discounts only partially compensated by a gold stock increase and Federal Reserve open-market purchases of securities. Member bank borrowing decreased sharply as discount rates fell, indicating a pronounced shift to the left in the banks' demand for loans from the Fed. Table 4–2 shows data at half-yearly intervals to demonstrate the point.

While we have noted that the discount rate at the Federal Reserve Banks fell to all-time low levels in 1930, this fact needs to be viewed in the context of market conditions. Market interest rates were also very low in 1930 as business and other private loan demand dried up and as safe short-term market instruments were demanded. Actually, while the discount rate was certainly low in comparison with past levels or by "normal standards," relative to interest yields on "riskless" short-term securities, the discount rate was not low.

The rapid fall in the money stock after 1930 occurred despite a rise in

Table 4–2
Federal Reserve Discount Rates and Bills Discounted, Selected Dates, 1929, 1930

End of Month	Discount Rate, Federal Reserve Bank of New York	Holdings of Discounted Bills by Federal Reserve Banks
June 1929	5%	$1,037 million
December 1929	4½%	632 million
June 1930	2½%	272 million

Adapted from Board of Governors of the Federal Reserve System, *Banking and Monetary Statistics*. Washington, D.C., 1943, pp. 340, 441.

the monetary base. The gold stock increased to mid-1931 before the British departure from gold in September sparked an external drain. Banks then borrowed somewhat more heavily from the Fed for some months to offset the effects of the gold drain, but the main factor raising the monetary base in 1932 was Federal Reserve Bank purchases of securities on the open market. The phenomenon of a fairly steady increase in the monetary base coincident with an unprecedented fall in the money stock over a period of some two and a half years is explained by the pathological behavior of the public and the banks in their liquid asset preferences. The behavior of individuals, businesses, and banks was rational and justified from their own viewpoints, but from the viewpoint of the economy it was abnormal and indicated a malfunctioning system. Between June 1930 and February 1933 the monetary base rose by 27 percent at the same time that M1 decreased by 21 percent. The public demanded much more currency relative to demand deposits. By February 1933 currency held by the public had risen by over 50 percent but demand deposits were 33 percent lower. Putting it a little differently, in February 1933 the public held only about $2.50 in demand deposits for every $1 of currency, whereas in mid–1930 almost $6 of demand deposits were held per $1 of currency. The banks acted to defend their positions by holding a larger fraction of reserves to deposits, some 22 percent in February 1933 compared with 15 percent in June 1930. Various shifting relationships involving bank reserves and components of the money stock are summarized in Table 4–3.

Using the expansion formula for the banking system (below), the money

Table 4–3
Bank Reserves and Money Supply: Changes in Absolute and Relative Quantities, June 1930, February 1933

	June 1930	February 1933	Change, June 1930 to February 1933
C = Currency held by public	$ 3.7 billion	$ 5.6 billion	+51%
D = Demand deposits	$21.6 billion	$14.4 billion	−33%
M1 = C + D	$25.3 billion	$20.0 billion	−21%
R = Bank reserves	$ 3.2 billion	$ 3.2 billion	—
R/D = Reserve to deposit ratio	.15	.22	+47%
C/D = Currency to deposit ratio	.17	.39	+129%
D/R = Deposit to reserve ratio	6.7	4.5	−33%
D/C = Deposit to currency ratio	5.8	2.6	−55%
MB = Monetary base	$ 6.9 billion	$ 8.8 billion	+27%

Adapted from Milton Friedman and Anna Jacobson Schwartz, A Monetary History of the United States 1867–1960, a study by the National Bureau of Economic Research. Princeton: Princeton University Press, 1963, tables A–1, A–2, and B–3.

stock is related to the monetary base, the reserve/deposit ratio, and the currency/deposit ratio.

$$MB \times \frac{1 + C/D}{R/D + C/D} = M1$$

$$6.9 \times \frac{1.17}{.32} = 6.9 \times 3.66 = 25.3$$

$$8.8 \times \frac{1.39}{.61} = 8.8 \times 2.27 = 20.0$$

We have noted that the Federal Reserve Bank of New York moved quickly to lower its discount rate at the time of the stock market crash. It also bought government securities. In doing so it acted on its own initiative for its own account by an amount well above the limit for purchases of securities that had been approved for the Open Market Investment Committee by the Federal Reserve Board. The New York Fed was free to act in this independent manner under the agreement of 1923 that established the Open Market Investment Committee, yet most board members, including Governor Young, considered such action as a challenge to the board. Some further tugs in the ongoing tug of war for control of policy took place between the Federal Reserve Bank of New York and the Federal Reserve Board. The board decided to make its approval of a lower discount rate contingent on the agreement by the New York Fed to refrain from further open-market purchases of securities without prior board consent. Subsequently (except briefly in early 1933) the Federal Reserve Bank of New York did not again buy government securities for its own account. It did advocate using open-market operations as well as lower discount rates to offset the decline in discounts, but had little success in persuading the Federal Reserve Board or the majority of other Federal Reserve Banks to this course of action.

In March 1930 the five-member Open Market Investment Committee was transformed into a twelve-member Open Market Policy Conference with a representative from each Federal Reserve Bank. In terms of its prominence, and its experience and expertise gained in the financial center of the country, the Federal Reserve Bank of New York was equipped to play a leading role in the conduct of monetary policy. Without the forceful Benjamin Strong's influence, however, the New York Bank failed to win support for a more expansionary policy, despite the efforts of Strong's successor, Governor George L. Harrison. Federal Reserve credit outstanding fell steadily along with the monetary base from the time of the crash until the end of 1930. The Federal Reserve Board considered its policy at this time to be one of monetary ease, but that was a highly dubious description. Throughout the period until the new situation brought about by Britain's departure from the gold standard, the same pattern generally prevailed. Harrison, on behalf of the Federal Reserve Bank of New York urged a more expansionary policy involving substantial purchases of securities. In September 1930 Eugene Meyer succeeded Roy Young as governor of the Federal Reserve Board, and while he, like Harrison, supported a more vigorous open-market purchase policy, the two decision-making bodies, the Open Market Policy Conference and the Federal Reserve Board, successfully resisted such urgings.

When Britain severed its gold link in September 1931 and gold began leaving this country, the Federal Reserve Bank of New York, the acknowledged authority for dealing with international monetary matters, assumed the mantle of leadership. It quickly tightened credit conditions by raising the discount rate. The traditional first duty of the central bank, defense of its currency's gold value, was considered paramount, a position generally supported within the system and outside it as well. So once again, as in 1920, external stability took priority over domestic requirements. With gold outflows draining their reserves, banks found it necessary to go to the discount window in the face of steeply increased discount rates.

The system's actions constricting credit were a response to the "free gold" problem. Federal Reserve notes outstanding required a reserve of 40 percent in gold plus 60 percent collateral in eligible paper or gold. The system obtained eligible paper chiefly by lending to member banks. To meet the public's demand for currency, the Federal Reserve Banks had greatly expanded their notes outstanding; the low level of bank borrowing from the Federal Reserve Banks meant that the eligible paper on hand was insufficient to meet the 60 percent requirement, thus requiring that gold be pledged. The result was to reduce the amount of free gold reserves, that is, gold not legally required to be held. The Federal Reserve Board saw itself in a bind. It wanted to ease credit conditions, but it feared that if it bought larger amounts of securities on the open market the banks would repay their indebtedness to the Federal Reserve Banks, thereby cutting down on available eligible paper. The result would be to reduce or even eliminate the free gold stock, making it difficult or even impossible to adhere to the gold standard. In February 1932 the Glass–Steagall Act removed this technical difficulty by permitting government bonds as well as eligible paper to meet the 60 percent collateral requirement. This unlocked the door to open-market operations—the very purchase of government securities would augment the assets available to serve as collateral. The Glass–Steagall Act enlarged the power of the Federal Reserve Banks in another way by permitting them to make advances under specified conditions to member banks on their promissory notes secured by any assets deemed satisfactory by the reserve banks.

For several months, from April to July 1932, the Open Market Policy Conference, prompted by the Federal Reserve Bank of New York, authorized a substantial open market purchase program. System holdings of government securities rose by about $1 billion and Federal Reserve credit increased considerably, although it fell back somewhat during the remainder of the year. The willingness of the conference temporarily to sanction an expansionary policy is explained in part by congressional attitudes. By 1932 Congress was anxious for a more stimulative policy, and proposals for new and radical legislation toward that end were under consideration. The governors, very conscious that Congress was looking over their collective shoulder, were willing to carry out a moderate expansionary program to forestall what they feared would otherwise be a dangerous monetary experiment by congressional mandate. Soon after Congress adjourned in July, the conference's ardor for expansion cooled; no further net additions were made to system holdings of government securities from August until the middle of the next year.

This episode raises the question of why the Federal Reserve System, putative guardian of the national financial system, was so reluctant to undertake a vigorous program of reflation at this time. Why did it dance briefly to Congress's tune but not follow through on open-market purchases although it seems obvious that the economy desperately needed stimulation? An investigation of the episode by Gerald Epstein and Thomas Ferguson that puts fresh light on the subject some fifty years after the events took place concludes that two sets of conflicting interest "help account for the Fed's notorious failure to arrest the Great Contraction."[5] One was internal to the system, and the other placed the needs of the system opposite the needs of the economy.

The Epstein–Ferguson explanation of why the open-market purchase program of 1932 was abandoned so soon has three main elements:[6]

1. Commercial banks were becoming unprofitable as their loans outstanding shrank drastically and were replaced by safe (but extremely low-yielding) short-term government securities. Open-market purchases by the Fed tended to drive up the prices and lower the yields on government securities. The squeeze on bank earnings was uneven among the Federal Reserve districts, and in those most affected, Chicago and Boston, the Federal Reserve banks were quick to express opposition to the expansionary program.

2. Following the adoption of the Glass–Steagall Act early in 1932, the Federal Reserve System as a whole seemed to have an ample supply of gold, yet each individual Federal Reserve bank had to maintain a gold cover of 40 percent for its notes. The way the gold was distributed among them was therefore a factor determining their attitudes. Since the banks still claimed independence from the Federal Reserve Board, they very likely would have refused to share their gold to provide cover for other banks. Individual banks stopped cooperating in a program of reflation when their gold stocks began to approach the legal requirement.

3. Foreign holders of bank balances in the United States withdrew large portions of them, particularly from banks in New York City, putting such banks in jeopardy. Federal Reserve open-market purchases of securities might

have compensated for this deposit drain, but the deposit outflow was immediate and large, whereas the Fed's securities purchases were of uncertain duration and amount. Furthermore there was a major renewed outflow of gold. In these circumstances there were complaints from the bankers that the Fed's policy was having a demoralizing effect, and opinion within the system shifted, bringing the program to an end by mid-year.

Early in 1933, in the midst of the chaotic situation leading up the national bank holiday, the system's open-market policy evaporated; it was deemed an inappropriate time for the Open Market Policy Conference to meet and the Federal Reserve banks reverted to acting individually.

The New Deal Phase

After finally ending its fall in the first quarter of 1933, the economy grew rapidly in real terms to its next peak in the second quarter of 1937. This cyclical expansion of fifty months is one of the longest in American history. But the economy had sunk so low that despite an average real rate of growth of 12 percent per annum in net national product over four years, the rate of unemployment averaged over 14 percent in 1937.

It is interesting to compare descriptions of this period. Friedman and Schwartz: "These are extraordinary rates of growth." Chandler, however, considers the recovery to have been puny: "The recovery that began in 1933 was woefully slow and faltering." Friedman and Schwartz look at the high absolute rate of growth and then put it in the context of the depression. They point out that since the population had grown nearly 6 percent, per capita output was actually lower at the peak in 1937 than in 1929, leading them to conclude that the incompleteness of the revival was even more notable than its rapidity. Chandler finds the expansion unimpressive because he focuses on actual output in relation to potential Gross National Product (GNP).[7]

Although recovery was far from complete by 1937, national income fell sharply from the peak in the second quarter of that year to a trough in the second quarter of 1938, and the unemployment rate rose to 19 percent for all of 1938. The recovery that began in mid-1938 gained momentum with the outbreak of World War II in 1939 and was sustained by American participation in the war for six and a half years until early in 1945 as the end of the war approached.

With this general sketch of economic performance in mind, let us look at the developments, policies, and ideas of these turbulent years.

Banking and Monetary Reforms

Experience (the perennial winner of the best teacher award) had taught a harsh lesson. The nation needed to understand what went wrong and to make appropriate changes to correct the mistakes of the past and prevent their recurrence. In this section the major banking and monetary reforms enacted during the New Deal administration of Franklin Roosevelt are considered. A little later the new theoretical approaches that grew out of the experience of the depression will be discussed.

The insurance of bank deposits by a federal agency, the Federal Deposit Insurance Corporation (FDIC), is the most basic structural change in the banking system to emerge from the Great Depression. The concept was far from new—bills to establish a federal system of deposit insurance had been introduced into Congress for almost half a century, and various states had tried their own plans with unsatisfactory results. Widely viewed as an idea whose time would never come, deposit insurance was not part of the New Deal agenda. Congressional perseverance brought it about in the face of opposition by the new president and the organized banking community, a combination not otherwise noted for their similarity of viewpoint. A Republican, Senator Arthur H. Vandenberg, added a bank deposit guarantee amendment to a banking bill in the spring of 1933. Senate and House conferees retained the amendment despite Roosevelt's request that they reject it. The American Bankers Association, to whom the guarantee proposal was "unsound" and "dangerous," fought hard against it, and leading Federal Reserve officials also opposed it. Eventually Roosevelt came to accept it, hoping to use it to unify the banking system, for the law originally required state banks to become members of the Federal Reserve System after 1936 to qualify for deposit insurance. Deposit insurance has since come to be regarded as a great accomplishment of the first hundred days of the New Deal era, and Roosevelt publicly referred to it as a fine achievement of his administration.[8]

Deposit insurance became effective on January 1, 1934, under a temporary plan provided by the Banking Act of 1933; it was succeeded in August 1935 by the present permanent system under the Banking Act of 1935. At the outset the insurance covered a maximum of $2,500 of deposits per depositor. By 1950 the limit had risen to $10,000. As a result of inflation and economic growth over the next third of a century, the insurance limit has risen to $100,000. To people living in the thirties this sum, forty times the original insurance maximum, would have appeared truly staggering; of course, the increase is not as impressive in real terms. Consumer prices by 1984 were roughly seven and a half times as high as in 1934, making $100,000 the equivalent of about $13,333 in 1934 dollars. If the original protection had been kept in real terms, insurance coverage would have risen to about $18,750.

At long last the nation found a remedy for bank failure epidemics. In view of the dismal historical record, and especially after the failure of over 9,000 banks in the four years 1930–1933—almost incredibly, 4,000 banks suspended operations in 1933 alone—the introduction of deposit insurance brought a new era to American banking. By the end of 1933 the number of banks was 15,015, compared with 24,633 four years earlier, a reduction of 39 percent. Some of the banks disappeared for reasons other than forced suspension, by merger, for example. From the point of view of the evolution of institutions, it is a striking fact that the virulent plague of bank deaths was cured by the modest FDIC after proving resistant to the much more majestic Federal Reserve System designed twenty years earlier to solve the problem of banking panics. Bank failures ceased to be a serious national problem after 1933, although in the mid-seventies and early eighties some large and more numerous failures had the effect of raising questions about the adequacy of the regulatory system.

Another issue that was resolved in the mid-thirties was the question of the location of the decision-making power within the Federal Reserve System. Heretofore the twelve Federal Reserve Banks vied with the board; and the *primus inter pares* of the banks, the Federal Reserve Bank of New York, sought to exert special influence vis-à-vis the board and other banks. Now the crown was placed on the collective head of a reconstituted and renamed board.

The Banking Act of 1935 converted the old Federal Reserve Board into the Board of Governors of the Federal Reserve System. Instead of eight members consisting of two ex officio members (the secretary of the treasury and the comptroller of the currency) plus six appointed members with terms of ten years, the new Board of Governors of seven would all be appointed for terms of fourteen years. The purpose of the change was to increase the independence and power of the board. The Banking Act of 1933 established the Federal Open Market Committee (FOMC), consisting of the heads of the twelve banks, to replace the Open Market Policy Conference. The Banking Act of 1935 made a significant change in the composition of the FOMC by making it consist of all seven members of the Board of Governors plus five members from the Federal Reserve Banks. This legislation also prohibits the several banks from engaging in open-market operations in government securities for their own account without the approval of the FOMC.

In our political system the office of president is higher than that of governor, but it is just the opposite in the Federal Reserve System. The Banking Act of 1935 took away the title of governor from the chief executive officers of the twelve Federal Reserve Banks and made them presidents. All members of the Board of Governors were given the title of governor, not just the executive head of the board, who now became chairman of the board. Thus the tradition of designating the chief executive of a central bank as its governor is preserved for its ruling oligarchy.

In addition to restructuring the Federal Reserve System, the Banking Act of 1935 increased its powers. The theory was that the system had failed to hold the economic contraction in check and to avert a banking panic because it lacked the necessary means of doing so.

In order better to control the money supply, the board was empowered to vary the reserve requirement percentages between the fixed 7, 10, and 13 percent set for net demand deposits of country banks, reserve city banks, and central reserve city banks, respectively, by an act of June 1917, and twice those percentages. In addition, the power of the Federal Reserve Banks to lend to member banks, which had been expanded in 1932 under the Glass–Steagall Act for emergency advances, was broadened on a permanent basis to permit advances on any security considered to be satisfactory. Thus the limitation of central bank discounting to eligible commercial paper to insure the productive use of credit, once looked upon as the means of implementing the real bills doctrine and thereby regulating the money stock, had gone completely out of the official rule book of the Federal Reserve System. The original concept of a central banking organism that would respond automatically to the needs of commerce, industry, and agriculture had turned out to be an environmental misfit.

A new type of control was given to the Federal Reserve System to regulate the use of credit. The Securities Exchange Act of 1934 empowered the Federal Reserve Board to regulate the amount of credit that banks and brokers might make available to their customers to buy and carry registered securities. From this authority come the margin requirements, Regulation U which applies to loans on stocks by all banks, nonmember as well as member, and Regulation T which applies to loans on stocks and bonds by members of national security exchanges. The "selective" credit control power is a direct result of what is generally considered to have been the inability of the Federal Reserve Board in the late twenties to cut off the flow of credit used to fuel the stock market without causing the rest of the economy to run out of gas. Certainly this sort of control over the allocation of credit was foreign to the thoughts of the writers of the Federal Reserve Act. The one type of credit control that was originally included, and indeed was prominent, was the eligibility requirement, and we have just seen how it met its fate.

In yet another area, that of regulation of banks, new rules were promulgated. The Banking Act of 1933 prohibited the payment of interest on demand deposits by member banks, and the Banking Act of 1935 extended the prohibition to all insured banks. The Banking Act of 1933 gave the Federal Reserve Board the power to set a maximum rate of interest that member banks could pay on time and savings deposits. The Banking Act of 1935 extended the coverage of this control power by giving it to the Federal Deposit Insurance Corporation to apply to insured nonmember banks. Again, the justification for these statutory changes is to be found in the experience of the banks in the late twenties. It was thought that competition among banks to attract deposits led them to pay excessive amounts of interest; to increase their earnings to meet their high interest costs, they might allow their reserves to become too low, and they might be led to acquire risky loans and investments. The rationale for these limitations was seriously challenged thirty years later, and by the early eighties they were in the process of being eliminated.

Additional steps to keep banks from again contributing to a speculative stock market binge were taken at this time. The notorious investment affiliates of commercial banks were dealt with summarily by being prohibited; restrictions were placed on interlocking directorates of commercial banks and investment companies. To prevent member banks from again serving as conduits for funds flowing into the stock market, they were no longer permitted to act as agents of whose wishing to make security loans.

The pledge of allegiance to the gold standard taken by the United States in 1900 and honored faithfully until 1933 was now largely renounced. It is true that the rules of the game of the gold standard were not always adhered to during the twenties when the rising gold stock called for a more expansionary monetary policy than was adopted. Yet American policy was deeply committed to keeping the dollar convertible into gold at its fixed price of $20.67 an ounce, and the monetary authorities undeniably acted to encourage the postwar restoration of the gold standard abroad. When the crunch of defending the convertibility of the dollar came after World War I and again in the fall of 1931, the central bankers did not hesitate to bite the bullet of tight money. But by 1933 the world economic environment was in a new dark phase: a debilitating worldwide depression threatened the social fabric and the political institutions of this and other countries, and the international gold standard had become a financial wreck to which only a handful of European countries clung. The conflict between domestic and international economic policies—between reviving the nation's economy and passively complying with whatever the external balance might require or permit—became obvious. However sound American money linked to gold might be in the abstract—and however blessed by the financial patriarchs and economic pundits—that golden link would have to be broken if it kept economic policy from putting people back to work.

Acting under the authority of the Emergency Banking Act of March 9, 1933, President Roosevelt took the United States off the gold standard as an emergency measure. Within a period of three months, steps were taken that greatly reduced the domestic role of gold. Gold and gold certificates were called in from all holders except the Federal Reserve Banks. Congress abrogated gold clauses in all contracts—they were declared to be "against policy"—a step that was challenged in the courts. Gold clauses, quite common in private and government debt contracts alike, typically required the debtor to pay in gold dollars of the weight and fineness that existed at the time of the contract originated, or their equivalents in nongold dollars. If the official price of gold were raised, debtors would have to pay more dollars; should the price of gold be doubled, a debtor who owed $1,000 would be obliged to pay $2,000. It would not be feasible policy for the government to raise the price of gold substantially under such circumstances. Rather than abandon freedom of maneuver on gold policy, Congress declared the gold clause void. Irate creditors, enraged that the sanctity of contract was not absolute, took to the courts. The controversy was put to rest in February 1935 by a five-to-four decision of the Supreme Court that upheld Congress. Since the general level of prices had fallen drastically, debtors at this time were paying more valuable dollars than they had borrowed anyway without the extra burden that the gold clauses would have required.

During 1933 our international gold policy was in a state of flux and uncertainty. For some weeks the suspension of gold payments was viewed as temporary and the dollar, although free to fluctuate, retained its value in terms of other currencies. Depreciation began in May; the exchange value of the dollar was again stabilized by the adoption of the Gold Reserve Act of January 30, 1934. During June and July 1933 an international economic conference was held in London. An effort by some European delegates to get commitments to the gold standard was rebuffed by a message from Roosevelt, who wanted to preserve freedom of monetary action for economic recovery. Beginning in September the secretary of the treasury, followed in October by the RFC, bought gold at gradually higher prices. The dollar was being deliberately depreciated against foreign currencies, with the intention of reversing the previous trend of appreciation resulting from the depreciation of foreign currencies. A cheaper dollar in terms of foreign currencies was intended to aid U.S. exports and curb imports, and so contribute to economic recovery. Although the depreciation of the dollar could be justified as correcting the previous excessive appreciation, foreigners tended to view it as a means by which the United States sought to achieve recovery by exporting deflation. In other words it was part of the overall pattern of competitive exchange depreciation, a kind of cutthroat competition in which countries acted individually in their own national interest with a macro result of uncertainty, instability, and declining trade for the world economy.

By the end of January 1934 the New Deal's definitive gold policy appeared in the form of the Gold Reserve Act of 1934. This replacement for the Gold Standard Act of 1900 established the framework for the new gold policy; under its provisions the policy took the following forms.

1. The official price of gold was raised from $20.67 to $35.00 an ounce, an increase of 69 percent. The content of the dollar was reduced from 23.22 to 13.71 grains of gold, a devaluation of the dollar in terms of gold of 41 percent. (There are 480 grains in an ounce, so $480/23.22 = 20.67$ and $480/13.71 = 35$). A side effect of devaluation was a profit to the Treasury of $2.8 billion—its 196 million ounces of gold were instantaneously increased in value by $14.33 each.

A stabilization fund of $2 billion was created and placed under the control of the secretary of the treasury for use in maintaining the stability of the dollar in the foreign exchange market.

2. All gold, including even that held by the Federal Reserve Banks, was nationalized. Domestically held currency was no longer redeemable in gold or gold certificates.

3. Gold would no longer be coined for domestic use; existing coins would be made into bars.

4. Gold might be held or transferred only in accordance with regulations prescribed by the secretary of the treasury. These permitted gold to be imported or exported freely, but domestically gold could be held or dealt in only for "legitimate" commercial, industrial, artistic, and scientific purposes.

The net result was the adoption of a limited or international gold-bullion standard in place of a full gold-coin standard, with the dollar devalued by 41 percent from its historic value established a century earlier. Although transformed in major ways, the monetary standard of the United States still qualified as a type of gold standard because the dollar was defined in terms of gold, gold could move freely in and out of the country, and U.S. money was convertible into gold for international purposes. The final break with the gold standard did not come until nearly forty years later, in 1971.

The monetary standard of the United States that resulted from the gold policy adopted in 1934 is not easily described. Clearly not a true gold standard, until 1971 (with exchange rates generally fixed) the system nevertheless was influenced by gold flows. A description provided by Friedman and Schwartz is helpful in bringing this hazy picture into better focus.

> It is not a gold standard in the sense that the volume of gold or the maintenance of the nominal value of gold at a fixed price can be said to determine directly or even at several removes the volume of money. It is conventional to term it—as President Roosevelt did—a managed standard, but that simply evades the difficult problems of definition. It is clearly a fiduciary rather than a commodity standard. . . . In principle, the Federal Reserve System has the power to make the quantity of money anything it wishes, within broad limits. . . . [The Federal Reserve System] clearly is not unaffected in its actions by gold flows. So long as the exchange rate between the dollar and other currencies is kept fixed, the behavior of relative stocks of money in various countries must be close to what would be

produced by gold standards yielding the same exchange rates, even though the mechanism may be quite different. Perhaps a "discretionary fiduciary standard" is the best simple term to characterize the monetary standard which has evolved. If it is vague and ambiguous, so is the standard it denotes.[9]

The devaluation of the dollar marked the end of the road for the American effort to reestablish a full-fledged international gold standard. For ten years after World War I the gold standard had laboriously been restored in the world economy, only to crumble in the first few years of the thirties. The United States was not forced to devalue by a shortage of gold reserves; the ratio of the nation's gold stock to its money stock was the highest since 1914.

In the spring of 1933, when many members of Congress were impatient for monetary expansion, it seemed possible that legislation would be enacted requiring the president to take specific action. Proposals were made to create money by a variety of means, including monetization of silver and issuing greenbacks. Roosevelt rather astutely kept his options open by persuading Congress to grant him a smorgasbord of permissive powers. In the "Thomas Amendment" to the Farm Relief Act of May 12, 1933, the president was empowered to enter into agreements with the Federal Reserve Board and banks for the latter to buy government securities, issue greenbacks, proclaim a new gold value of the dollar, reestablish bimetallism by providing for the unlimited coinage of silver as well as gold at fixed ratios, and accept silver from abroad in payment of war debts by foreign governments. No use was made of the provisions regarding the Federal Reserve or the greenbacks, and we have seen what eventually happened concerning gold. The silver policies remain to be considered.

The one tangible result of the London Economic Conference of mid–1933 was an international agreement to take steps to raise the price of silver. The effect was that the United States undertook to buy its annual domestic output of silver for monetary purposes, and the Treasury began purchasing silver in December 1933. Then the Silver Purchase Act of 1934 required Treasury purchases of silver in the United States and abroad until the stock of silver was equal in value to one-third of the value of the monetary gold stock or the price of silver reached its monetary value of $1.29 an ounce. By the end of 1941 about $1.6 billion was spent for the purchase of silver, a considerable sum but far short of the objectives of the Silver Purchase Act.

The purchase of silver was quite unnecessary for the achievement of the objective of monetary expansion. A revival of the silver movement of the 1890s is largely responsible. The severe deflation rekindled the old belief of the agrarian West and South that silver was the preferred way to expand the money supply. Joined to this broad movement were the silver-mining interests and the senators from the silver-producing western states. When united as a special interest group, the influence of the latter was politically very potent. One thinks of William Jennings Bryan as the silver movement's patron saint, but his eloquence was no longer available, for he died in Dayton, Tennessee, in 1925 following his successful prosecution of John Scopes for teaching evolution contrary to state law. The key man in "doing something for silver," the negotiator of the silver agreement in London, was Senator Key Pittman of Nevada. One may surmise that Bryan, an ardent prohibitionist, would have been chagrined to see Pittman, "whose sprees had shamed his own delegation and scandalized London," as silver's champion.[10]

In its domestic effects the silver-purchase program was essentially a price-support program for the commodity silver, quite similar to the price supports for cotton, wheat, peanuts, and so on. It also resulted in the stockpiling of silver. Silver certificates, which formed part of the circulating money supply, were printed as silver bullion was acquired, but the net effect on the money stock was relatively minor.

The Money Stock, Interest Rates, and Monetary Policy

The M1 money stock rose from $19 billion in April 1933 to $31 billion in March 1937, a rise of 63 percent in only four years. The monetary base increased slightly faster, by 67 percent. The surge in the monetary base resulted from a huge addition to the nation's gold stock, the so-called golden avalanche. The rise in the price of gold from $20.67 to $35.00 an ounce increased the profitability of gold mining substantially. Some of the additional gold came from domestic mines and from scrap, but much larger amounts came from other countries. A large-scale flight of capital to the United States from Europe developed as a result of the rise of Hitler and the growing anticipation of war, and it continued right through 1941. The result of the devaluation of the dollar in 1933–1934 plus the increased quantity of gold was a tripling of the value of the nation's gold stock between 1933 and 1937, from $4 billion in December 1933 to $12.7 billion by the end of 1937. Four years later, at the time of Pearl Harbor, December 1941, it was $22.7 billion. The main significance of all this is that the rising gold stock created high-powered money in abundance. The Federal Reserve System was more a spectator than a participant in the monetary expansion; from 1933 to 1937 Federal Reserve credit was virtually unchanged.

One of the main reasons why the money stock had fallen from 1930 to 1933, the trend of a lower deposit/currency ratio, was now reversed. The public became more willing to hold money in the form of bank deposits. Renewed confidence came with the fresh approach to economic problems by the new administration; after the banks were reopened in March 1933 following the national bank holiday, deposits increased relative to currency held by the public. Further impetus to the rise in the deposit/currency ratio was provided by the introduction of deposit insurance at the beginning of 1934, and the upward trend continued until late 1935 when the ratio became stable. Of course this development tended to cause M1 to rise faster than the monetary base; we need to account for the fact that the opposite was in fact the case.

The factor that kept the money growth below its potential was a decline in the ratio of deposits to bank reserves. As gold flowed in, the banks gained reserves, giving them the opportunity to convert these additional cash assets into other forms, that is, loans and investments. To the extent that the banks chose to do this, the result for the system would be an expansion of the stock of money as well as a rise in total bank assets. The banks, however, chose not to expand in proportion to their increased reserves but at a much slower pace, with the result that they accumulated a large volume of "excess reserves." Such excess reserves averaged about $2.5 billion in 1935 and 1936 or about 48 percent and 42 percent of total reserves respectively, rather startling fractions when one reflects that banks are profit-making (in addition to "money-making") institutions, and excess reserves imply less than maximum profits. Excess reserves diminished in 1937, but they soared to higher levels in the next few years, peaking at an average of $6.3 billion in 1940. The excess reserves were widely interpreted as an indication that the banks were so awash with funds that they did not have any use for them; they were simply an unneeded surplus. According to this view the excess reserves demonstrated the existence of extremely easy-money conditions. The private demand for loans was low as a result of business depression, and the yield on investments was remarkably low. From the viewpoint of the banks, the low demand for credit by the public limited the supply of assets available for bank acquisition. At the same time, however, a very important shift occurred in the asset preferences of banks, for they now preferred a much more liquid portfolio composition than before the Great Depression. The banks deliberately chose a higher ratio of cash assets (with zero returns) to total assets. Among their earning assets they shifted toward the highly liquid short-term government obligations. By 1935 and 1936 the yield on Treasury bills was not much more than .1 percent, and later in 1940 it fell to an incredible .014 percent. At this time banks had a strong preference for assets that could be converted into cash quickly without any significant loss of value. This preference for liquidity was a major factor in driving short-term interest rates to their extraordinarily low levels.

After its rapid growth from 1933 to early 1937, the M1 money stock fell by about $2 billion to mid–1938, after which it entered a long period of expansion. The monetary base, after a pause in 1937, resumed its growth to 1940. The deposit/currency ratio held steady, but the deposit/reserve ratio continued to fall until 1940.

From its low point in April 1933 at the start of the New Deal to September 1939 when World War II began, the M1 stock grew by 85 percent and M2 by 69 percent. As we have noted, the growth was interrupted by a fall during the recession of 1937–1938.

In contrast to the major expansion of money from 1933 to 1939, velocity showed only minor change. A modest increase by 1937 was followed by levels closer to those of 1933. Velocity fluctuated moderately within a range well below that of the 1920s. Money stock and velocity data are shown in table 4–4.

The period 1933–1939 is notable for its low interest rates. High-grade short-term obligations such as commercial paper and Treasury bills yielded less than 1 percent, much less after 1937 as noted above. Long-term bond yields were low too, in the range of 3 to 3.5 percent for high-grade corporate bonds. Interest rates were not only remarkably low but during the economic upswing of 1933–1937, contrary to normal behavior, they fell further; the growth of demand for borrowed funds associated with increased production was easily accommodated by a rapidly increasing supply of loanable funds that was swollen by the capital inflow.

The Federal Reserve System was equipped with the rediscounting mechanism at birth and by 1923 had assumed its second major credit control instrument, open-market operations. With these two means of controlling the monetary base, the system went forth into the post–World War I era with the intention of exerting a strong influence on economic activity. Now, twenty years after its creation, the system put aside these methods of monetary control: from 1933 to 1939 Federal Reserve credit was essentially unchanged. Open-market operations did not cease, but they were carried out to influence the rate of return on securities rather than to raise or lower total credit. After playing the leading public policy role in the economic drama from 1922 to 1933, the Federal Reserve System was now reduced to a character part. It did not have much to do with the development of the

Table 4–4
Money Stock and Velocity of Money, 1933, 1937, 1938, 1939

Money Stock	April 1933	March 1937	May 1938	September 1939
M1	$19.0 billion	$31.1 billion	$29.1 billion	$35.1 billion
M2	$29.7 billion	$45.5 billion	$43.9 billion	$50.2 billion
Velocity[a]	1933	1937	1938	1939
M1	2.19	2.47	2.30	2.21
M2	1.38	1.67	1.53	1.52

Adapted from Milton Friedman and Anna Jacobson Schwartz, *A Monetary History of the United States 1867–1960*, a study by the National Bureau of Economic Research. Princeton: Princeton University Press, 1963, pp. 714–715, 774.

[a]Velocity refers to money income divided by the money stock.

plot. Fiscal policy took center stage, while other new public actors were also introduced, such as the Tennessee Valley Authority (TVA) and, in temporary roles, the Works Progress Administration (WPA) and the Civilian Conservation Corps (CCC).

Rediscounting at the Federal Reserve Banks became trivial after 1933; it was like a flame flickering and almost out. The banks were "saturated" with reserves in excess of their requirements—if a bank did need additional reserves it was cheaper for it to sell some low-yielding short-term assets than to pay the higher cost of borrowing from the Fed, although the discount rate was hardly usurious. From 3.5 percent in March 1933 the discount rate stepped down four times to 1.5 percent in February 1934 and then to 1 percent in August 1937, where it remained undisturbed until 1942.

The phrase *monetary ease* was used by the Federal Reserve System to describe its general policy between 1933 and the start of World War II. It might well be called *permissive* or *passive* because essentially the Federal Reserve System allowed the inflow of gold to have its full monetary effect. The pronounced rise in the monetary base and the accumulation of excess reserves by the banking system created an inflationary potential but no imminent danger; the Federal Open Market Committee therefore did not employ open-market sales to negate the effects of the gold inflow. For a time the Treasury stepped in to sterilize the gold inflow. Ordinarily when the Treasury bought gold, it paid for it from balances set up on the books of the Federal Reserve Banks on the basis of deposits of gold certificates representing the gold purchased. In other words, the gold paid for itself, and the result of the Treasury's purchase was to add to the reserves of the banking system when the Treasury's checks were collected. During the first three quarters of 1937 the Treasury borrowed funds to pay for the gold, a procedure comparable to open-market sales of securities by the Federal Reserve Banks. Since in this case gold certificates were not printed, the gold was rendered "inactive," at least temporarily. The effect was to counteract or neutralize the increase in the monetary base that would otherwise result if the "normal" method were used. In using this sterilization procedure, the Treasury took a leaf from the book of the Federal Reserve, which used open-market sales for the same purpose in the 1920s.

Although the Federal Reserve System abstained from using its traditional open market and rediscounting instruments, it made full use of the power to vary the reserve requirements of the member banks given to the Board of Governors under the Banking Act of 1935. Between August 15, 1936, and May 1, 1937, the reserve requirement percentages were doubled in three steps. The purpose of this steep increase was not to put on the monetary brakes but, in view of the unprecedented amount of excess reserves in the banking system, to take in slack so that the central banking authorities would be better able to deal with a future need to apply the brakes. After allowing excess reserves to accumulate, the system decided to eliminate a large block of them through conversion into required reserves, on the supposition that they were not needed and might give trouble later. The rationale was that so large a volume of excess reserves did not serve any economic purpose but merely indicated that the banks did not have sufficient loan demand or investments available to them to employ all of their funds. Like newlyweds who receive six toasters as wedding presents, the banks were seen as not knowing what to do with the excess. Banks might well want to hold more excess reserves than they did before the banking panics of the early thirties, but there is a limit to everything, and there was thought to be an excess of excess reserves. The Federal Reserve could have sold securities on the open market to soak up the excess reserves, but the amounts involved were so large that the Federal Reserve Banks would have been deprived of most of their income. The system did not want to take action that would be considered to be a contractionary policy shift while the economy was still severely depressed. Like a patient recovering from a debilitating illness, the economy was still weak and might easily suffer a relapse. The Federal Reserve System, as in 1928–1929 and 1931, again saw itself locked into a position which it considered untenable with respect to the use of its traditional general credit control powers. Open-market operations were ruled out because of the large amounts that would be involved, and the discount rate was useless at a time when the banks were not borrowing. Under the circumstances the Board of Governors reached for the newly acquired tool of changing the reserve requirements. By this means the excess reserves could be rendered harmless— by jacking up the reserve requirements in a few steps the banking situation could be placed in a position which would again make open-market operations feasible. Changing reserve requirements was a blunt tool that could not be used to fine-tune the money supply but was useful on infrequent occasions to effect the kind of major pruning now required. Once the excess reserves had been reduced to "reasonable" levels, the flexible tool of open-market operations would again be brought into use on a continuous basis. It was recognized that raising reserve requirements involved risk; it was a new device and might have an undesired inhibiting effect on bank credit expansion. The risk was taken beginning with the August 1936 increase in reserve requirements, which was explained as a precaution against uncontrollable credit expansion in the future, and not a departure from the easy-money policy. Two further increases were put into effect on March 1 and May 1, 1937. By early 1937 economic activity was rising rapidly, prices were increasing, and the stock market was out of its coma and on the move again.

In 1937–1938 the recovering economy suffered a relapse that was distinctly painful although thankfully brief. The cyclical peak came in the second quarter of 1937, by the autumn the slump was obvious, and the trough

occurred in the second quarter of 1938. The combination of reserve requirement increases (August 1936 to May 1937) and the sterilization of gold by
the Treasury (January to August 1937) was expected by the Board of Governors to result in the shrinkage of excess reserves without banks selling off
securities or restricting loans, and hence without a rise in interest rates. But
interest rates did rise slightly. More important, a rather dramatic change
occurred in the money stock: from a peak of $31.1 billion in March 1937
it fell to $29.1 billion in May 1938. This unintended restrictive effect was a
result of underestimating the demand by the banks for the most liquid of
assets, excess reserves. The diuretic was powerful, draining excess reserves
by $1.25 billion from $2 billion early in 1937 to $750 million in August.
To regain some of this lost liquidity, the banks became more restrictive in
their lending practices and sold some investments.

For the year beginning in the spring of 1937 the recession—within a
depression—brought a drop of one-third in industrial production. For all of
1938, unemployment averaged 19 percent, up by a third over 1937; GNP
in real terms was 5 percent lower in 1938 than in 1937. The Federal Reserve
cannot escape blame for this sharp economic setback, but on the other hand
it can hardly be held solely responsible for it. In particular, federal fiscal
policy played a role by shifting toward restriction in 1937 as expenditures
for goods and services as well as transfer payments were cut and new social
security taxes were collected. The combined budgets of federal, state, and
local governments were "shifted from a deficit of $3.1 billion in 1936 to a
surplus of $300 million in 1937. These were indeed large shifts of fiscal
policies in the direction of restriction."[11] For the whole period 1933–1939
federal fiscal policies were no more than slightly expansionary. In a later
examination of the period it was concluded that "fiscal policy seems to have
been an unsuccessful recovery device in the 'thirties—not because it did not
work, but because it was not tried."[12]

The restrictive policies were replaced by expansionary policies in the
latter part of 1937 and 1938: the Treasury desterilized inactive gold; member bank reserve requirements were lowered; federal government expenditures were increased. In the late spring of 1938 economic recovery again got
started and continued into the period of the war. By 1939 real GNP was
slightly higher than in 1929, but with an unemployment rate in excess of 17
percent the economy was still severely depressed; real output has been estimated to have been 22 percent below its potential. The gold inflow continued, and the reserves of the banks grew as a consequence. The Federal Reserve
did intervene in the government securities market, not to regulate the money
stock but to prevent or limit "disorderly" conditions in that market. The
objective was to stabilize the prices of securities to assist the Treasury in its
financing, and to protect the banks' bond portfolios from disturbing fluctuations.

Keynes and Some Central Bankers

> In the perspective of history, a revolution in thought takes on the appearance of inevitability. In the flood tide of current events, however, it is difficult to ignore the element of chance in the process. It was a most unlikely series of accidents that led to Marriner Eccles, a banker, who had been strongly influenced by Foster and Catchings, being placed at the head of the monetary system, with me, an equally unorthodox ex-Canadian economist, as his assistant (nominally Assistant Director of Research). Rarely have two people with such different backgrounds or aptitudes which complemented each other so well been so suddenly catapulted into a strategic spot at a critical moment which enabled them to make an impact.
>
> Lauchlin Currie[13]

> The success of the Keynesian revolution in economic thought led to a temporary eclipse of the quantity theory of money. . . . It became a widely accepted view that money does not matter, or, at any rate, that it does not matter very much.
>
> Milton Friedman[14]

John Maynard Keynes's innovations in the analysis of monetary and fiscal policy—the field of study known as macroeconomics since the 1940s—are generally recognized as the most important developments in economic thought in the twentieth century. In marking the centenary of his birth (June 5, 1983), *The Economist* observed that "his economic views have been more influential than any other economist of his time, perhaps of all time."[15] The views of two Nobel laureates from the United States support this evaluation. Paul Samuelson considers Keynes "one of history's political economists—in the top class with Adam Smith. . . . The Keynesian revolution did indeed create a new branch of economics. . . ."[16] Milton Friedman, who led a counterrevolution against Keynesian economics, directs his criticisms of Keynesian doctrine more to Keynes's followers than to Keynes himself, whom he regards as "one of the great economists of all time—to be listed in the pantheon of great British economists" and "truly a remarkable scientist." This despite Friedman's view that Keynes caused economics to head in the wrong direction for some decades.[17]

It may be a slight exaggeration to say that there was no macroeconomics before Keynes; "the neoclassical quantity theory of money was, in fact, what we now call macroeconomics."[18] But as a macroeconomic theory, the quantity theory of money was unimpressive; it was used mainly to explain price fluctuations and did not serve to guide the capitalist world out of the bog of depression. What Keynes did in his *General Theory of Employment Interest and Money* was to provide a comprehensive new framework of analysis, a whole new approach explaining how the gross national product and level of employment are determined. It is the spring from which modern macroeconomics flows. The intense, persistent depression of the 1930s called into question the neoclassical paradigm and the laissez-faire economic policies associated with it. This historical event, the depression, precipitated the Keynesian revolution. Keynes offered what he considered to be a total break with orthodox economics. He rejected the orthodox view that unemployment was voluntary, that workers could get jobs by taking a wage cut. Neoclassical theory failed to understand the role of money and missed the point that changes in money wages and changes in real wages were not always the same. The orthodox view that a cut in the general wage level would relieve the unemployment problem was unwarranted and might even worsen the situation by reducing aggregate demand. Keynes's insight stemmed from his recognition of a dichotomy in neoclassical economics between the theory of value and distribution (microeconomic theory, the main body of neoclassical thought) and the theory of the price level (explained by the quantity theory of money). Value theory, that is, the theory of relative prices, was explained without regard to money or the absolute level of prices; money was brought in only to explain the absolute general price level. This division was viewed by Keynes as a basic weakness in prevailing economic theory, and he undertook in *The General Theory* "to escape from this double life and to bring the theory of prices as a whole back to close contact with the theory of value."[19]

By acquiescing in Say's Law (for the economy as a whole, supply automatically generates its own demand), orthodox economists could ignore the macroeconomic questions of the determination of demand and supply for total output. It was thought that all income would necessarily be spent on output, because income saved would not be held idle but would be channeled into spending for investment goods. The rate of interest would fluctuate to bring the necessary balance between the amount society saved and the amount it invested. Keynes attacked Say's Law and maintained instead that national income and employment were determined by aggregate effective demand. Consumption spending depends upon the level of income, generally a fairly stable relationship defined by the consumption function. Investment spending is explained by the marginal efficiency of capital (the expected rate of profit) in conjunction with the rate of interest. Investment spending is volatile because it depends on expectations of future revenue flows and costs. Uncertainty and changing expectations play major roles in the Keynesian view of how investment spending is determined. A new theory of the rate of interest, the liquidity preference theory, is presented in which the rate of interest depends upon a liquidity preference schedule showing how much money people want to hold at each interest rate, and the quantity of money. The bottom line of the new approach was the conclusion, at the time a shocking conclusion, that the invisible hand was a figment; the economy was not necessarily destined to move relentlessly toward full employment equilibrium if left to itself but was likely to find an equilibrium some distance below its potential. In fact, full employment equilibrium was but a special case in the "general theory."

Let us now move from this capsule summary to consider more deliberately the role of money and its implications for monetary policy. Before Keynes made his revolution, the quantity theory (recall Irving Fisher) held sway. Keynes (before he became a "Keynesian") followed his great teacher, Alfred Marshall, who had adhered to the quantity theory using the Cambridge or cash balance equation ($M = kPQ$ where $k = 1/V$) for relating money to output and prices instead of the equation of exchange used by Fisher, but this was a technical and not a substantive difference. So Keynes was a good quantity theorist himself until the 1930s (just as Luther was a good Catholic until 1517). The revolution came from within the economic establishment.

In an important book written in 1923, Keynes says of the quantity theory of money that it is fundamental and its "correspondence with fact is not open to question." Then, significantly, he adds that "it is often misstated and misrepresented . . . by careless adherents of the quantity theory. . . ." The error consists in stating that a percentage change in the money stock must cause the same percentage change in the price level. In other words, the velocity of spending is assumed to be constant, although, Keynes points out, everybody knows that this is not true, at least in the short run. In the long run he grants that it probably is true, and then adds one of the most frequently quoted statements in economic literature: "But this *long run* is a misleading guide to current affairs. *In the long run* we are all dead. Economists set themselves too easy, too useless a task if in tempestuous seasons they can only tell us that when the storm is long past the ocean is flat again."[20]

What Keynes described as an error was accepted for all practical purposes as the rule. Monetary theory up to the early thirties took V as highly stable in the equation $MV = PQ$. If the economy fluctuated in the short run it was because of changes in M, and if prices rose or fell over the long run it was because of changes in M. Monetary policy was available to stabilize the economy by the use of open-market operations and the discount rate. As we have seen earlier, there was in the twenties a high degree of confidence in the ability of the Federal Reserve System to use its monetary control powers to maintain economic prosperity in this manner.

Keynes had identified the central problem of monetary analysis. The question of velocity, the heart of the quantity theory, is crucial to understanding monetary theory. Mark Blaug has shown that during the neoclassical period from 1870 to 1930 quantity theorists were not satisfied with just the long-run implications of the theory. We have noted in chapter 1 that Fisher, who is often taken to have been a rigid quantity theorist, actually dealt fairly extensively with "transition periods" when V and T are subject to change. According to Blaug, this was general: "The striking characteristic of quantity theorists in this period was the emphasis on short run problems, on the instability of V in the short run rather than the proportionality of money to prices in the long run."[21] Richard T. Selden agrees that the principal quantity theorists did not maintain that V is constant over time, and refers to misleading "textbook caricatures" of them.[22] Perhaps Fisher and others were misunderstood, their treatments of changes in V taken to be mere minor qualifications of the main thesis, or as disclaimers in fine print to be ignored. Fisher was mistakenly interpreted by many to have considered V an institutional datum. A recent example demonstrates the point. The author states that "the quantity of money is linked rigidly to the value of transactions" in Fisher's version of the quantity theory, adding that the constancy of V was explained by the fact that in the short term, payments practices and the structure of the economy could be regarded as fixed.[23] Regardless of what the quantity theorists actually said, they were generally thought to have said that V was virtually constant:

> In monetary theory, [Fisher's] analysis was taken to mean that in the quantity equation $MV = PT$ the term for velocity could be regarded as highly stable, that it could be taken as determined independently of the other terms in the equation, and that as a result changes in the quantity of money would be reflected either in prices or in output.[24]

In *The General Theory*, Keynes offered his income–expenditure analysis to explain changes in national income ($C + I + G = \text{GNP}$) as an alternative to the quantity theory approach relating the stock of money to national income. He held that in an economy operating below the full employment level, the value of V (or k) was not at all stable but would generally adapt to changes in the money stock or the level of income. This does not dispute the validity of the equation of exchange, a logically unassailable formal relationship, but the quantity theory lost its usefulness as a policy guide. Keynes argued that a rise in M might well be offset by a fall in V, so that prices and output would not be affected. Similarly, if for some reason the level of income should rise autonomously with M constant, then V will rise. Instead of being more or less constant, velocity easily adapts itself to or accommodates autonomous changes in the other variables. The rationale for this behavior derived from Keynes's analysis of the demand for money, that is, the amount of money people choose to hold (liquidity preference). He separated the demand for money into two main categories: (1) the M_1 demand for transactions and precautionary motives, and (2) the M_2 demand for the speculative motive. The M_1 segment was presented as a fairly stable fraction of income, so it was consistent with the quantity theory approach. But the M_2

demand was explained as inversely related to the current rate of interest. It was an unstable relationship, because it was affected by uncertainty concerning the future level of the interest rate.

Keynes's analysis was distinguished from that of Fisher's by its treatment of interest rates. An especially significant feature of the liquidity preference function applied when unemployment was rife and interest rates very low. The interest rate could reach a floor—the M_2 demand for money would be perfectly elastic or horizontal at some very low positive interest rate. If additional money were created it would be held as idle balances. Why so? If it were used to buy bonds, the price of bonds would rise and the interest rate would fall even lower. This would be an unacceptable option—it would be preferable to hold the money. Why surrender a perfectly liquid asset (money) to gain only a tiny interest return with the accompanying high risk of a future capital loss on the bonds ominously on the horizon? Sooner or later the market interest rate would rise and the bonds would fall in value. These conditions, described as absolute liquidity preference, allowed M to change without affecting income, and conversely income could change without affecting M! Was this explanation realistic? Strictly speaking, no; Keynes himself said he did not know of an example and referred to it as a limiting case. Yet Keynes and many others thought that the low interest rates of the thirties hovered only slightly above the level of absolute liquidity preference, so for practical purposes, for policy-making purposes, it was relevant and important.

To conclude, it was Keynes's contention that the *quantity* of money was unimportant under conditions of economic depression. It is the *spending* of money for output, aggregate demand, that is important. The key to economic recovery was autonomous spending, chiefly business investment spending and government expenditures for goods and services. It was important to have ample money to keep interest rates low in order to encourage investment spending, but if businessmen are pessimistic and the profit outlook bleak, then investment spending would be inadequate and monetary policy ineffective. It was in the collapse of investment spending that Keynes found the explanation for capitalism's ills. The depression virus entered the economic system via a loss of productive investment opportunities, and spread into a wider general loss of income for the system as a whole through the multiplier process. The result was the conclusion that monetary policy was unimportant, a weak support in time of trouble. Money should be kept plentiful and cheap, for it provided suitable growth material if used, but it could not initiate expansion. It was necessary to generate spending for output, and for this purpose fiscal policy was advocated. Thus the practical policy result of the Keynesian revolution was to elevate fiscal policy into the prime policy role and to demote monetary policy.

The most prominent person in the monetary field in the United States in the 1930s was a commercial banker and industrialist from the inter-mountain West who became head of the Federal Reserve System, Marriner S. Eccles.[25] A Mormon, Eccles came from an extraordinary family back-ground: his father, David Eccles, attended no school, came as a boy of fourteen to Utah from the slums of Glasgow, died leaving an estate valued at $7 million consisting of a variety of business enterprises, and was survived by two wives and twenty-one children. Marriner followed his father as a very successful entrepreneur in banking, construction, sugar refining, and other enterprises, and in embracing the ethos of laissez-faire capitalism. A leader of the western business establishment and a Republican who staunchly supported Hoover in 1928, he accepted the consensus view of businessmen that a new era of economic progress had come and that depression and panics were relics of an earlier time.

Marriner Eccles was in his early forties when the Great Depression struck. While able to keep his chain of banks free of failure, he keenly appreciated his own vulnerability and the desperate national situation. A period of self-examination led to rejection of the belief in self-corrective economic forces and to recognition that individual bankers were not able to halt deflation. A self-made man with little formal education—he had not completed high school—Eccles came to recognize his lack of economic understanding and reached out for new ideas. In 1931 he became acquainted with the "under-consumptionist" theory developed by William T. Foster and Wadill Catch-ings which attacked Say's Law, and interpreted the theory in terms of his own experience in banking and other businesses. This led to recognition of the need for government action to raise purchasing power. By 1932, several years before the Keynesian revolution began to be felt, Eccles began pro-moting the concept of a compensatory fiscal policy, much to the conster-nation of his fellow bankers. In February 1933 he presented to the Senate Finance Committee a program for economic recovery involving deficit fi-nancing—in contrast to the testimony of a long list of prominent leaders of finance, industry, and other fields of endeavor, whose only recommendation was to balance the budget and hope for the best. Two years later, when comparing Eccles's suggestions before the committee with the economic pro-gram of the New Deal administration, the poet/author Archibald MacLeish observed that Eccles "was not only a Mormon but a prophet."[26] In January 1934 Eccles accepted an appointment as assistant to the secretary of the treasury, intending to serve in Washington for a maximum of sixteen months. He remained for seventeen years, returning to private life in Utah in 1951. The change in plans resulted from a major and unanticipated leadership role in the Federal Reserve System.

In mid-1934 Eugene Black resigned as governor of the Federal Reserve Board and was succeeded by Marriner Eccles in November. Eccles had made a strong impression on administration officials; his credentials as a successful banker and industrialist with "enlightened," well-articulated views gave him high standing among the liberal intellectuals. When Roosevelt broached the subject of an appointment as governor of the Federal Reserve Board, Eccles replied that he would be interested only if the president would work for legal changes to correct serious deficiencies in the Federal Reserve System. The paramount problem was the relative impotence of the Federal Reserve Board and the powerful but concealed influence of private banking interests. The Open Market Committee provided for in the Banking Act of 1933 consisted of one member from each reserve district. Since members were designated by the Federal Reserve Bank boards of directors, each with a majority of private bankers, private interests had enormous yet unobtrusive influence over policy. Also, each Federal Reserve Bank continued to have the right to refuse participation in transactions recommended by the Open Market Committee. The body with ultimate responsibility, the Federal Reserve Board, could approve or disapprove the policies of the Open Market Committee but could not initiate open-market operations. The Open Market Committee could not itself execute its policy. The directors of the Federal Reserve Banks could obstruct policy but could not make it. These administrative arrangements seemed designed to avoid responsibility and maximize ineffectiveness. President Roosevelt gave his support to Eccles on banking reform legislation and announced his appointment as governor of the Federal Reserve Board.

A protracted and bitter legislative struggle ensued until a new banking law, the Banking Act of 1935, was adopted in August 1935. It was the biggest battle in Washington for Eccles, who was a willing combatant with an imperious manner. Senator Carter Glass, who played a vital role in the passage of the Federal Reserve Act in 1913 and was the Senate's resident authority on the Federal Reserve System, was not consulted by either Roosevelt or Eccles, and became hostile to both Eccles's confirmation as governor and the principal reform proposals. The governor of the Federal Reserve Bank of New York, George L. Harrison, joined Glass in opposing important legal changes; the reforms would shift power from the New York reserve bank to the board in Washington. Numerous prominent economists (including Oliver Sprague of Harvard, Edwin Kemmerer of Princeton, and H. Parker Willis of Columbia) and bankers (among them Winthrop W. Aldrich of Chase, James H. Perkins of National City, and James P. Warburg of the Bank of Manhattan) testified against Title II of the banking reform bill, which contained Eccles's reform proposals. Irving Fisher, however, gave the banking bill his enthusiastic support. Finally a new law, the result of much political strategy, pressure, and bargaining, emerged from the legislative process. A brief recapitulation of the reordering of central banking powers in the Banking Act of 1935 is in order.

1. A seven-member Board of Governors of the Federal Reserve System would replace the eight-member Federal Reserve Board on February 1, 1936.

Neither the secretary of the treasury nor the comptroller of the currency would serve as ex officio members of the new board.

2. The Federal Open Market Committee would be reconstituted on March 1, 1936, with a membership consisting of the seven members of the Board of Governors plus five representatives of the Federal Reserve Banks, to be selected by the boards of directors of the Federal Reserve Banks according to a schedule of rotation.

3. The chief executive officers of the Federal Reserve Banks would be designated as president and first vice-president on March 1, 1936. Their appointments by the boards of directors of each Federal Reserve Bank became subject to the approval of the Board of Governors.

4. The Board of Governors was authorized to set reserve requirement percentages for member banks between the existing prescribed amounts and twice the prescribed amounts.

5. The power of Federal Reserve Banks to make loans to member banks was broadened by authorizing them, under the regulations of the Board of Governors, to make advances not only on eligible paper but on any paper considered to be satisfactory.

Marriner Eccles was confirmed by the Senate as governor of the old Federal Reserve Board in April 1935 after surviving a close call in Senator Glass's subcommittee. Early in 1936 the nominees for the new Board of Governors, Eccles as chairman, were confirmed without hearings. The Board of Governors soon employed its newly acquired power to vary member bank reserve requirements. As noted earlier, the reserve requirement percentages were increased (once in 1936 and twice in 1937) to neutralize the enormous amounts of excess reserves held by the banks; although the economy was still operating far below its potential, there was fear of incipient inflation. The 1937–1938 recession that followed was subsequently fully debated and continues to be a subject of dispute. Blame has been placed on the increases in reserve requirements, following which the money stock shrank.[27] Eccles exonerated the increases in reserve requirements by maintaining that they did not cause money rates to rise more than fractionally and did not cut off credit to the economy. It was three months after the final increase in reserve requirements became effective that the production downturn developed, and private credit began to contract at the end of 1937 only after the recession started. Eccles saw the causation running opposite to what later came to be called the monetarist view: instead of credit contraction causing the recession, he contended that credit contracted as a result of the recession. In Eccles's view the blame belonged mainly on fiscal policy. The federal budget shifted from a $4 billion deficit in 1936 to a small surplus for the first nine months of 1937, in part because of the introduction of social security taxes.

While fiscal policy was a new and controversial instrument which Eccles believed to be important and valuable, he of course appreciated the vital role of the money stock. It was just at this time that the theory of a compensatory fiscal program, put forward by Eccles and a group of government economists, began to gain allies in the academic community. The publication of Keynes's *General Theory* in 1936 had a bracing effect on the economics profession, particularly upon the younger faculty members and graduate students.[28]

When Eccles began his career in government at the Treasury in 1934, his ideas were far from polished and benefitted greatly from the help of a bright young economist named Lauchlin Currie, a recent refugee from Harvard, who joined the Treasury at about the same time and who shared Eccles's views.[29] Currie had lost faith in the efficacy of monetary policy under depressed economic conditions after the abortive business upturn in early 1930, and began advocating deficit spending. The senior and strictly orthodox Harvard economics faculty frowned on such heresy; by joining other young Harvard instructors early in 1934 in supporting New Deal policies, Currie made himself persona non grata. At that time the influence of what came to be called Keynesian ideas on the economics profession was insignificant. Keynes made the case for expansionary policies in *The Means to Prosperity* (1933), in a widely read open letter to the president in *The New York Times* on December 31, 1933, and in a visit to Roosevelt in the summer of 1934, but it was not until the publication of *The General Theory* in 1936 that his thesis, in full theoretical regalia, caught fire in the profession and then gradually spread to the corridors of power.

When Eccles took over as governor of the Federal Reserve Board in November 1934, he took Currie with him to be assistant director of the Division of Research and Statistics. From then until 1939, Eccles and Currie had a close partnership, linked with other New Dealers, to apply expansionary policies. Eccles was the "outside" man who made speeches and did the talking to win support for the policies. Currie was the "inside" man who provided the research and analysis, discussed the ideas with Eccles and others in the inner circle of liberal advisers, and did the writing. Eccles was the practical man who had met payrolls, thought himself allergic to theory, and never read Keynes. Currie was the brilliant academician who had to some extent anticipated Keynes. Each on his own had reached conclusions similar to those of Keynes regarding fiscal policy. The appearance of *The General Theory* provided them with assurance and confirmation. Galbraith points out that through them the Federal Reserve was the point of entry for Keynes's ideas into Washington.[30] In 1939 Currie's reputation as an effective analyst resulted in his appointment as the first professional economist on the White House staff, where he served as economic adviser to Franklin Roosevelt until 1945.

Currie developed the theoretical case in support of the New Deal macroeconomic policies. He argued that incentives for investment needed artificial stimulation and that government deficits were needed to propel the economy forward. He presented numerical estimates of the amounts of stimulus needed and suggested preferred types of spending for maximum effectiveness. Monetary and fiscal policies were necessary and complementary means for achieving economic growth and stability.

The recession of 1937–1938 was a stinging setback requiring reevaluation of New Deal policies. By the fall of 1936, at the time of Roosevelt's reelection, the economy was recovering rapidly. When the economy began suddenly to collapse in September 1937, with a particulary sharp fall in industrial output, and accompanied by a plunging stock market, the recovery program was attacked for too much or too little intervention. Currie's analysis led him to conclude that insufficient planning had been done. He viewed the recovery in 1936 as too rapid, due particularly to the large size of the net federal contribution, which was exaggerated by the bonus paid to veterans of World War I over the president's veto, and to private inventory accumulation. Then in 1937 there were declines in the elements that had been expansionary, most notably a drastic decline in the government's net contribution as tax collections rose under the Social Security Act, along with a higher level of private savings.

In his analysis of the recession of 1937—1938 Currie dealt at some length with the monetary policy explanation, the thesis that the increase in reserve requirements together with the sterilization of gold inflows by the Treasury caused or contributed to the decline. He pointed out that from 1933 to 1936 the money stock expanded rapidly. By 1936, with excess reserves exceeding $3 billion, it was prudent for the body responsible for preventing injurious credit expansion to take the precautionary step of raising legal reserve requirements. It was desirable to remove the fear of monetary inflation and inventory stockpiling. He examined the argument that the higher reserve requirements led banks to sell bonds, and then, with bond prices weak, new bond issues were discouraged and thus capital investment declined. This case fell for lack of supporting evidence. In the end Currie found monetary policy innocent of causing or abetting the recession. He admitted that, as matters turned out, the rise in reserve requirements could perfectly well have been postponed, but this was hindsight and was not evident in May 1937 when the last of the increases in reserve requirements became effective. This view that monetary policy in 1937 was not responsible for the recession is of course diametrically opposed to the interpretation of many others, including Friedman and Schwartz, who found it to have had a serious deflationary effect.

One final point. The Great Depression has been widely interpreted as demonstrating the failure of monetary policy. Not so, say the Friedmanites;

it was not tried (or not used correctly). Perhaps then it showed the failure of fiscal policy. Not so, say the Keynesians, it was not tried (or not used correctly).

Retrospective Evaluations

The events of the 1930s fundamentally altered economic thinking and policy-making. The way the Great Depression came to be understood led to a more active interventionist governmental role in economic life. With the passage of time, the depression decade has been revisited by economists, and it seems safe to say even after half a century that the work of reexamination has not ended. In 1963 Friedman and Schwartz presented a thorough study and reinterpretation of the period, challenging the views then generally accepted. In the 1970s Charles Kindleberger and Peter Temin disputed some of the Friedman/Schwartz conclusions. In 1981 papers sponsored by The Center for Research in Government Policy and Business at the University of Rochester were published under the title *The Great Depression Revisited*. Our purpose here is to pluck some of the salient points from the store of understanding and disputation to provide some indication of the recent state of informed opinion.[31]

The question of causality between money and income—do changes in money cause changes in the economy (monetary hypothesis) or do changes in the economy cause changes in money (spending hypothesis)—is the central issue addressed by Friedman and Schwartz in their study of the 1929–1931 contraction. They point out that the experience of those years strongly enhanced the view that money follows the course of business activity. It was clear that the Federal Reserve System, contrary to its intention, failed to keep the money stock from declining sharply. The system saw itself and was seen by many others to be overwhelmed by nonmonetary forces; it was considered powerless to prevent the steep decline in the money stock that resulted from the collapse of the economy. The Keynesian income–expenditure theory was advanced to explain the economy's miserable performance and to account for the failure of monetary policy. This interpretation—that money is not the causal factor but a consequence of income changes—is quite wrong according to Friedman/Schwartz.

The main conclusion reached by Friedman and Schwartz is that the 1929–1931 contraction actually strengthens the line of causality running from monetary changes to economic changes. They assert that during the contraction the Federal Reserve System could have pursued policies to keep the money stock from falling or to raise it. Such policies had been provided for when the system was founded and had been carried out in prior years. The failure to carry out such policies in a timely and sufficient manner is attributed to the problems of bureaucracy, division of power, and personalities within the Federal Reserve System. Friedman/Schwartz maintain that until late 1931 a truly expansionary monetary policy would not have conflicted with the policy of adhering to the gold standard. In their view the situation would have been better handled in the absence of the Federal Reserve System as in 1907. Initially the reaction to the bank failures would have been greater and banks would very likely have restricted convertibility of deposits into currency, but the crisis would have been shortened and economic recovery would have been possible in a few months. The experience of the 1929–1931 contraction is seen as consistent with the totality of the Friedman/Schwartz study of the whole period from 1867 to 1960. They are careful not to exaggerate the main point, but they insist on the main point.

> While the influence running from money to economic activity has been predominant, there have clearly also been influences running the other way, particularly during the shorter-run movements associated with the business cycle. . . . Changes in the money stock are therefore a consequence as well as an independent source of change in money income and prices, though, once they occur, they produce in their turn still further effects on income and prices. Mutual interaction, but with money rather clearly the senior partner in longer-run movements and in major cyclical movements, and more nearly an equal partner with money income and prices in shorter-run and milder movements—this is the generalization suggested by our evidence.[32]

In 1976 Peter Temim asked, "Did monetary forces cause the Depression?" His answer was no with respect to the crucial two-year period from the October 1929 crash to the September 1931 British departure from gold. Temin warned against drawing firm conclusions from the theories used to explain the experience of the Depression because they rely heavily on variables which cannot be observed, such as the effect of bank failures on confidence which discouraged business investment and increased the risk of holding long-term securities, and caution by businessmen induced by rapidly falling raw materials prices. He is not impressed by the Friedman/Schwartz contention that the Federal Reserve could have mitigated the severity of the Depression substantially if only it had pumped out enough high-powered money. He observes that to claim that a policy was not used does not prove that it would have been successful. On the basis of the available data, Temin undertook to compare the two main theoretical approaches and found the Keynesian spending hypothesis to be a better fit than the Friedman/Schwartz money hypothesis: "It is more plausible to believe that the Depression was the result of a drop in autonomous expenditures, particularly consumption, than the result of autonomous bank failures."[33] While Temin favors the spending hypothesis, his emphasis on a shift in the consumption function as the key element is a noteworthy variation on the Keynesian theme.

Critics of Temin consider his version of the Friedman/Schwartz monetarist hypothesis to be in the straw person category.[34] Friedman/Schwartz contend that the Depression would not have been so severe if the Federal Reserve had increased the monetary base sufficiently to compensate for the drop in the deposit/currency ratio. But this is not what concerns Temin, so he largely ignores it—his question is the direction of initial causation. Temin is faulted for misunderstanding the monetary hypothesis by falsely assuming it to hold that explicit restrictive action was taken from 1929 to 1931, something that Friedman/Schwartz clearly deny.

The range and complexity of the analytical discussion of the period of the Great Depression precludes an attempt to summarize the present state of the controversy. In the hands of specialists the field is esoteric and requires substantial theoretical preparation. It is possible, however, to give some indication of the broad picture.[35]

The monetary (monetarist) explanation makes the money stock the prime mover of shifts in aggregate demand. Changes in velocity are fully acknowledged but it is emphasized that any major change in velocity is almost certainly preceded by a prior change in money; that is, if the rate of growth of M rises, then V will rise; if the rate of growth of M falls, or if M decreases, then V will fall. The responses of velocity to changing monetary conditions vary through time due to changes in socioeconomic conditions, including random fluctuations. If the Federal Reserve authorities had responded to the stock market crash by pressing firmly and persistently on the money accelerator, they could substantially have mitigated the decline in velocity. Leading advocates of the monetary account take the position that it gives a better explanation than the nonmonetary account, although it has not been able to provide a complete understanding. The various nonmonetary factors are not considered to have been demonstrated as valid, so while they have not been proven wrong they are not accepted.

A diametrically opposed viewpoint rejects monetary influences during the 1929–1931 period and makes nonmonetary causes responsible for the economic collapse. According to this thesis, autonomous declines in spending on output caused a decrease in velocity. Then, as a result of the nonmonetary shocks to the economy and the fall in V, there followed an endogenous reduction in M.

An intermediate or eclectic view incorporates both monetary and nonmonetary factors in causal roles. A relatively small decline in the money stock during the early stages of the Depression was accompanied by a considerably larger drop in velocity. Changes in M fail to provide an adequate explanation; it is necessary to recognize and identify autonomous changes in spending to interpret the economy's performance satisfactorily, for an exogenous change in velocity requires an explanation in terms of nonmonetary variables. The quantity theory alone is inadequate or insufficient; to explain nonmonetary forces it is necessary to study categories of expenditure, a process for which the Keynesian income—expenditure approach was designed.

A full explanation may be beyond the grasp of researchers. One reason why the explanations are incomplete may be the failure to allow for international monetary influences through changes in the exchange rate, capital flows, and liquidity crises.[36] The idea that the Federal Reserve authorities were powerless to influence economic events has been rejected. That the Federal Reserve was solely responsible for the Depression is also a highly doubtful thesis. In other words, money mattered, but it was not all that mattered.

5
Financing World War II, 1939–1945

> In a national emergency of this magnitude, sound banking principles, like many peacetime freedoms and immunities, are likely to be subordinated to the paramount national purpose.
>
> E.A. Goldenweiser[1]

Between September 1, 1939, when World War II began with the German land and air assault on Poland, and December 7, 1941, when the Japanese attacked Pearl Harbor and the United States entered the war, monetary policy did not change significantly. During the period of active United States war participation of three years and nine months—V–E (Victory in Europe) Day was on May 8, 1945, and V–J (Victory over Japan) Day was on September 2, 1945—ordinary monetary policy was suspended as the Federal Reserve System volunteered to serve the war effort as a sort of financial supply corps for the Treasury. World War II required a much longer and greater national effort than World War I. In World War I the United States remained neutral for the first thirty-two months and participated as a belligerent for nineteen months, whereas in World War II the period of neutrality was twenty-seven months and that of active participation forty-five months.

When war broke out in 1939, the monetary gold stock of $16.6 billion was more than double what it was immediately ater the devaluation of the dollar on January 1, 1934 ($7.4 billion). War brought a more rapid inflow of gold, raising the gold stock to $22.7 billion by the end of 1941. Member bank excess reserves were more than $5 billion late in 1939, rose to an all-time peak of almost $7 billion at the end of 1940, and, even after a decline due partly to a rise in reserve requirements to the legal maximum in November 1941, were $3 billion at the time the United States entered the war. The M1 money stock grew rapidly from $35 billion in September 1939 to $48 billion at the end of 1941, due to the rise in the gold stock; Federal Reserve Bank credit was essentially flat. On the whole the open-market and gold policies begun in 1933 were continued until the attack on Pearl Harbor. There is similarity between the periods of neutrality in both world wars, for the bulk of the growth in the money stock during the neutrality period of World War I was also due to an increase in the gold stock.

Although the Federal Reserve System did not use open-market operations for the purpose of affecting member bank reserves to any important extent during the period of neutrality, it intervened in the market to prevent large fluctuations in the prices of government securities. The maintenance of an "orderly market" was not a new objective—it had been on the Federal Reserve's agenda since the mid-thirties, and some securities were purchased in 1937 for this purpose. With the threat of war growing stronger, the Federal Open Market Committee got ready to intervene to maintain orderly market conditions by authorizing its executive committee in April 1939 to buy as much as $500 million of government securities if there should be a severe market disturbance. Following the outbreak of war, the system did buy securities of nearly this amount during September to steady the market. The securities were sold off during the remainder of 1939. Similar but much smaller support operations were carried out in the spring of 1940 when German forces invaded Denmark, Norway, and the Low Countries, and again right after Pearl Harbor. The policy of maintaining orderly market conditions kept the bond portfolios of banks from falling very much and also helped to maintain a generally stable capital market in the interest of encouraging economic recovery.[2]

When the war started, the danger of inflation was minimal, for there were still nine million unemployed and real national output was only some 5 percent above 1929. Wholesale and consumer prices were stable and still well below the levels of a decade earlier. A huge amount of unutilized productive capacity was available waiting for increased demand to put it to use. The impact of the war on the economy was modest until the German attack on western Europe in the spring of 1940 and the subsequent fall of France in June. War orders then poured in, mainly from Britain, and at the same time the United States overcame its hesitation about rearming and set in motion a large defense program. With this strong increase in demand, industrial production and real national income rose rapidly as idle human and material resources were absorbed in the formation of what was to become, in Roosevelt's words, "the great arsenal of democracy." To pay for their imports from the United States the British used up over $2.5 billion of gold, dollar balances, and U.S. securities. To enable the British and allied governments to sustain their purchases, the United States began a program of lend–lease in March 1941 through which the United States government eventually paid for about $50 billion of exported war materiel. Unlike the government loans that met a similar need during World War I, lend–lease obviated the problem of war debt repayments that had embittered international relations after World War I. The start of lend–lease marked the end of the gold inflow to the United States. As productive capacity began to be approached in certain industries and as bottlenecks appeared in the supply of various factors of production, pressure on prices began to be felt; by 1941 price inflation became a matter of concern. Inflation was not seen as a serious imminent threat, however, for the long depression has accustomed people to deflation, and the new "theory of secular stagnation" advanced by Professor Alvin H. Hansen, the influential American convert to the new economics of Keynes, held that a chronic lack of demand would make frequent artificial monetary/ fiscal stimulants necessary in the future to keep the economy from running down. However, as the pace of inflation quickened, the large amount of excess monetary reserves posed a potential threat to central bank policy. In response to this situation the Federal Reserve took several steps. It absorbed a small amount of bank reserves in the second half of 1940 by selling securities. On September 1, 1941, the Board of Governors, acting under an executive order of the president, imposed Regulation W, a means of controlling consumer credit by applying minimum down payments and maximum maturities to installment loans on certain goods such as automobiles, refrigerators, and so on, the production of which would divert resources from military purposes. Then on November 1, 1941, the board raised reserve requirements to the maximum level under the existing law.[3] These actions by the Federal Reserve System did not appreciably restrict the expansionary monetary potential.

With the entry of the United States into the war, a new and fundamentally different monetary policy was adopted and then adhered to for the duration of the conflict. The theme was announced the day after Pearl Harbor by a statement of the Board of Governors:

> The System is prepared to use its powers to assure that an ample supply of funds is available at all times for financing the war effort and to exert its influence toward maintaining conditions in the United States Government security market that are satisfactory from the standpoint of the Government's requirements.[4]

The key step to implement the wartime support policy came in March 1942 when the Federal Open Market Committee, as a result of a conference with Treasury officials, agreed to provide the reserves necessary for financing the war. The chosen method of providing the reserves and thereby facilitating Treasury financing was open-market purchases of government securities sufficient to maintain "about the then existing curve of rates." In other words, the Federal Reserve System undertook to peg the market for government securities so that the market prices of securities could not fall below the desired level. By buying the securities, the Federal Reserve added to member bank reserves, enabling the banks to purchase government securities for their own account. Such purchases then added to bank deposits, thereby making funds available to nonbank investors for subscriptions to offerings of Treasury obligations.[5] In addition to open-market operations, the Federal

Reserve was authorized to make direct purchases from the Treasury up to a ceiling of $5 billion under legislation adopted in 1942 and subsequently extended. Unlimited authority to make such purchases, given in the original Federal Reserve Act, had been eliminated in the Banking Act of 1935.[6]

By committing itself to a policy of supporting the government securities market, the Federal Reserve System abandoned control of the money supply. The initiative in the open-market operations, no longer held by the system, was now in the hands of the holders of government securities. This meant that bank reserves would be created whenever the holders of government securities sold them to the Federal Reserve Banks, whose demand for them was perfectly elastic at the support price. Thus the process added a flow of excess reserves to the banking system, on the basis of which a multiple amount of bank deposits was created. The Federal Reserve System was well aware of the inflationary potential its policy was creating, but it gave first priority to meeting the financial needs of the Treasury. It could not have been otherwise, for the nation would hardly have accepted a policy that denied funds required to finance an all-out war seen as necessary for national survival. Inflation was an evil but clearly the lesser evil compared to a limited war effort and possible defeat. Although inflation could not be avoided, neither could it be ignored. The Board of Governors identified the principal weapons against inflation as taxation, savings, and direct controls over goods, prices, and wages.

The Treasury had a tremendous need for funds to carry out the war effort. To appreciate the magnitude of federal financial operations, it helps to relate them, as Lester Chandler has done, to previous experience:

> During the six years following June 1940 the federal government spent $383,372 million. This was more than twice as much as it had spent during the preceding 150 years, nearly 100 times as much as it spent during the Civil War, and 10 times as much as it spent during World War I. Its annual spendings at the peak of the war effort were greater than total spendings for output during any year between 1929 and 1940.[7]

The extent to which war financing is inflationary depends on the methods used. The following list of sources of funds ranging from least to most inflationary provides the basis for the strategy underlying the approach taken by the Treasury in consultation with the Federal Reserve System.

1. Taxation. Spending by government replaces spending by the public, to the extent the public would have spent. No new money is created.

2. Borrowing of money income that the public would have spent. Similar to taxation except that lenders have a future claim for repayment.

3. Borrowing of money that would have remained idle. No new money is created but velocity rises.

4. Borrowing from commercial banks. New money is created.

5. Borrowing from the central bank. Bank reserves as well as new money are created.[8]

How did the Treasury raise the huge sums it needed? Of the total of roughly $380 billion, 40 percent was raised by taxes, 35 percent came through borrowing from nonbank sources, and 25 percent by borrowing from banks, including the Federal Reserve System. Between December 1939 and December 1945 Federal Reserve Bank credit expanded from $2.6 billion to $25.1 billion.[9]

Interest rates were kept low throughout the war. The Federal Reserve System maintained a pattern of yields on government securities ranging from ⅜ of 1 percent on ninety-day Treasury bills to 2½ percent on long-term bonds. The fact that these securities could be sold at the support price made them perfectly liquid and the equivalent of interest-bearing money. The rate of 2½ percent was agreed upon by the officials of the Treasury and Federal Reserve as the crucial rate in the pattern. Most of the officials wanted to have a public statement establishing the rate for the duration of the war, but Secretary of the Treasury Morganthau vetoed the idea.[10]

The discount rate at the Federal Reserve Bank of New York was left at 1 percent, with a special rate of ½ percent on advances secured by short-term government securities. This was of no importance; the banks could readily get reserves by selling off government securities and had no incentive or need to go into debt.

The M1 money stock increased from September 1939 to December 1941 by 37 percent and more than doubled (111 percent increase) during the period of active U.S. participation in the war. Over the six years from September 1939 to September 1945 the M1 money stock nearly tripled. Increases in M2 were not quite as pronounced for the six year period. Velocity of spending increased rather moderately between 1939 and 1942 as the money stock increased, but during the remaining war years it dropped steadily. In 1945 the M1 and M2 velocities were about 25 percent lower than in 1942. Money stock and velocity data are shown in table 5–1.

As in the first World War, during World War II the Federal Reserve System served as the Treasury's agent for selling newly issued securities and used its powers of money creation to insure its success. The tactics were different but the effect was the same in each case. During World War I the system provided reserves to the banks by discounting bills of the member banks (usually secured by government securities), but it held few government securities itself. During World War II the system increased its outstanding

Table 5–1
Money Stock and Velocity of Money, 1939, 1941, 1942, 1945

Money Stock	September 1939	December 1941		September 1945
M1	$35.1 billion	$48.2 billion		$101.8 billion
M2	$50.2 billion	$64.1 billion		$131.0 billion
Velocity[a]	1939	1941	1942	1945
M1	2.21	2.17	2.37	1.75
M2	1.52	1.61	1.84	1.37

Adapted from Milton Friedman and Anna Jacobson Schwartz, *A Monetary History of the United States 1867–1960*, a study by the National Bureau of Economic Research. Princeton: Princeton University Press, 1963, pp. 715–717, 774.

[a]Velocity refers to money income divided by the money stock.

debt primarily by purchasing government securities, with only small amounts of discounts. The result again was to expand the monetary base, providing the basis for a large rise in the money stock. In addition to adding to the reserves of the banking system, the increase in Federal Reserve credit served to meet the public's demand for more coin and currency and to offset a gold outflow of $2.7 billion. The excess reserves of the member banks fell to about $1 billion during the war. The desire of bankers to hold large amounts of excess reserves now ended. As the banks bought government securities they acquired income-earning assets which did not constitute legal reserves but which were as liquid as money and readily convertible into reserves.[11]

During the World War II years the deposit/reserve ratio rose, adding to the money stock, while the deposit/currency ratio fell, having the opposite effect. While the direction of movement in these ratios was the same as in World War I, their relative importance differed substantially. In World War II the deposit/reserve ratio was the much more significant factor.[12]

War is notorious for its inflationary effects, but these need not be concurrent with the period of hostilities. Prices rose more gradually during the war years than during the years immediately before and after. The inflationary impact of World War II was largely delayed until the postwar period. During the period of U.S. neutrality (1939–1941), wholesale prices rose 23 percent, compared to 14 percent for the longer period of war participation. On an annual rate basis the rise from August 1939 through November 1941 was 9 percent, or double the 4 percent annual rate for the period from November 1941 through August 1945.[13] Viewed in the context of the period from 1939 to mid–1948 when the war-induced inflation peaked, the rise in prices during the war was surprisingly modest. From May 1942 to the end of 1945, the cost-of-living index went up only sixteen points, or about a fifth of the total rise for the whole period. For wholesale prices the proportion was only about one-tenth.[14] The inflation that was building through the financing of massive deficits was repressed by wartime direct controls over resources, rationing of scarce goods, and price and wage controls. Income receivers added to their liquid assets of money balances and securities because many consumer and producer goods were simply not available. Government price controls provided assurance that money would retain its value reasonably well throughout the dark night of wartime. Money balances accumulated during the war would be available to spend for all sorts of goods that would again become available when at last the sweet day of peace arrived. With life and liberty more secure, it would be most agreeable to have some money with which to pursue happiness. To some extent the price indexes understated the degree of the inflation, due to the lower quality of some goods and to practices designed to escape the price control rules either legally or illegally (black market).

In 1945 Congress reduced the monetary authority of the executive branch. It eliminated the extraordinary powers granted in 1933 to the president, acting through the Treasury, to change the value of gold and silver and to issue $3 billion of United States notes.

6
Post–World War II Adjustment, 1945–1951

The coming of peace brought the opportunity for a fresh approach to our nation's economy after the trauma of depression and war. A new attitude, based on the belief that the market economy would respond favorably to a policy of enlightened government intervention of a limited and pragmatic nature, became prominent and provided the intellectual and political climate for legislation proclaiming a positive role for public policy. Reflecting the ideological shift away from laissez-faire induced by the experience of the 1930s, and apprehensive of how the economy would perform if government withdrew more or less completely from the economic playing field now that hostilities were over, Congress enacted the Employment Act of 1946. For the first time in our national history the government assumed responsibility for the management of the economy with particular emphasis on the maintenance of employment.

> The Congress declares that it is the continuing policy and responsibility of the Federal Government to use all practicable means consistent with its needs and obligations and other essential considerations of national policy, with the assistance and cooperation of industry, agriculture, labor, and State and local governments, to coordinate and utilize all its plans, functions, and resources for the purpose of creating and maintaining, in a manner calculated to foster and promote free competitive enterprise and the general welfare, conditions under which there will be afforded useful employment opportunities, including self-employment, for those able, willing, and seeking work, and to promote maximum employment, production, and purchasing power.[1]

The act created new governmental structures for monitoring, analyzing, and reporting on the economy, with the expectation that policies would be forthcoming appropriate to future needs and circumstances. Congress provided itself with the Joint Economic Committee, and the president was given a Council of Economic Advisers. Since the Employment Act of 1946 states objectives for the nation, the Federal Reserve System is implicitly bound by it, but the objectives, of a broad and general nature, did not add to or subtract from the central bank's role in any noticeable way.

In the five-year period immediately following World War II, monetary policy was constrained by the fiscal/monetary policies that had been used to finance the war. Before a transition to a new peacetime mode could be effected, the start of the Korean War in June 1950 added a strong new dimension and urgency to monetary issues. The result was a major controversy between the Federal Reserve System and the Treasury in 1950–1951 that culminated in a landmark decision called the Accord which was announced on March 4, 1951, and which marked a major turning point in monetary policy.

There were two principal monetary legacies from World War II. One was inflation stemming from the huge war-induced accumulation of liquid assets; by mid-1948 this inflationary storm had blown itself out. The second legacy was the continuation of the pegging policy by the Federal Reserve System. With the start of the Korean War the system faced up to the inflationary potential of continuing its policy of support of the market for government securities dating from 1942, and went to the mat with the Treasury over this crucial issue. It is around these core problems that the following discussion is organized.

The 1946–1948 Surge of Inflation

At the beginning of 1945, as the end of World War II approached, economic activity peaked and then contracted slightly until October; a strong three-year expansion followed until November 1948. Contrary to widely held expectations, no depression occurred. The Office of War Mobilization and Reconversion projected unemployment of between 7,400,000 and 8,300,000 in 1946,[2] but unemployment kept below 2,500,000. Instead of sinking into the economic equivalent of Bunyan's Slough of Despond, economic activity turned out to be vigorous. It had been thought that the drastic decline in government war expenditures would bring on a painfully sluggish transition period until private expenditure could be rallied, but in fact expenditures for consumption, private investment, and exports were much greater than anticipated. Contrary to previous postwar experiences—the sharp collapse of 1920–1921, for example—the transition from war to peace was surprisingly smooth.[3]

The postwar inflation started slowly: by June 1946 the cost of living index was a mere 3 percent higher than the V–J Day level. Prices had been held in check during the war by direct controls which were in the process of gradual relaxation. It would of course take time for the production of civilian goods to fill the shortages resulting from years of lost output when resources were directed to military purposes. But with the war over, there was public and congressional impatience with controls, and Congress allowed most wage and price controls to expire on June 30, 1946. After this the smouldering inflation quickly flared up as people sought to convert money and near-money into goods and services. Wholesale prices during 1946 increased more than for all of 1939–1945. The inflationary means were created during the war, but the effects were largely delayed until after the war, with a peak in prices coming in August 1948.

> In short, more than 60 percent of the entire increase in the cost of living between 1939 and late 1948, and nearly 70 percent of the total rise of wholesale prices, occurred after the end of the war when government spendings had fallen far below their wartime levels and federal deficits were changed to surpluses.[4]

During the war, people saved an unusually large share of their incomes; basic consumer goods were rationed to provide for equitable distribution and there was not much else to buy.[5] By the end of the war, liquid asset holdings of the private sector (excluding financial institutions) were more than triple the prewar level, as shown in table 6–1.

The Washington economists responsible for forecasting postwar economic activity used prewar data to derive a consumption function, computed a multiplier, and made estimates for investment spending, government spending, and so forth. Their GNP prediction for 1946 proved to be far below the actual level, much to the benefit of the nation but embarrassment

Table 6–1
Estimated Liquid Asset Holdings of Individuals and Businesses,[a] 1939, 1945
($ billion)

	1939[b]	1945[b]
Currency	5.8	25.5
Demand deposits	20.9	60.2
Time deposits	26.3	47.7
Savings and loan shares	4.0	7.2
U.S. government securities	12.0	86.9
Total	69.0	227.5

Adapted from Lester V. Chandler, *Inflation in the United States 1940–1948.* New York: Harper and Brothers, 1951, p. 79.

[a]Holdings of banks and other financial institutions are excluded.

[b]End of year.

of the forecasters. With the benefit of hindsight their big mistake became apparent: the consumption function had shifted upward as people drew on their vast holdings of liquid assets. The pent-up demand for consumer goods made consumer spending much larger relative to income than in prewar years for which data were available.

Considering the circumstances, the postwar inflation might have been considerably greater than it was. The rise in prices and incomes between 1946 and 1948 was attributable more to a modest rise in velocity than to a growth of the money stock in those years. V1 grew by 14 percent from its extraordinarily low level of 1946 but still in 1948 was far below the rates of the thirties; M1 was only 4 percent higher in June 1948 than in June 1946. Since the Federal Reserve System had not regained control of the money stock, its slow growth seems rather unexpected, perhaps even mysterious.

> The foremost monetary puzzle of the immediate postwar period is why the money stock did not grow at a very much more rapid pace. This sharp difference from its behavior after World War I, when the most rapid rate of increase in the stock of money came after the end of the wartime deficits, does not reflect any fundamental difference in monetary policy. After both wars, the Reserve System continued the wartime policy of providing all the high-powered money demanded at a fixed rate: in World War I, through maintaining an unchanged discount rate; in World War II, through supporting the price of government securities at unchanged levels. And the reversal of the gold flows, from an outflow after World War I to an inflow after World War II, should have fostered a more rapid rate of monetary expansion after the later war.[6]

Both the low rate of increase in M1 and the small rise in V1 indicate that the public was willing to hold large amounts of liquid assets at low rates of interest. If the public had wished to sell off more of its income-earning liquid assets, the prices of government securities would have tended to fall, causing the Federal Reserve to buy more of them, thus boosting the monetary base and the money stock. If the public had wished to part with more of its money balances by spending for output, velocity would have risen more. But why should people have been content to hold an abnormally high ratio of liquid assets to income? More precisely, why was the public willing to reduce the ratio of its money and other liquid assets to its income so gradually? If it had been impatient to do so, the increases in the money stock and inflation would have been more pronounced. One reason the public did not spend more was the substantial government cash surpluses of $5.7 billion and $8.0 billion in calendar years 1947 and 1948. A second reason was the expectation of a major postwar slump accompanied by falling prices. Although inflation was indeed rife from mid-1946 to mid-1948, it was widely viewed as the ride up on the roller coaster which would soon come hurtling down. If one thinks that prices will soon be plunging and jobs will be hard to get, there is good reason to hang on to cash balances and other liquid assets. Inflation during 1946–1948 caused concern, but deflation was expected to follow, and this expectation moderated the inflation.[7]

Removing the Peg

Adoption of the policy of supporting the government securities market in 1942 was quickly and easily done, and tended to create a harmonious "partnership" between the Federal Reserve System and the Treasury. Ending that policy after the war was a slow process that became an acrimonious struggle before a denouement was reached in the form of the Accord of March 4, 1951. In its later stages the dispute between the Treasury and the Federal Reserve System involved the president and Congress—it was an acute, even dramatic, struggle over the restoration of monetary control to the central bank. We will trace the relationship between the Federal Reserve and the Treasury from 1945 to 1951 to see how it was affected by changing circumstances until the Federal Reserve once again was in a position to carry out a flexible monetary policy of its own making.

During the war and for a time afterward, the Federal Reserve System willingly supported the government securities market, viewing its cooperation with the Treasury as necessary to meet urgent political and economic requirements of the times. But inflation and the specter of much worse inflation concerned the Federal Reserve authorities, understandably so of course, since they are traditionally and primarily responsible for preserving the value of the dollar. A central banker who isn't concerned about inflation is like a physician who isn't concerned about infection.

Early in the postwar period the Federal Reserve moved gingerly away from its wartime stance, inching its way toward a more independent policy, with the Treasury urging caution.[8] In April 1946 the Federal Reserve System, against the wishes of the Treasury, eliminated the preferential discount rate on bank borrowings collateralized by government securities. On July 10, 1947, the first change was made in the pattern of rates on government securities when the Treasury bill rate was allowed to rise above its posted ⅜ percent level. The Treasury agreed with this move apparently because the Federal Reserve System, on April 23, 1947, adopted a policy of paying about 90 percent of the net earnings of the Federal Reserve Banks to the Treasury.[9] Shortly thereafter the rate on certificates was also raised. These relatively minor rate changes were adjustments in and not a repudiation of the policy of a fixed pattern of rates. The long-term 2½ percent rate was still sacrosanct. In 1948 Allan Sproul, president of the Federal Reserve Bank of New

York, testified in favor of continued support of the market, and in 1949 the chairman of the Board of Governors, Thomas B. McCabe, confirmed the policy before a congressional committee.[10]

Continuation of the pegging policy clearly suited the Treasury's needs by holding down the interest cost on the national debt and easing the problem of rolling over (refinancing) the debt. But why, in view of its need to regain control over the money stock to ward off inflation, was the Federal Reserve willing to continue the wartime policy for some years into peacetime? Briefly and starkly put, the central bankers did not want to risk precipitating an economic collapse. The system's leaders maintained that they still had multiple objectives to meet, one of the most important being stability in the market for government securities. If market participants were to conclude that government securities would fall in value, financial institutions would experience an erosion of their assets, with the danger of a wave of bankruptcies. Credit might become extremely tight and costly. It was not primarily to assist the Treasury in its refunding operations that the Federal Reserve authorities continued to be so "cooperative," but to avoid serious damage to the national economy. They feared that a serious decline in production and employment would follow from a vigorous policy of credit contraction. Their statements imply no middle way between (a) supporting the market at stable prices and (b) withdrawing support regardless of what might happen to government securities prices and interest rates. It was a case of all or nothing. Presumably a policy of raising long-term interest rates gradually was viewed as inadequate to halt inflation but more than adequate to frighten bondholders into massive selling.

In August 1948, after the surge in the price level, Congress gave the Federal Reserve System temporary authority to increase reserve requirements and to restore direct control over consumer credit. Since prices peaked that same month, the timing was hardly ideal. The following year when Chairman McCabe asked Congress for authority to continue these powers, and to extend the reserve requirements to all insured banks, Congress turned thumbs down and allowed the temporary authority to lapse on June 30, 1949. By then prices were falling, so Congress saw no need to allow the Federal Reserve to keep the special inflation-fighting gear which had been provided when inflation was perceived as a present danger.

With the economy weakening in 1949, the Federal Reserve System shifted to a policy of increasing the supply of money. Now, for a time, the system could support lower interest rates; the Federal Open Market Committee announced that it was no longer committed to a fixed pattern of rates, meaning that rates could fall. But while the Federal Reserve would be flexible in allowing rates on government securities to fall during recession, would it pursue a symmetrical policy involving tighter money and higher interest rates when the economy became bullish again? Senator Paul Douglas of Illinois, a distinguished University of Chicago economist, conducted searching hearings on monetary policy in 1949 and questioned Chairman McCabe concerning the extent to which the Federal Reserve System's new policy meant "flexibility both ways." McCabe said that the Federal Reserve System did indeed mean flexibility both ways, but he made it clear too that the continuing partnership between the Treasury and the Federal Reserve System required the Federal Reserve to convince the Treasury of any future need for rising rates. Yet while Treasury–Federal Reserve agreement and cooperation were stressed in public statements, basic considerations were driving a wedge between the two agencies. The Treasury's needs regarding debt management inhibited the Federal Reserve System from utilizing open-market operations to carry out its fundamental responsibility of controlling credit. This caused the system to be increasingly restive, and by 1950, as we shall see, it decided that it was necessary to break free of its bonds (or of the Treasury's bonds!).

The economic contraction that began in November 1948 did not develop into a depression or severe recession; the serious postwar slump had not just been late in arriving, it never materialized. By October 1949 the mild recession touched its low point, and a vigorous four-year recovery began. In 1950, however, a deus ex machina appeared: North Korea invaded South Korea on June 25, and three days later United States forces were ordered to aid South Korea.

The outbreak of the Korean War had a profound shock effect on the American economy. Coming when the memory of World War II was still green, and with the possibility that it might escalate into World War III, it touched off a speculative boom as consumers and producing firms, anticipating future shortages, bought all sorts of items—finished goods, intermediate goods, and raw materials. Wholesale prices rose by 16 percent from June 1950 to February 1951. Velocity rose rapidly as holders of liquid assets used them to add to their stocks of physical assets. As noted earlier, before 1950 the widespread anticipation of a major fall in prices had acted to restrain spending. As time passed, and with only a slight fall in the price level during the recession of 1948–1949, the basis for this expectation was eroded. The start of the Korean War led instead to expectations of scarcity and rising prices, so the psychological inhibitions against parting with liquid assets were replaced by incentives to do so. The surging demand triggered by the new war became the basis for severely strained relations between the Federal Reserve and the Treasury.

The officials of the Federal Reserve and the Treasury now had to set policy to finance the government's activities under obviously inflationary circumstances as military action expanded rapidly in an atmosphere of great uncertainty. The nation's resources were close to full employment in mid–1950, unlike the situation in 1939–1940. The two agencies could not reconcile their approaches: the result was serious disagreement that became public in August 1950 and persisted until March 1951. The Federal Reserve authorities decided that they could no longer subordinate monetary policy to the financing and debt-management needs of the Treasury by supporting a fixed pattern of interest rates. In effect they issued a declaration of independence. The discount rate was raised in August 1950 and at the same time the Board of Governors and the Federal Open Market Committee announced their readiness "to use all the means at their command to restrain further expansion of bank credit consistent with the policy of maintaining orderly conditions in the government securities market."[11] They added that restraint was essential in the area of monetary and credit policy. The Federal Reserve timed its announcement shortly before the Treasury was to announce the terms of a large refunding operation, thereby putting pressure on the Treasury to set higher rates on the new securities than on the maturing securities. When the Treasury refused to be swayed and maintained the existing rates for its new securities, the Federal Reserve felt compelled to buy a major fraction of them to avoid having the Treasury offering overwhelmingly rejected by the market, but at the same time the Federal Reserve sold comparable securities from its large portfolio at higher yields. The dispute was thus evident in the market—the Fed had not backed down but had forced the controversy into the open. The "partners" could no longer settle their differences unobtrusively behind closed doors. As yet, however, the Federal Reserve limited itself to a moderate rise in short-term rates and held firmly to maintaining the 2½ percent rate on the longest-term bonds. Relations between the Treasury and the Federal Reserve continued to be strained for the remainder of 1950.

By early 1951 the key 2½ percent rate became a pivotal issue. After a meeting early in January of Treasury Secretary Snyder and Chairman McCabe with President Truman, Snyder stated publicly that the 2½ percent rate had been agreed upon for future Treasury financing. Shortly afterward both Sproul and Eccles openly expressed objections. Snyder was roundly criticized in the financial press for trying to intimidate Federal Reserve officials. The leading figures in the two agencies became deadlocked in a hostile atmosphere, unable to resolve their differences as the Treasury faced major funding needs. President Truman intervened by meeting with the Federal Open Market Committee at the White House on January 31, 1951. A White House press release followed, stating that the Federal Reserve authorities had pledged to support the stability of government securities for the duration of the emergency, meaning (according to a Treasury statement) stabilizing the market prices of government securities at existing levels. Some members of the Federal Open Market Committee, notably Eccles, made known that they had a different interpretation. The FOMC sent a letter to the president stating that they had assured him of their cooperation with the Treasury so as to maintain public confidence in the securities but omitting reference to a pattern of rates. Press discussion continued around a theme of emasculation of the Federal Reserve's independence, and the mood continued to be rancorous. Then on February 19 Chairman McCabe took the bull by the horns by advising the Treasury that the Federal Reserve was "no longer willing to maintain the existing situation in the Government security market."[12] Congress, with Senator Douglas in the lead, indicated support for the Federal Reserve. The president set up a new ad hoc study committee, but the Federal Reserve and the Treasury avoided "outside" interference by reaching a settlement on their own in the form of the statement below issued on March 4, 1951. The accord is of great significance because it brought an end to Federal Reserve support of the government securities market at pegged prices and enabled the Federal Reserve to resume a truly independent monetary policy. Just what policies would emerge remained to be worked out, as we shall see in the next chapter.

> The Treasury and the Federal Reserve System have reached full accord with respect to debt-management and monetary policies to be pursued in furthering their common purpose to assure the successful financing of the Government's requirements and at the same time, to minimize monetization of the public debt.[13]

The buying binge and price inflation associated with the start of the Korean War subsided early in 1951. Consumer prices rose much more gradually and wholesale prices fell as anticipated shortages did not appear. Perhaps also, inflationary expectations were diminished by the well-publicized behavior of the Federal Reserve System as related to the accord.

To summarize the general behavior of the money stock over the five years beginning in mid–1946 it is convenient to divide the period into three parts. During the first eighteen months (June 1946–January 1948) M1 grew by 5.4 percent. It fell gradually for (almost) two years (January 1948–January 1950) by approximately 2 percent. Then for the last eighteen months (January 1950–June 1951) it rose by 6.6 percent. Between 1946 and 1948, velocity of M1 rose by roughly 14 percent, fell by 3 percent from 1948 to 1949, and increased by 19 percent between 1949 and 1951. For the whole five years from June 1946 to June 1951, the M1 money stock increased by only 10 percent; between 1946 and 1951 the velocity of M1 increased by 32 percent. Table 6–2 presents the data.

Table 6–2
Money Stock and Velocity of Money, 1946–1951

Money Stock	June 1946		January 1948	January 1950		June 1951
M1	$106.8 billion		$112.6 billion	$110.3 billion		$117.6 billion
M2	$139.3 billion		$147.9 billion	$146.3 billion		$154.0 billion
Velocity[a]	1946	1947	1948	1949	1950	1951
M1	1.52	1.62	1.73	1.68	1.89	2.00
M2	1.16	1.23	1.31	1.27	1.43	1.53

Adapted from Milton Friedman and Anna Jacobson Schwartz, *A Monetary History of the United States 1867–1960,* a study by the National Bureau of Economic Research. Princeton: Princeton University Press, 1963, pp. 718–719, 774.

[a]Velocity refers to money income divided by the money stock.

7

An Era of Relative Calm, 1951–1965

In retrospect, the period 1951–1965 was one of relative calm. Compared with the preceding and succeeding periods—with the earlier problems associated with World War II that culminated in the Accord of 1951, and with the later difficulties let loose by the escalation of the Vietnam War—this decade and a half overlapping the Eisenhower and Kennedy years was quite tractable. These years have come to be viewed nostalgically as highly successful for overall economic policy and performance. The combination of a good rate of economic growth with relatively low unemployment and inflation provided strong evidence of the restored health of capitalism. An economic system seen as seriously (by some even fatally) flawed in the thirties now demonstrated fresh vitality in the United States and in Europe as well. "The twenty years from 1948 through 1967 may well be celebrated by historians as the most benign era in the history of the industrial economy, as also of economics."[1]

Yet there was considerable contention over monetary policy during these years, and many an arrow was aimed at the Federal Reserve System. The economy grew in a moderately undulatory manner not unlike its performance from 1922 to 1929, but of course without falling off a cliff as in 1929. There were three cyclical peaks and troughs in the 1951–1965 era, with the peaks coming in July 1953, August 1957, and April 1960. A disturbing feature of the pattern of growth was the progressive reduction in the length of the expansion phase of the cycle.

By 1960 the trend of shortening expansions became a matter of national concern. Even though the economy was growing most of the time and the contractions were relatively mild, growth lagged relative to that of major foreign countries. The advice of the legendary baseball pitcher Satchel Paige not to look back because someone might be gaining on you was not generally thought sage. Particular attention in the economic regatta was focused on the race between the USSR and the United States. The USSR, although far behind, was rowing fast and rowing continuously, whereas the United States would row for a while, then rest on its oars for a while, with an "unfavorable" trend in the row–rest ratio. "Until the 1960's, the Soviet economy grew rapidly, and some feared that the Soviet Union would overcome and surpass American economic production by 1980."[2] The fact that between 1956 and 1961 the real GNP of the USSR grew at a rate estimated to be triple that for the United States made Khrushchev's threat to bury us economically seem credible. Such fears turned out to be groundless as the Soviet tempo later tailed off, but at the time the outcome was not clear.

The Fed Returns to the Driver's Seat

With their freedom to conduct monetary policy restored by the accord, the Federal Reserve authorities had to decide how best to use their power. They were anxious to effect a smooth transition that would avoid potential problems. The system quickly abandoned fixed price supports for government securities but did not withdraw completely from the market. Sudden and complete withdrawal might have resulted in panicky collapse, which in turn could well have spread to the market for private obligations and so undercut the economy. Nor could the Federal Reserve ignore the Treasury's financing operations to the point of failure of a new issue and possible default on a portion of the national debt. Therefore the Federal Reserve moved cautiously toward greater market flexibility from March 1951 to March 1953. Immediately after abandoning pegging, it described its policy as one of maintaining an orderly market, which was succeeded by a policy of greater tolerance of market fluctuation, referred to as preventing a disorderly market. The Federal Reserve thus extricated itself gradually from market participation except as necessary to provide an adequate monetary base and meet emergency situations.

Under the leadership of William McChesney Martin, Jr., who succeeded McCabe as chairman of the Board of Governors on April 2, 1951, the system chose to limit itself as much as possible to one policy instrument, open-market operations, and to limit itself further by concentrating on Treasury bills in what came to be known as the "bills only" or "bills preferably" policy. This policy was adopted by the Federal Open Market Committee in March 1953 and was revealed to the public under the banner of "The Transition to Free Markets" in a speech by Chairman Martin.[3] In taking this course the Federal Reserve authorities sought to implement the concept that a central bank should minimize its interference with the credit market; the market should be as free as possible to allocate available funds among alternative uses through competition. Open-market operations by the Fed would have one purpose only, that of controlling the amount of bank reserves to promote economic stability and growth. Thus two years after the Federal Reserve System had regained its freedom, under the accord, fully to exercise control over open-market operations, it decided to restrict its transactions to short-term securities, preferably Treasury bills.

For the next eight years, until 1961, the system stuck with, or as critics of the policy viewed it, was stuck with, the "bills only" doctrine.[4] The initial reason for "bills only" was to improve the performance of the market for government securities. It was pointed out that market participants had been forced to contend with uncertainty as to when and to what degree the Fed might enter the intermediate and long-term sectors of the market, as a result of which intermediaries were reluctant to take positions and make continuous markets. The market was said to suffer from a lack of depth, breadth, and resiliency. An unfavorable psychology on the part of professional operators in the market was considered sand in the market mechanism which could be removed by having the Fed keep hands off all but the short end of the market. It seems unlikely, however, that the "bills only" policy did in fact improve the performance of the government bond market.

> The available statistical evidence and the view of market participants suggest that, despite the "bills only" policy and contrary to Chairman Martin's assertions, the Government bond market in recent years has been thin and artificial. Thus the "bills only" policy would seem to have failed in one of its main purposes.[5]

Although the case for "bills only" was originally made on technical grounds of improving bond market performance, it was later defended in terms of its effectiveness in implementing monetary policy. Its proponents held that monetary policy could be fully effective via "bills only" because market linkage would transmit the policy's impact throughout the full range of maturities. But in arguing that purchases or sales in the short end of the market would very quickly spread to the medium and long-term segments of the market, the system contradicted its argument that "bills only" minimized the impact of open-market operations on longer-term securities, for that case rested on poor linkage and hence poor transmission. In other words the objective of a bond market free from outside interference was thwarted even though the Fed adhered to "bills only."[6]

Another motive for "bills only" was to avoid a return to the pegging policy of 1942–1951. If the Fed dealt in longer-term securities it would obviously influence the terms of Treasury borrowing in the relevant maturity ranges. There was thought to be a danger that in a time of credit restraint, as the Treasury's interest costs rose the Federal Reserve might be pressured to reduce interest rates. Thus the Fed might get trapped in a situation similar to the one that existed prior to the accord in which it would be restrained from using its powers for stabilization of the economy. Having fought free of pegging, it is understandable that the central bankers would be sensitive on the issue. There was negligible support for a return to pegging within the economics profession or in Congress, although the idea that the system should exercise its influence to keep interest rates generally quite low was not uncommon. In justifying "bills only" on the threat of pressure to return to pegging, the system may have been overly defensive and circuitous, for clearly the prime and strong case against pegging is the straightforward one that it handcuffs the central bank in the exercise of monetary policy.

As the "bills only" policy was carried out during the 1950s it came under fire. During periods of credit ease, the short-term markets were inundated with liquidity in order that some of it would spill over into longer-term markets, making more credit available at lower interest rates to encourage spending for construction, plant and equipment, and local government projects—to encourage investment a depressed economy required flooding of the money market. Later, when the economy began to revive, there was excess liquidity to be pumped out of the financial system before monetary policy could begin to be effective in controlling the expansion. The Federal Reserve System was widely criticized for excessive ease, and its leading officials came to recognize the validity of the criticism. During periods of credit restraint the effect of monetary policy carried out through "bills only" on bond yields was also unsatisfactory. Bond yields reacted unreliably, responding either too much or too little to credit policy.

> There seems to be very little doubt that monetary policy did create too much liquidity in the 1954 and 1958 recessions and that the policy of "bills only" was a major reason why this happened. For, as noted earlier, the way "bills only" works is to saturate the short-term markets with funds and then allow some of the excess liquidity to seep into all other sectors of the market. And it is also clear that much of the difficulty which monetary policy had in imposing restraint on the economy in a timely fashion can be traced to the necessity to absorb such excess liquidity before restrictive measures could take effective hold.
>
> Thus while open market operations, restricted to "bills only," were able to ease the capital markets sufficiently to stimulate long-term borrowing and spending and to reverse recessionary trends, the price was the creation of so much liquidity as to severely impair the ability of monetary policy to restrict credit in succeeding periods of business recovery and expansion.[7]

Pneumonia was once known as the old man's friend because it carried off those for whom life had run its course. The gold standard, more specifically an outflow of gold from the United States in the fall of 1960, served to carry off the "bills only" doctrine. Low bill yields in New York relative to those in London and other European financial centers caused gold to leave the United States. At this juncture the Fed wanted relatively low long-term rates to encourage the domestic economy but relatively high bill rates to encourage the holding of dollar balances. To achieve this, the system needed to buy long-term securities and sell (or at least abstain from buying) short-term securities. The "bills only" doctrine, now clearly inappropriate, was officially laid to rest on February 20, 1961, when the following announcement was made.

> The System Open Market Account is purchasing in the open market U.S. Government notes and bonds of varying maturities, some of which will exceed five years.
>
> Authority for transactions in securities of longer maturity has been granted by the Open Market Committee of the Federal Reserve System in the light of conditions that have developed in the domestic economy and in the U.S. balance of payments with other countries.[8]

The "bills only" policy was considered by economists generally to be a mistake because it unnecessarily restricted the powers of the central bank. From the point of view of the control of the money stock, the *kind* of securities bought or sold is not significant; the effect on the monetary base depends solely on the *amount* of open market operations. But from the point of view of the "credit" effects of monetary policy (apart from the "monetary" effects), that is, the determination of the pattern or structure of interest rates, the kind of securities is important particularly because of the influence of the long-term interest rate on investment spending. "The major criticism levied against the bills only policy was that the System was denying itself an instrument, considered potent by the critics, for affecting economic activity, namely, affecting the relative yields on long- and short-term securities."[9]

During the 1950s, for the first time since the 1920s, the Federal Reserve could use its monetary control powers under "normal" conditions, that is, without the distortions of depression or war. Here, in capsule form, is what happened to the economy.

1. The economy entered the 1950s with an expansion which brought it close to capacity levels by early 1953. To forestall the emergence of inflation the Fed allowed credit to tighten and raised the discount rate from 1¾ to 2 percent.[10] By mid-1953 a mild recession began. The Federal Reserve responded by buying securities, reducing member bank reserve requirements, and lowering interest rates. The public and the banks became highly liquid and the economy began to grow again by mid–1954.

2. From the second quarter of 1954 to the third quarter of 1957 the economy expanded rapidly. GNP rose by 24 percent, with a 41 percent growth in gross private investment. Consumer prices were remarkably stable until the spring of 1956—at the same level as late 1952—but then rose by 5.4 percent in eighteen months. From the perspective of the 1970s and 1980s

this inflation is closer to a molehill than a mountain, but it was not lightly regarded when it occurred. It was the first significant inflationary problem since before World War I that could not be blamed on war financing. The Federal Reserve held a defensive posture from early 1955 until the latter part of 1957, keeping M1 virtually constant. As the investment demand schedule shifted to the right and expenditures on output increased, the demand for money rose, driving up interest rates to their highest level in twenty-five years (3.6 percent for three-month Treasury bills and 3.7 percent for long-term Treasury bonds). The expansion was launched on the easy credit conditions of 1954, but during the last two years of the expansion the Fed was very stingy with its credit. Yet once the economy got up a head of spending steam it maintained its momentum by virtue of an increase in the income velocity of spending. The banks assisted in the rise in V by selling off a large chunk of their holdings of Treasury securities to the public. The public's holdings of deposits therefore diminished but were quickly replenished as the banks expanded their loans to borrowers who of course were eager to spend. By this means, and as interest rates rose, increased demand for transactions balances could be accommodated as "speculative" or "asset" balances decreased.

3. From mid-1957 to the spring of 1958 the economy went through a brief recession which the Federal Reserve System countered with a liberalization of credit by again using all three general credit control powers. The Consumer Price Index (CPI) continued to rise, albeit slowly.

4. The 1950s ended with a two-year recovery that began in May 1958. It was not a robust recovery. The unemployment rate ratcheted upward: only 3 percent in 1951–1953, it averaged 5.5 percent for 1959–1960. Consumer prices were inching up at a rate of only 1.5 percent per annum, but, in the context of sluggish economic growth and the failure of prices to fall during the previous recession, there was spreading fear that inflation was becoming chronic. In this inflation-wary climate, and trying to keep the economy on a short monetary leash, the Fed shifted to a restrictive policy as soon as the economy started to move up. As it had in 1955–1957 the system held bank reserves taut (the Fed favored the expression "leaning against the wind") and interest rates rose to thirty-year highs.

In 1960, looking back over the decade of the 1950s, the record seemed good, but not good enough. The fact that no major depression had occurred in the postwar period was clearly a cause for deep satisfaction. But the shining hopes for rapid growth, low unemployment, and price stability were not being realized. For the years 1951–1960 the real rate of growth of GNP was 2.8 percent per annum. The unemployment and inflation rates were pressing persistently upward.

We have noted in connection with the "bills only" doctrine that the Federal Reserve System was faulted for creating excessive amounts of liquidity during the recessions of 1953–1954 and 1957–1958. In view of the relatively unimpressive growth rate and the disappointing unemployment trend, much criticism was also directed at the system for following an excessively restrictive policy. The mainstream Keynesian economists who exercised influence in the Kennedy and Johnson administrations from 1961 through 1968 were highly critical of Federal Reserve policy in the 1950s for retarding growth through tight money. The Fed was seen by them as having been guided by outdated theory and by a failure to set high enough goals for employment and output.[11] These combined criticisms conjure up an image of the Fed as a poor driver who periodically jazzes the engine to get moving but then applies the brake as soon as the car gets up some speed. The central bank had regained its independence in the 1950s but without receiving the kudos in exercising it that it had enjoyed in the 1920s. In feeling its way it began tentatively in these years to pay a little attention to the growth of the money stock per se rather than focusing entirely on credit conditions and interest rates, but the operating targets for its policy were money-market conditions and net free reserves.

During the 1950s a major development occurred concerning the way inflation is perceived that was important for monetary policy. Inflation traditionally was viewed as caused by excessive aggregate demand, a monetary phenomenon. As the post–World War II period began, inflation was seen in this familiar light, and the possibility that inflation could occur simultaneously with substantial unemployment was hardly recognized. Both neoclassical and Keynesian theory attributed inflation to excessive demand ("demand-pull inflation"). But the failure of prices to fall and then their rise during the recessions of the 1950s led economists to expand their understanding of inflation to include cost-push or sellers' inflation, so that thereafter inflation became a disease with more than a single cause. From 1951 on, it was contended that cost-push inflation was operating and the dichotomy between demand-pull and cost-push inflation gained acceptance. Cost-push was widely interpreted to mean wage-push to a great extent, although it applied to monopoly elements generally, not to unions alone.[12] Cost-push inflation posed a serious dilemma for the monetary authorities. When wages and prices were pushed up, output and employment tended to decline unless the money supply was increased enough to generate the additional demand necessary to take the goods off the market at the higher prices. If the central bank refused to provide the additional money, it would be blamed for allowing output and employment to fall, but if it did create additional money it "validated" the higher prices and so sanctioned and sustained inflation. Since the macroeconomic objectives of the nation included high and growing production, low unemployment, *and* stable prices, the Fed was widely seen as having an impossible task—it was damned if it did and damned if it didn't expand the money supply to match the higher prices. Some economists thought that if the Fed would just remain true to the traditional central banking objective of preventing inflation, then the market participants, both labor and management, would soon get the message and learn in their own self-interest to reach "fair" wage bargains with overall stability in prices.[13] But many others thought that the pain of unemployment and lost output would be too great and that monetary and fiscal policy alone were not enough. The growth of economic thinking about inflation did not stop with the introduction of the cost-push concept. Soon the demand-pull/cost-push dichotomy was seen as too simple and inadequate, and in the 1960s a flowering of inflation theory took place, including structural and expectational inflation.

In their 1963 article, "Survey of Inflation Theory," Martin Bronfenbrenner and Franklyn D. Holzman pointed out that cost-push theories existed historically but were looked upon as new in the 1950s in reaction against the reigning demand-pull orthodoxy. It is a striking fact that during the 1930s both John Maynard Keynes and Joan Robinson anticipated the dilemma of most western countries after World War II: the impossibility of achieving full employment and price stability simultaneously without price or wage controls.[14]

President Eisenhower appealed to unions and management to exercise restraint lest in their eagerness for bigger slices of pie they should bring on policies that would shrink the pie. In other words the concept of an incomes policy was being broached by presidential counseling in the 1950s. This appeal to responsible market behavior in the general interest was too general to be effective. An attempt to provide a more specific incomes policy appeared in the January 1962 Annual Report of the Council of Economic Advisers which set forth guideposts for responsible wage–price behavior. They were subsequently embraced by presidents Kennedy and Johnson, who used them as means of education and persuasion to try to restrain the market power of strong unions and businesses in order to keep a wage–price spiral at bay. They were designed to provide overall price stability. Increases in wage rates were to be kept equal to the average national increase in productivity, which would maintain stable labor cost per unit of output for the economy. Individual prices were expected to rise in industries with below-average advances in productivity and fall in industries with above-average productivity advances. The extent to which the guideposts were responsible for the low rate of inflation from 1961 to 1965 is not clear. It is clear that they could not cope with the powerful demand-pull inflation that developed after 1965. This is no reflection on their effectiveness, however, for their advocates clearly presented them as complements to and not substitutes for a sound monetary/fiscal policy mix.

The Promised Land—Almost

> It was like the spectacle which greeted the eyes of Moses from the summit of Pisgah, and, in the warm glow of their feelings, they cried out, "It is the promised land!"
>
> —William Hickling Prescott[15]

The quotation above may overstate the euphoria felt by the economists of the (Kennedy) New Frontier in the heady days of the 1960s—but not by much. Walter W. Heller, chairman of the Council of Economic Advisers, 1961–1964, made this assessment in 1966:

> Economics has come of age in the 1960's. Two Presidents have recognized and drawn on modern economics as a source of national strength and Presidential power. Their willingness to use, for the first time, the full range of modern economic tools underlies the unbroken U.S. expansion since early 1961. . . .
>
> The paralyzing grip of economic myth and false fears on policy has been loosened, perhaps even broken. We at last accept in fact what was accepted in law twenty years ago (in the Employment Act of 1946), namely, that the Federal government has an overarching responsibility for the nation's economic stability and growth. . . .
>
> These are profound changes. What they have wrought is not the creation of a "new economics," but the completion of the Keynesian Revolution—thirty years after John Maynard Keynes fired the opening salvo.[16]

Arthur Okun, chairman of the Council of Economic Advisers under President Johnson, observed in 1969 that "The persistence of prosperity has been the outstanding fact of American economic history of the 1960s. The absence of recession for nearly nine years marks a discrete and dramatic departure from the traditional performance of the American economy." But it was the first half of the decade that was truly satisfying. Okun added, quite prophetically it now seems: "The high-water mark of the economist's prestige in Washington was probably reached late in 1965."[17]

A prominent feature of the Kennedy economic program was the large tax cut of 1964, the proposal for which came out of the economic textbooks of the postwar period with their "new" Keynesian cast.[18] It was undertaken in accordance with the view that "In 1961, once recession had turned into recovery, nothing was more urgent than to raise the sights of economic policy and to shift its focus from the ups and downs of the cycle to the continuous rise in the economy's potential,"[19] that is, a steady growth model was substituted for a cyclical model. The thrust of policy was to propel the economy upward on a track that would maximize production, employment, and purchasing power continuously through time. While the major weapon of the Kennedy administration was fiscal policy, monetary policy played an important complementary role. In contrast to its policy in the 1950s, when its sensitivity to the danger of inflation resulted in aborted recoveries, the Federal Reserve System did not attempt deflation during the expansion from 1961 to 1965. As it met the expanding credit needs of the economy, the cost of long-term borrowing rose gradually. The monetary and fiscal authorities maintained close cooperation during these years. To help achieve a coordinated macroeconomic policy, the chairman of the Board of Governors of the Federal Reserve System met regularly with the heads of the Treasury, the Bureau of the Budget, and the Council of Economic Advisers. The foursome was dubbed the quadriad in the Kennedy administration, and President Kennedy usually attended the meetings. Such coordination had been established previously in the latter years of the Einsenhower administration under the leadership of Secretary of the Treasury Robert B. Anderson. Following the death of Kennedy the quadriad atrophied—it did not fit the style of the Johnson administration.[20] It has been very plausibly argued that the fight against inflation during the Eisenhower years (1953–1960) purged the economy of inflationary expectations and so set the stage for rapid growth with only minor inflation from 1961 through 1965.[21]

It was noted earlier that the "bills only" policy was terminated early in 1961 in an attempt to stem an outflow of gold. The incoming Kennedy administration introduced what was called Operation Twist (or Operation Nudge), a policy intended to twist the term structure of interest rates, raising short-term rates to halt the outflow of capital and so to solve the balance-of-payments problem, and lowering, or at least stabilizing, long-term rates to encourage domestic private investment. To accomplish this the Fed could buy long-term securities and the Treasury could shorten the average maturity structure of the national debt by increasing the relative supply of Treasury bills and other short-term securities. Between 1961 and 1965 the actual behavior of interest rates conformed to the goal of the policy, yet the policy itself received little credit for the result. The reasons are that (1) the behavior of interest rates was explained by other factors; (2) the Fed's net purchase of long-term securities was small and the Treasury failed to shorten its debt structure.[22] The policy was talked about more than it was acted on, and after 1965 it disappeared from view. Subsequently the concept itself came in question on the grounds that international capital flows and private investment spending are functions of interest rates in general, which would make twisting the term structure unimportant.

Before leaving the period 1951–1965, some indication of the overall performance of the economy may be gained by a few summary statistics for the subperiods 1951–1960 and 1961–1965, as shown in table 7–1.

For the period 1951–1960, M1 grew by 19 percent and its income

Table 7–1
Comparative Output, Price, and Unemployment Data, 1951–1960, 1961–1965

	1951–1960	1961–1965
Average annual increase in real GNP	2.8%	5.3%
Average annual increase in CPI[a]	1.5%	1.3%
Average annual rate of unemployment[b]	4.5%	5.5%

Adapted from *Economic Report of the President, 1979*, pp. 185, 217, 244.
[a]Consumer price index
[b]The unemployment rate was 3% for 1951–1953 and 5.2% for 1954–1960.

Table 7–2
Money Stock and Velocity of Money, 1951, 1960, 1961, 1965

	1951	1960	1961	1965
Annual Average M1 ($ billion)	119.2	141.6	143.9	163.8
Velocity (GNP/M1)	2.78	3.58	3.65	4.22

Adapted from *Historical Statistics of the United States*, Part 2, 1975, p. 992, and *Economic Report of the President*, 1985, p. 232.

velocity by 29 percent. The faster rise in *V* than in *M* in financing the growth of GNP in the 1950s is explained by the fact that commercial banks were not competing for time and savings deposits. The banks were not expanding at the pace of the economy—GNP grew four times as fast as demand deposits. Nonbank financial intermediaries expanded their credit instruments (savings and loan shares, for example) rapidly to finance economic growth. Nonbank credit instruments increased much faster than bank demand deposits, the velocity of which had to increase. From 1961 to 1965, M1 grew by 14 percent and its income velocity by 16 percent. The money stock grew gradually over the entire decade and a half, with some acceleration after 1963. Table 7–2 shows the quantity of money and its velocity for selected years.

The Banks Stir Themselves

> The acceptance of the idea that commercial banking would have to buy deposit funds through the time and savings deposit route instead of merely relying on free checking-account deposits brought a major change in the industry.
>
> —Paul S. Nadler[23]

Banking has been important both as an intermediary between savers and investors and as a creator of new money. Along with providing credit to the economy, banks have provided services, notably the clearing and collection of checks. In carrying out their important functions, bankers largely followed traditional methods of operation and were essentially passive and predictable. Prestigious and often powerful but unimaginative, banking was not a vocation with an image of innovation and challenge. Bankers generally exemplified thrift, probity—and stodginess.[24] In the 1950s circumstances developed that provoked a fundamental change in the way banks operate. Bank management was galvanized into new modes of behavior, and "aggressive" banking resulted.

From 1933, when interest on demand deposits was prohibited and interest on time and savings deposits became regulated, until the mid–1950s, banks did not need to compete to attract time and savings deposits. As noted earlier, the banks had reserves in abundance until the end of World War II, and until 1951 they could readily get additional reserves by cashing in government securities. But during the 1950s, notably with the boom of 1955–1957, interest rates began to climb.[25] As market interest rates rose, corporations began to transfer surplus funds from bank demand deposits to short-term securities which were capable of earning substantial returns, and individuals transferred funds from commercial banks to savings and loan associations and savings banks. As this trend developed, individual banks found that their deposits, hence reserves, were being drained away. For the banking system as a whole it became clear that as the economy grew, the nonbank financial institutions were outstripping the relatively static banks in volume of business.

Early in the 1960s the commercial banks began to respond to the challenge with a new management strategy known as liability management. The accepted strategy up to this time gave relatively little attention to the sources of bank funds, which of course are chiefly bank liabilities. Bank deposits were viewed primarily as a function of the wealth of the community in which the bank operated, supplemented by some marketing effort. Since bank management had little influence on the amount of deposits, it gave most of its attention to managing assets. The art of banking consisted mainly of acquiring the composition of assets that would earn satisfactory profits while preserving the liquidity and solvency of the bank. To provide liquidity for the bank, it was necessary to hold short-term assets (secondary reserves), primarily government securities. From time to time, member banks might tap their Federal Reserve Banks for a discount to obtain some additional funds. During the 1960s the whole concept of bank management shifted.[26] Banks came to take a targeted growth of assets as their starting point and adjusted their liabilities to meet the needs of their growing assets. Instead of relying mainly on liquid assets to satisfy their need for liquidity, they now went into the money market to borrow (to "buy money"). Under this mode of operation the banks could expand along with the growth of the economy. As borrowers increased their demands for loans, the banks in turn increased their capacity to lend by drawing in funds on the liabilities side of their balance sheets. The suction power for this was higher interest, implemented by a new credit instrument admirably designed for the task, the negotiable certificate of deposit, or CD.

The negotiable CDs that large money-center banks began to issue early in 1961 were already employed by some regional banks outside New York and Chicago. Their new significance sprang from the fact that the really big banks now offered them, plus the development of a secondary market for them in New York which provided the liquidity of a true money market instrument.[27] By their use, banks were able to reach out from their local areas to tap the national pool of money market funds. Corporate deposits, attracted in huge amounts, brought in funds which the banks could funnel into short-term loans. The flow of funds through the banks' balance sheets could be adjusted to respond as the demand for loans fluctuated. Within six months of their introduction, the negotiable CDs of New York City banks reached the $1 billion level. Total negotiable CDs outstanding at large commercial banks in the United States rose steadily to almost $25 billion in 1968; their growth thereafter was interrupted drastically by recessions, but the upward trend brought them to $100 billion by 1980.[28]

Negotiable CDs were the most striking of the new sources of funds open to banks in return for their paying the going interest rate. Another was the federal funds market. Federal funds had been used as a way of meeting a deficiency in a bank's reserve position, but now they were seen also to be a source of lendable funds. One result was that the Federal Reserve's discount rate ceased to be a ceiling rate on federal funds, for banks eager for funds were often motivated to bid up the federal funds rate above the rate the Fed charged for discounting. Still another new source of funds used to draw on the national market was the subordinated debenture. Of course, traditional time and savings deposits were a steady source of funds, but unlike the newer sources they lacked flexibility. As bankers became accustomed to their power to attract money from the impersonal money market as long as they paid enough for it, they questioned the need for large secondary reserve positions and began to reduce them.[29]

8
Inflation Lifts Off, 1965–1969

All too soon, Vietnam blew the economy off course.
—Walter W. Heller[1]

The progress made during the first half of the 1960s suggested the possibility that the "new economics" had provided the knowledge to cure the economy of the old bane of the business cycle, just as medical science had recently eliminated the scourge of polio. The expansion that began in February 1961 at the start of the Kennedy administration continued until December 1969 in the first year of Nixon's presidency, a total of 106 months, or almost nine years, easily breaking the record for the longest span from trough to peak. But something happened on the way to the promised land of steady economic growth, full employment, and stable prices. In the late 1960s, inflation, which had been held in check since the end of the Korean War in 1951, broke out due to demand-pull pressure caused by the Vietnam War. In addition to the problem of inflation, the financial markets suffered bouts of tightness that bordered on crises and that introduced a new type of ailment with the label of disintermediation. These problems placed a heavy burden on monetary policy. We turn to an examination of inflation, credit squeezes, and the responses of the monetary authorities as they sought to improve their performance.

The Resurgence of Inflation

The war in Vietnam produced what is widely recognized as the greatest blunder in Government economic policy since World War II.
—Edwin L. Dale, Jr.[2]

The statement quoted was made in 1973 by a leading writer on economics of *The New York Times*. In July 1965 U.S. combat troops were sent in force to Vietnam just as the economy was nearing the full employment level, so that the additional spending on the war threatened to drive aggregate demand above the supply potential of the economy. The inflationary danger was well understood by the chairman of the Council of Economic Advisers,

Gardner Ackley, and other economists of the administration. Yet even though the danger was foreseen and there was ample time to prepare a policy to avoid it, the opportunity to do so was missed. What occurred instead has been called the Great Botch of 1966.[3] President Johnson blundered by rejecting the advice of his economic advisers to ask Congress for a tax increase early in 1966, thereby missing a "key block" that allowed inflation to gain momentum. A year later, in January 1967, the president did ask for a tax increase, and Congress finally enacted one in July 1968, two and a half years after the advice was originally given. As 1966 began, Johnson had domestic (Great Society) legislation pending in Congress which would have been put at risk by a recommendation for higher taxes. It was also possible then to hope that the war effort would be brief and not overly costly—wishful thinking, as events soon showed. Eventually Johnson realized that he was mainly to blame for the debacle.[4]

The inflation set in motion at the end of 1965 became a major issue in the last half of the 1960s. Since taxes were not raised until 1968, it fell to monetary policy to provide the primary brake on the booming economy. Consumer prices, which had risen by 1.9 percent during 1965, rose by 4.7 percent during 1968, a more rapid increase than in any year since the Korean War. In 1969 the increase was 6.1 percent, slightly higher than during the Korean War years.

Federal Reserve Policy—The Bucks Are Stopped Here

> The Federal Reserve probed, tested, and reacted. It shot in the dark in some instances. Yet the Board put on an outstanding performance in 1966, making wise judgments and, most of all, having the courage to act promptly and decisively on them. The objectives could not have been carried out if the Board had been frozen by timidity or hogtied by rigid rules about the growth of the money supply, the level of interest rates, or any other criterion of monetary policy.
> —Arthur M. Okun[5]

Presidents can turn their thumbs down to the advice of their economists but not to the decisions of the Federal Reserve. The Board of Governors raised the discount rate from 4 to 4.5 percent on December 3, 1965, a "provocative" act that led to a direct confrontation with President Johnson and immediately resulted in congressional hearings with abundant media coverage.[6] The discount rate was raised because of war-induced pressure of excess demand and because the balance of payments was in continuing deficit. The board chose the discount rate increase at this time, after some internal debate, because of its announcement effect. The commercial banks had been deterred from raising the prime lending rate by presidential pressure despite a heavy demand for credit at the existing rate. The board also raised the Regulation Q ceilings on time deposits by a percentage point, with the intention that they would then be too high to have an effect on the market. In this way the Fed acted in accordance with free market philosophy; the market would be able to determine how credit would be distributed, and the central bank would be concerned solely with the total amount of credit, not with its allocation among the sectors of the economy.[7] We shall soon see, however, that less than a year later the system found direct intervention to be expedient.

The Federal Reserve gradually increased monetary restraint during the first eight months of 1966 in a clearly overheated economy.[8] The M1 money stock was held constant from April until the year ended. Although the discount rate was kept constant at the level set in December 1965, market interest rates rose sharply to new post–World War II highs as intense competition developed in the credit markets. In response to an extremely heavy demand for borrowed funds, the credit flow shifted markedly toward business. The banks, anxious to meet the large demand of their customers for accommodation, scrambled for funds. They increased their borrowings from the Federal Reserve, but that of course was a limited source. Funds were attracted in the form of CDs until mid-year, when the rates paid on competing money market instruments became more attractive than the 5.5 percent ceiling under Regulation Q. As sales of large-denomination CDs fell, the banks pushed small-denomination CDs in an effort to attract consumer savings, but to a large extent all they did was draw down their own passbook savings accounts, an exercise not unlike climbing a greased pole. It was evident that liability management did not produce an ever flowing stream of funds. With CDs running off as market rates rose, banks turned to quite costly sources by borrowing federal funds and Eurodollars (dollar-denominated deposits against banks located outside the United States). They also sold U.S. government and municipal securities at sacrifice prices. By late summer, as the credit squeeze turned into (in the jargon of the day) crunch, and with interest rates at levels not seen for four decades, signs of disorderly market conditions appeared: the climax was at hand. "With no apparent end to the demand for funds and the upsurge in interest rates, conditions in the financial markets seriously deteriorated in August and some observers even saw the threat of a financial panic."[9] In other words there was apprehension that those seeking liquidity by selling bonds would fail to find buyers at more than disastrously low prices, a feeling remotely akin to that felt by a sky diver uncertain about his parachute. At this critical juncture the central bankers, deeply concerned about both the dicey conditions in the securities market and with the growth in business loans, decided to resort to "moral suasion," that is, to give some fatherly advice to the banking community. A letter was sent on September 1, 1966, by each Federal Reserve Bank president to all of the member banks in his district pointing out that the national interest required them to (a) moderate the rate of expansion of business loans, and (b) reduce their liquidation of securities. The banks were very politely given to understand that the discounting privilege was not to be used for further expansion of business loans. Predictably, the response of the commercial bankers was that the Fed would cripple the economy with such quantitative controls, but a calming effect was felt in the security markets, and interest rates soon began to subside. Other steps were taken that contributed to stabilizing market conditions, such as presidential action to reduce nondefense spending and to suspend both the tax credits on machinery and equipment and the accelerated depreciation allowances on new buildings. By October it became clear that the pace of economic activity was moderating, and the Federal Reserve relaxed the degree of restraint on the banks somewhat. Near the end of the year the Federal Reserve signaled that it considered the storm to be over by announcing that the letter of September 1 no longer applied.

Monetary policy during 1966 curtailed the total demand for goods and services, but its impact upon different sectors was distressingly uneven. Housing, small business, and local government were leading victims of tight money—by October housing starts fell by 50 percent compared with the previous December. The financial institutions closely associated with the housing industry, the thrifts, suffered severe problems as the flow of funds, like a diverted river, changed direction. Funds were withdrawn from the financial intermediaries, a malfunction soon known as disintermediation. The hardest hit, the savings and loan associations, experienced net outflows during four months. Without an inflow of funds, and with the possibility of massive withdrawals, their ability to finance the residential construction industry was severely impaired.

A closer look at the problem of the savings and loan institutions begins with the point that rising interest rates subjected them to competition from the money and bond markets. Since savings and loans lent long on mortgages, the slow turnover of their assets kept them from competing for deposits when interest rates rose. When the Fed raised the Regulation Q ceiling to 5.5 percent in December 1965, it made commercial banks more competitive vis-à-vis the savings and loans. As noted earlier, the big banks were able to attract funds to lend to their major corporate borrowers for inflationary capital goods spending, while simultaneously building construction was depressed. As the squeeze worsened, the several types of thrift institutions pressed for a return of the interest rate ceiling to its pre-December level, but the system rejected a rollback on the grounds that money would not flow to the thrifts from the banks but from both of them to the market. In a climate of grave uncertainty concerning the viability of the thrifts, the

Board of Governors authorized the Federal Reserve Banks to make emergency loans to nonmember depository institutions if that should become necessary—the "lender of last resort" was prepared to come to the rescue. In September, after months of intense lobbying and debate, Congress passed the Interest Rate Adjustment Act of 1966, which authorized the Fed to set differential interest rate ceilings by deposit size. The board immediately reduced the ceilings on time deposits of less than $100,000 from 5.5 percent to 5 percent, while leaving unchanged the 5.5 percent rate on the large CDs. The new law also extended deposit rate ceilings to the thrifts for the first time, but the ceilings set for them were higher than for the banks, providing an advantage over commercial banks in attracting deposits and easing the pressure on the beleaguered thrifts.

After slowing down in 1967, the economy surged upward during the first half of 1968 as GNP expanded at an annual rate of 10 percent and unemployment dropped to 3.5 percent. With serious inflation and a run by foreign governments on the nation's gold reserves recognized as imminent dangers by the business community, Congress finally agreed to Johnson's urgings and passed a 10 percent income tax surcharge in June 1968. At this time, as the long-delayed tax increase began to bite, the big question for the Federal Reserve was the extent to which spending would be depressed. Unfortunately its forecast (and others) exaggerated the braking power of the tighter fiscal policy.[10] Instead of the fiscal "overkill" that was expected by many, inflationary psychology asserted itself in the summer and fall, and the economy maintained a fast second half despite the fiscal restraint. Opinion within the Federal Open Market Committee gradually shifted from October to December toward restraint, until by mid–December the system turned decisively toward restraint. While many economic forecasts for 1968 were not very accurate, the monetarists' were quite good. This is a matter of some significance, for the monetarists were working their way toward greater acceptance during the 1960s; their record in 1968 added to their credibility and contributed to their rise to prominence in policy-making, a point soon to be elaborated.[11]

A reading of the annual reports of the Federal Reserve Bank of New York for the late 1960s reveals the year-by-year struggle to slow down inflation without precipitating a recession or financial collapse. The year 1966 was described as one of "difficult problems and decisions," and 1967 was called "a trying year." The report for 1968 thought that the combination of monetary and fiscal restraint in effect at the end of the year should bring the economy under control in 1969, but it was far from confident.[12] As it turned out, 1969 was (without overstatement) "a difficult year."

Throughout 1969 the Federal Reserve System maintained a policy of intensive restraint as inflationary forces remained strong. The discount rate was raised to its highest level in forty years, reserve requirements were raised, and system open-market operations kept pressure on bank reserve positions. In large measure 1969 was a replay of 1966. The growth of the M1 money stock for the second half of 1969 was at a rate of only 1.5 percent per annum. As in 1966, disintermediation hurt the housing market and threatened the solvency of many thrift institutions; as short-term market interest rates rose well above the Regulation Q interest rate ceilings, deposit balances set off in hot pursuit. The highest inflation rate since the Korean War went hand-in-hand with high interest rates. The large banks saw a massive runoff of negotiable CDs—a $12 billion net outflow—and responded by trying every tactic they could think of to escape from the Fed's regulations in order to maintain their earning assets. They drew in nondeposit funds via Eurodollars, repurchase agreements, and sales of commercial paper by bank subsidiaries and affiliates. The banks were nimble in finding nondeposit gaps in the Fed's regulations, and the Fed responded with more complex regulations. The large corporations were able to bypass the banking system and go directly to the open market to obtain funds. At last, as 1969 came to a close, the long period of excessive aggregate demand that began in 1965 ended, as did the expansion of the economy that began in early 1961. December 1969 marked the topping out of the cycle.

The year 1966 also saw the emergence of the one-bank holding company concept, previously used as a device to control small banks, as a means by which large banks could elude Regulation Q ceilings on negotiable CDs. By the legal device of forming a holding company, a bank could in effect borrow money free of an interest rate limitation. A teenager unable to buy liquor at the club can imbibe if his dad buys it for him. In this case the bank legally creates its own holding company "dad" which is able to tap the money market by issuing CDs or otherwise borrowing free from Federal Reserve regulation. It took a few years before the Federal Reserve could get Congress to amend the Bank Holding Company Act, but in 1970 the Federal Reserve was given power to regulate one-bank holding companies. The banks had been like sturgeon in spawning one-bank holding companies in the late 1960s, and these continue as a prominent feature of the American banking scene.

Questioning the Adequacy of Federal Reserve Operating Procedures

> I call the pre–1966 period the age of innocence because it was possible at that time to think of monetary policy in very simple terms.
> —Sherman J. Maisel[13]

The Federal Reserve operating targets from 1951 until 1970 were linked to money market conditions—a money market strategy. In this post-accord era, high priority was given to maintaining stability in financial markets. It was considered vital that interest rates and securities prices should change gradually, for financial institutions held large amounts of government securities and were vulnerable to a rapid rise in interest rates that would seriously depress government securities prices. The prevailing view was that investment spending was insensitive to interest rate changes, so that an interest rate change large enough to have an effect on aggregate demand would cause turmoil in financial markets. Keynesian theory relied on fiscal policy to deal with the business cycle; monetary policy was needed to expand the money stock as the economy grew and to be "on call" to prevent incipient financial crises from derailing the real economy. Acting within this structure of ideas, the Federal Reserve System used interest rates as its operating target and as its intermediate target as well. These targeted objectives of course were transmission mechanisms connecting the money supply with the ultimate goals of real output and stable prices. Interest rate targets are effective in meeting a disturbance in financial markets or a money supply disturbance, but when spending disturbances predominate, then interest rate targets can be perverse, leading to procyclical price and output movements. Federal Reserve operating procedures came under fire by outside critics in the early 1960s. The inflationary pressures that began in 1965 forced the issue, and the Federal Open Market Committee began to modify its targeting procedures.[14]

When Sherman Maisel became a governor of the Federal Reserve System in 1965 he was disappointed to find that no description of how monetary policy was made or how it operated existed. Apparently it was all considered self-evident. Chairman Martin described monetary policy as leaning against the winds of inflation and deflation with equal vigor. If inflation was a problem, then the Fed should supply only part of the money that the public demanded, but if recession was imminent then the Fed should supply more money than was demanded. Looking back on his tenure on the Board of Governors, Maisel concluded that semantic confusion was not uncommon: "Frequently, members of the FOMC argued over the merits of a policy without ever having arrived at a meeting of the minds as to what monetary policy was and how it worked."[15]

Here is how the Federal Reserve's money market strategy used money market conditions as a target. The manager of the Open Market Desk would buy and sell securities so that the banks would have a net reserve position as set by the Federal Open Market Committee at each meeting. For example, the target might be net free reserves of $100 million or perhaps net borrowed reserves of $200 million.[16] As the commercial banks make loans or buy securities, they create deposits and so determine the reserves they require. If the Fed does not on its own initiative create additional reserves to match the pace of bank expansion, the banks must borrow at the discount window, so if the banks create deposits faster than the Fed pumps out reserves to them, the result is an increase in net borrowed reserves. The manager of the open-market account in the Federal Reserve Bank of New York has the information to carry out his instructions effectively—he is well able to control net borrowed reserves on a weekly basis. Next, the link between the level of net borrowed reserves and the federal funds rate is quite consistent,[17] so that control over net borrowed reserves gives control over the federal funds rate. So far so good, but while this procedure allows the Fed to control the level of net free or net borrowed reserves, *the Fed does not have control over the total amount of reserves and therefore of the money supply*. As a result of lending and creating deposits, the banks require more reserves, so they borrow more from the Fed. It follows that to keep to the net reserve target, the manager of the open-market account must create additional reserves. Furthermore the money market strategy considered the level of net reserves to serve as a measure of monetary policy. When the Fed wanted to tighten monetary policy it did so by firming money market conditions: the banks had to borrow more. Then the Fed could jack up the discount rate above market rates or require the banks to reduce their deposits as a condition of loan renewal. Over time, interest rates would rise until credit expansion stopped.

In 1966 adherence to the money market strategy led to serious trouble. The root of the problem was that monetary policy was measured solely by money market conditions. As inflationary pressure mounted, it was obvious that a restrictive monetary policy was needed. The discount rate was raised and market interest rates rose but no real restraint was exercised. How could this be? It was profitable for the banks to lend money and then run to the discount window for borrowed reserves. The manager of the open-market account was constrained to hold net borrowed reserves at the level specified in the FOMC directive, which required him to purchase securities in increasingly larger amounts, thereby increasing the level of total reserves. To a considerable extent the Fed was deceiving itself by adhering to a policy of tightening that did not tighten.

> To those who adhered to the traditional doctrine and saw money market conditions tightening, the Fed was doing its part to fight inflation. But to those of us who saw the fast growth of the monetary aggregates and the rapid creation of money and credit, it seemed that the Fed, far from combatting inflationary forces, might even be adding to the inflation.[18]

During the spring of 1966 one group within the FOMC wanted to adopt monetary aggregates and reserves as a measure of policy in addition to the level of net borrowed reserves. After much discussion, in June a compromise was adopted under which the committee instructed the manager as usual in terms of money market conditions, but a secondary set of targets was added based on reserves (or, later, on the growth in bank deposits at member banks—the "bank credit proxy"). If the secondary targets were not being hit, then the manager was to switch to a different set of money market conditions. Thus if reserves (or bank deposits) rose faster or slower than the rate specified, the target for net borrowed reserves would be changed. The FOMC introduced a special clause directing that certain action should be taken "provided that" something else happened. For example, a target of net borrowed reserves of $200 million might be specified provided that if required reserves or bank deposits increased faster than expected then the net borrowed reserves target would be raised to $300 million, forcing the banks to borrow more and causing the federal funds rate to rise. Adoption of the proviso seemed at the time to be a significant change in operating procedure, but as it was interpreted it had little effect. Yet it presaged changes that were to come a few years later—the "real significance of the proviso lay in the fact that a majority of the FOMC had agreed that some improvements in operating procedures were necessary."[19]

In September 1968 another type of change in Federal Reserve operating procedures was adopted. Prior to the change, banks were required to hold reserves on a "contemporaneous" basis under which the amount of required reserves in a given banking week was based on average deposits in that same week. Under the new "lagged" basis, the banks' required reserves were determined by the weekly average of deposits two weeks earlier. The change, generally pleasing to the banking community, was quite controversial. It was looked upon with strong disfavor by economists who emphasized control of the money stock on the grounds that it resulted in greater fluctuations in the money stock than did contemporaneous reserve accounting.[20] The system eventually agreed with the critics of the lagged system and reverted to a version of the contemporaneous reserve accounting system in 1984.

9
The Tempest of the Seventies, 1970–1979

> The 1970s have been characterized by the worst of both worlds. High inflation and low levels of activity have become the norm.
>
> Alan S. Blinder[1]

> To begin making progress, we must face up to our lack of progress in the seventies. The economic record of the past decade is the second worst of the century—inferior to all but the horrible 1930s.
>
> Arthur M. Okun[2]

There is a certain morbid symmetry about our monetary experiences in the 1970s: the decade began and ended in an atmosphere of crisis, deflation, and reform of Federal Reserve methods of operation. The intervening years provided little reason for satisfaction and none for complacency. At times inflation flared to heights that were alarming and totally unexpected. Equally surprising, a comprehensive system of controls was for a time placed on the economy by a president who previously had proclaimed them to be abhorrent. The international monetary system, carefully planned at Bretton Woods in 1944 and confidently adopted in the bright days after World War II, collapsed. Supply-side "shocks," particularly the oil shortages of 1973 and 1979, required adaptive measures to contain the damage. One can imagine some of Charles Addams's ghoulish cartoon characters being nostalgic for the seventies.

From Martin to Burns

> Among the best stories of 1969–70—possibly even true—is a tale of Chairman Arthur Burns and Gaylord Freeman of the First National Bank of Chicago meeting in the men's room of the Cosmos Club and standing side by side. Freeman supposedly says out of the blue, "Arthur, would the Fed let what is essentially a well-run bank go under?" And Burns, pipe in mouth, shock of gray hair falling in his eyes, says through clenched teeth, "Maybe."
>
> Martin Mayer[3]

William McChesney Martin, Jr., holds the record for service as chairman of the Board of Governors, a period of almost nineteen years from April 1951 to January 1970. Elected as the first paid, full-time president of the New York Stock Exchange in 1938 at age 31, he was considered the boy wonder of finance. While still relatively young, in 1951 just after the accord was reached, he was chosen by fellow Missourian Harry Truman to chair the Board of Governors.[4] His tenure as chairman extended through the administrations of Eisenhower, Kennedy, and Johnson, by each of whom he was reappointed, plus one year of Nixon's.

Chairman Martin viewed money from a moral perspective. Governments had a proclivity historically to create excessive amounts of money, immoral behavior that depreciated the value of money. For two decades Martin was widely known as the symbol of monetary integrity. Personable and persuasive, he sought to strengthen the Federal Reserve System as an independent force for the public interest by promoting nonpartisan political support for it so that it would have allies when it had to take unpopular positions.[5]

Although Martin was widely perceived as generally favoring deflationary policies, the record of the Fed during the sixties does not support this contention. His position was that the system needed to provide the monetary means to accompany normal economic growth, although his approach focused first on financial markets and less directly or immediately on the performance of economy.[6] In making monetary policy Martin relied primarily on the tone and feel of financial markets—on an interpretation of events in the market and on psychological factors—more than on quantitative measurements. In common with other Federal Reserve chairmen, Martin was hard to pin down to precise goals. Since monetary policy manifestly has several major goals which often are in conflict to some degree, Federal Reserve spokesmen invariably choose not to concentrate on specifically defined goals by which their performance may be judged. This is understandable but exasperating to those trying to evaluate monetary policy. At one point Senator Proxmire, who respected Martin's ability, nevertheless compared his explanation of monetary policy to nailing a custard pie to the wall.

When Martin's tenure ended on January 31, 1970, one year into the Nixon administration, Arthur Burns became the tenth chairman of the Board of Governors of the Federal Reserve System. Dr. Burns, who had succeeded Wesley Clair Mitchell as research director at the National Bureau of Economic Research, was an authority on the business cycle and professor of economics at Columbia University, and a past president (1959) of the American Economic Association. He was also experienced as a government adviser, having served as the chairman of the Council of Economic Advisers in the first Eisenhower administration. A little later, as informal adviser to Vice-President Nixon, he warned that the policies of the Fed would bring on a recession in 1960 and so diminish Nixon's chances for the presidency. After his election to the presidency in 1968, Nixon installed Burns as his special counselor until he could appoint him to head the Fed at the expiration of Martin's tenure. Now that Nixon had "his man" at the Federal Reserve, harmony between the Fed and the White House seemed assured, but within a year a major policy split developed.[7] At the outset of Burns's tenure at the Board of Governors he was considered to be quasi monetarist, but by no means doctrinaire, and the terms eclectic and pragmatic seem entirely appropriate to describe him.

At the Brink

> Of particular importance were the actions of the Federal Reserve in connection with the commercial paper market. . . . This market, following the announcement on Sunday, June 21, of the Penn Central's petition for relief under the Bankruptcy Act, posed a serious threat to financial stability. The firm in question had large amounts of maturing commercial paper that could not be renewed, and it could not obtain credit elsewhere. The danger existed that a wave of fear would pass through the financial community, engulf other issuers of commercial paper, and cast doubt on a wide range of other securities.
>
> Arthur F. Burns[8]

The collapse of the huge Penn Central Railroad in June 1970 sent shock waves through the financial community that was already experiencing heavy precautionary demands for liquidity. It compounded the mood of uncertainty touched off several weeks earlier by the extension of the Vietnam War into Cambodia, the shootings at Kent State University, and the protests that erupted throughout the country. The conditions for a liquidity crisis were present—the stock market dropped to its lowest level in six years and long-term interest rates were at new highs. An old-fashioned rush for liquidity was getting under way, threatening distress selling of assets. Penn Central's default on $82 million of its commercial paper placed the commercial paper market in jeopardy. Suddenly and understandably, investors became much concerned about the credit worthiness of commercial paper issuers. As a result many corporations had trouble refinancing their maturing commercial paper.

The Federal Reserve System had shifted in January toward a somewhat less restrictive policy than in 1969, although not markedly so, because it wanted to lessen inflationary expectations. But with various financial institutions being squeezed, the demand for liquidity threatened to bring on a serious monetary crisis. To relieve the squeeze the FOMC voted late in May to provide whatever reserves might be needed by the financial markets. At the time of Penn Central's failure some $40 billion of debt was outstanding in the commercial paper market. Normally such paper is considered almost as safe as Treasury bills, but now the holders of commercial paper suddenly realized that they had assumed more risk than they had thought. With their minds thus concentrated, many withdrew from commercial paper posthaste and put the proceeds into safer securities. Would it be possible for the holders of commercial paper who did not choose to renew to be paid by the borrowers? As a rule, the borrowers have commitments from their banks for funds to pay off commercial paper not rolled over, but the demands for funds might be enormous and so raise the question of the ability and willingness of the banks to honor their commitments. Economic conditions had changed, the banks were worried about their own liquidity, and the solvency of some of the borrowers was uncertain. Borrowers unable to continue borrowing might fail and the failures might spread—a financial domino effect. Under these circumstances the Federal Reserve acted in the best central banking tradition as lender of last resort. In the words of a policy maker:

> At this point the Federal Reserve informed the major banks of the country that its discount window . . . was wide open. If they needed funds to make loans to their customers who were having difficulty in rolling over their commercial paper in the market, they were invited to borrow from the Fed. Further, to enable the banks to attract more money, the Board raised interest rates permitted to be paid on certificates of deposit (CDs).[9]

The sequel was that the banks borrowed quite heavily from the Fed in the next few weeks; over the next quarter bank CDs almost doubled, commercial paper outstanding declined significantly, and the Fed provided reserves at an annual rate of 25 percent. A slide into the abyss *à la* 1930 was averted in 1970 as the economy stabilized.

Monetarism Matters

> The monetarists are having their innings on the coat-tails of political events just as the fiscalists made hay in the first part of the 1960's.
> Lawrence R. Klein[10]

> In the twenty years since the initial appearance of *Studies in the Quantity Theory of Money* by Milton Friedman and associates (1956), a longstanding historical tradition of monetary theory that seemed to have been swept away into intellectual limbo by the "Keynesian Revolution" has reemerged under the description of "monetarism" to reemphasize the role of money in explaining fluctuations in economic activity and inflation.
> A. Robert Nobay and Harry G. Johnson[11]

Probably the longest continuous controversy in the field of economics in the post–World War II period has been the "Keynesian–monetarist debate."[12] It has been conducted exhaustively at various intellectual levels by many participants. One notable occasion was the dialogue between Milton Friedman and Walter W. Heller in November 1968 in which the speakers focused on the usefulness of fiscal and monetary policies.[13]

After having gained ground in the academic world in the late 1950s and 1960s, the monetarist school began in the 1970s to have a more direct effect on policy. President Nixon's economic advisers were essentially monetarist and the Federal Reserve, while not embracing monetarism, sidled in its direction. Monetarism concerns a principle of basic importance similar to Say's Law in that it can be stated briefly, as an aphorism really,[14] but its exegesis is vast when subjected to theoretical and applied scrutiny. As a result of the Great Depression and the Keynesian revolution, monetary policy was considered relatively unimportant, even insignificant, as a cause of economic fluctuations by the mainstream economists of the early post–World War II period. The "Chicago School" quantity theorists (known as the monetarist school since about 1968) asserted that this constituted a great misunderstanding, and they stressed that the quantity of money was of strategic importance; in short, money (really) matters. By the 1970s it was clear that monetarism mattered as well, that is, had become an influential force. How this came to pass is our present topic. A point worth keeping in mind is that while monetarism means more than just the quantity theory, monetarists are latter-day quantity theorists, for monetarism grew out of the quantity theory. Monetarism without the quantity theory would be like peanut butter without peanuts or a hamburger, whatever the condiments, without the beef. The quantity theory is the essence of monetarism.

Milton Friedman is regarded as the father of monetarism, but before discussing his role it is appropriate to recognize a relatively unsung hero of the quantity theory approach who "kept the faith" when (almost) all about were losing theirs. It would be too much to claim that Clark Warburton was the only important forerunner of monetarism, but a good case has been made that his is a "unique place in the development of the quantity theory since the Depression."[15] Most of Warburton's career was devoted to research for the Federal Deposit Insurance Corporation, which he joined in 1934 and from which he retired in 1965. During the 1940s and early 1950s he presented a series of papers that drew on National Bureau of Economic Research data to demonstrate the importance of money in determining economic activity, and he discussed many of the issues that constitute the monetarist position. His approach was inductive, and it treated the money supply as a basically exogenous force that is primarily responsible for the broad, important changes in economic activity. From a policy standpoint he favored a stable growth rate of the money supply—a monetary growth rule—and doubted that an active stabilization policy could improve economic performance. With respect to the Great Depression, Warburton blamed the Fed for the decline in the money supply in the early thirties and the subsequent decline in economic activity. He dismissed the argument of Federal Reserve officials that open-market operations were not feasible because of the "free gold" problem. The contraction of 1937 was blamed on the Federal Reserve also. Monetary policy in the 1930s was not "easy": beginning in 1928 the Fed turned to tight money and kept the tourniquet on throughout the thirties. For Warburton, the Great Depression did not demonstrate the instability of the market system but was the bitter fruit of misguided central bank policy. He criticized the Federal Reserve for relying on interest rates to denote monetary policy; setting an interest rate target resulted in an unstable money supply which in turn meant an unstable economy. Warburton clearly resisted the Keynesian tide concerning the role of money and interest rates. From the perspective of the late 1960s and later, Warburton was a man before his time, for his work was almost completely neglected.[16] Ironically his death occurred less than three weeks before the Federal Reserve System switched targets from the federal funds rate to the growth rate of reserves on October 6, 1979.[17] In their magnum opus, *A Monetary History of the United States 1867–1960,* Friedman and Schwartz acknowledge Warburton's work with great respect and pay him the high compliment that "time and again, as we came to some conclusion that seemed to us novel and original, we found that he had been there before."[18]

Milton Friedman is a "prophet of the old-time religion" in the sense that he holds fast to the (University of) "Chicago tradition of political conservatism and the ideology of laissez-faire."[19] Like Keynes before him, Friedman is a controversial figure who stands at the top of his profession; he clearly leads the monetarist forces.[20]

It is not true that once you have seen one monetarist you have seen them all. Monetarism comprises a school of economists who share certain propositions but who do not have identical positions. In a term favored by Friedman, monetarism is a counterrevolution to the Keynesian revolution, and he has provided a sequential account of its emergence and development from 1930 to 1970, a synopsis of which is presented here.[21]

1. Pre–Keynesian Orthodoxy

As of 1930 the quantity theory of money as expounded by Irving Fisher, using the quantity equation $MV = PT$, was the generally accepted doctrine. Velocity was considered to be highly stable and independent of the other terms, so that changes in M caused changes in P and/or T. Short-term fluctuations in the economy were due to changes in the quantity of money; long-term price trends reflected changes in the quantity of money. Monetary policy, consisting of changes in the discount rate and open market operations, provided the means for economic stabilization.

2. The Keynesian Revolution

The Great Depression was widely interpreted as demonstrating the ineffectiveness of monetary policy in coping with an economic decline, and it ended the doctrinal reign of the quantity theory of money. (This interpretation was utterly mistaken according to Friedman, for whom the depression is a testament to the effectiveness of monetary policy. The world drew the wrong conclusion from its costly experience.) The explanation for the failure of the quantity theory provided by Keynes was that velocity was not highly stable, as had been thought, but was adaptable, a will-o'-the-wisp. A rise in M is likely to be offset by a fall in V leaving PT (or PQ) unchanged. Therefore the quantity of money is not what matters. Instead the critical variable is autonomous spending on output, that is, private business investment and government spending. Thus the role of money was downgraded and largely dismissed. A further point was that prices are quite rigid and are mainly determined by labor costs which in turn are explained by institutional factors. Fiscal policy became the favored stabilization instrument, whereas monetary policy was seen as useful only in holding interest rates down to reduce the cost of financing government debt and to encourage investment spending. At the end of World War II, mainstream Keynesianism had become the new orthodoxy. An inference that came to be drawn by the 1950s was that since price increases are due to cost increases, to restrain inflation it is necessary to have an incomes policy. Friedman adds his belief that the application of Keynesian doctrine to policy reached its peak during the Kennedy administration, especially with respect to the tax cut of 1964.

3. The Monetarist Counterrevolution

By the 1960s Keynesian doctrine was in the process of gradually losing some of its influence. Keynesian analysis had led to the expectation of a depression after World War II, but instead of deflation the problem turned out to be persistent inflation. A reexamination of monetary policy during the Great Depression disclosed that the Federal Reserve was to blame for allowing the money stock to fall. The problem was not that monetary policy was ineffective but that the wrong policy had been carried out. The Federal Reserve System was created to provide liquidity when needed to stop a banking panic, but in 1930–1933 it failed to meet its responsibility.

Friedman's confidence in his interpretation leads him to the unequivocal statement that "if Keynes were alive today he would no doubt be at the forefront of the counter-revolution. . . . Monetary policy had not been tried and found wanting. It had not been tried. Or, alternatively, it had been tried perversely. It had been used to force an incredible deflation on the American economy and on the rest of the world. If Keynes . . . had known the facts about the Great Depression as we now know them, he could not have interpreted that episode as he did."[22]

Another important factor contributing to a loss of confidence in the Keynesian approach and in favor of a reborn quantity approach was the extensive empirical analysis showing that movements of velocity generally were in the same direction as changes in the money stock. Thus velocity reinforces changes in the quantity of money.

In the 1966 episode in which a tight money policy was combined with an easy fiscal policy the result was a slowing down of the economy which was reversed only after monetary policy became expansionary. Then in 1968 when the surtax was enacted and Keynesians expected economic growth to be arrested, the Fed expanded the money supply and the result was a continuation of the boom. In each case the "controlled experiment" supported the monetarists' view. This experience brought about a major change in professional and lay opinion. Friedman's belief in monetary policy is based on long-run historical evidence, so he considers the episodes of the 1960s as illustrations rather than demonstrations.

From being ignored at first, over time the small band of monetarist challengers to the orthodox Keynesian position gained both a hearing and a chorus of ridicule. Eventually, however, the monetarists became intellectually respected as the counterrevolution spread.

Monetarism is defined or explained in varying degrees of detail. Thomas Mayer, in his comprehensive *The Structure of Monetarism* (1978), states that he could find no complete list of all monetarist propositions so he constructed his own list of twelve items, four of which are "basic." In 1970 Milton Friedman provided a list of eleven "key propositions" covering four pages. What follows is a subset of selected quotations from Friedman's list, a "short list" of key propositions.[23]

1. There is a consistent though not precise relation between the rate of growth of the quantity of money and the rate of growth of nominal income.

2. This relation is not obvious to the naked eye largely because it takes time for changes in monetary growth to affect income, and how long it takes is itself variable.

3. On the average a change in the rate of monetary growth produces a change in the rate of growth of nominal income about six to nine months later.

4. The changed rate of growth of nominal income typically shows up first in output and hardly at all in prices.

5. On the average, the effect on prices comes about six to nine months after the effect on income and output, so the total delay between a change in monetary growth and a change in the rate of inflation averages something like twelve–eighteen months.[24]

6. In the short run, which may be as much as five or ten years, monetary changes affect primarily output. Over decades, on the other hand, the rate of monetary growth affects primarily prices.

7. It follows . . . that *inflation is always and everywhere a monetary phenomenon* in the sense that it is and can be produced only by a more rapid increase in the quantity of money than in output. However, there are many different possible reasons for monetary growth, including gold discoveries, financing of government spending, and financing of private spending.

A final note. Some monetarists, including Friedman, advocate an automatic policy—a monetary growth rule—providing for a steady rate of growth of the money stock over time. Others would vary the rate of growth of the money stock to offset nonmonetary destabilizing forces. The disagreement stems from different views of whether or not present knowledge is sufficient to make discretionary policy helpful. The general thrust is in the direction of a fairly stable growth rate of money.

Scrapping the Game Plan

> The rules of economics are not working in quite the way they used to. The problem of cost-push inflation, in which escalating wages lead to escalating prices in a never-ending circle, is the most difficult economic issue of our time.
>
> Arthur F. Burns[25]

President Richard Nixon brought an economic strategy or "game plan" with him when he entered the White House in January 1969. The major economic problem inherited from the Johnson administration was inflation, and the challenge was to reduce inflation without causing a severe recession. The game plan, worked out by the coaching staff headed by Nixon's first chairman of the Council of Economic Advisers, Dr. Paul W. McCracken, was based on gradualism. A "Friedmanesque" monetary policy was the core of the game plan. A pragmatic application of the concept espoused by Friedman was the guiding principle, not a rigid monetary growth rule. The fiscal policy approach which had been favored by the Kennedy–Johnson administrations was de-emphasized partly because tax rates and government spending lack flexibility of adjustment, but also because of a desire to reduce the role of government in the economy. It was thought that although higher taxes might restrain inflation, they would also tend to encourage undesirably high government expenditures; the way to an expenditure cut was through a tax cut. Direct intervention, whether wage-and-price controls or guideposts, was anathema to Nixon. He scorned the previous Democratic administrations for their intervention in the private sector and renounced the use of exhortation (jawboning) to influence labor or business leaders in their price and wage decisions. For two and a half years the game plan served as the basis for policy until suddenly one summer night, August 15, 1971, it was scrapped in a dramatic about-face.

During the first year of the game plan the Federal Reserve System was still under the leadership of Chairman Martin. It stood firm against inflation, slowing the growth of the money stock to almost nothing during the second half of 1969, following which the economy went into a contraction at the end of the year for almost a year. In 1970, with Nixon's appointee Arthur Burns now chairman of the Board of Governors, serious problems arose that prompted a rapid increase in the money supply. The recession was accompanied by very high interest rates, by the shocks of the Cambodian invasion by U.S. troops and the collapse of the Penn Central Railroad, and by the threat of a liquidity crisis, as previously discussed. By mid–1970 the unemployment rate rose to 5 percent from an average of 3.5 percent in 1969 while the rate of inflation declined slowly.[26] The stock market slumped, raising some fear of a replay of 1929. Under these circumstances the FOMC, while affirming its allegiance to a long-run policy of moderate expansion of money and credit, found it necessary temporarily to accelerate the growth of the money supply. In trying to cope more or less simultaneously with inflation, recession, and a liquidity squeeze, the Fed used the brake and accelerator to deal pragmatically with whatever problem seemed most urgent at the moment. However attractive the idea of a steady, moderate expansion of the money supply might be in theory, the monetarist medicine prescribed by Dr. Friedman was too much for the Fed to swallow. When the Republican party suffered at the polls in November 1970, further strain was placed on the game plan.[27]

The role of Arthur Burns was clearly a key element in the evolution of economic policy in 1970 and 1971. Prior to 1970 he had been severely critical of wage–price guideposts, but as events unfolded in these years his position changed. Here is the gist of some of his most noteworthy observations:[28]

May 18, 1970 (Conference, American Bankers Association, Hot Springs, Virginia): Monetary policy should be moderately expansionary, fast enough to keep the economic slowdown from cumulating but slow enough to avoid excess demand. Primary reliance in the battle against inflation requires monetary and fiscal policies working together. Incomes policies have not been very successful but should not be ruled out as a supplement to fiscal and monetary measures for the transitional period of cost-push inflation.

December 7, 1970 (Pepperdine College, Los Angeles, California): Monetary policy during 1970 has found a middle course between extreme restraint and aggressive ease. But because collective bargaining settlements have not responded to the anti-inflationary measures to date, it would be desirable to adopt an incomes policy to supplement monetary and fiscal policies.

July 23, 1971 (Joint Economic Committee): A year ago it was believed that the degree of underutilization of resources now prevailing would significantly moderate inflation. But this has not happened—"The rules of economics are not working in quite the way they used to." The problem of inflation combined with unemployment is beyond the ability of monetary and fiscal policies alone to solve as quickly as the nation demands; additional actions are needed to control wages and prices, and so allow the economy freely to use its resource potential.

In 1971 public dissatisfaction with the combination of recession and slow progress on inflation brought pressure on the government to intervene. Labor and management increasingly called for intervention of some kind in wage and price determination. In Congress, many who had previously authorized the president to impose controls under the Economic Stabilization Act of 1970—power he said he did not want—insisted on a formal incomes policy. The Nixon administration continued officially to deny that the game plan would be changed, although within the administration many joined privately with Burns who, as we have seen, publicly called for a new policy. Prices were rising in anticipation of the adoption of controls. Finally the decision was made at a weekend meeting at Camp David to adopt what President Nixon, in his address to the nation when he came down from Camp David on a Sunday night in mid–August, called "the most comprehensive New Economic Policy to be undertaken by this nation in four decades." A president whose political credo was nonintervention had come to adopt a price and wage freeze.[29] Until close to the fateful decision, loyal administration spokesmen continued staunchly to defend the game plan. In July 1971 Secretary of the Treasury John Connally denied that the president would create a wage–price review board or impose mandatory controls. For aficionados of irony, the case of Paul McCracken is a gem. His article in *The Washington Post* on July 28, 1971, excoriated John Kenneth Galbraith's testimony before the Joint Economic Committee in favor of freezing prices, saying that "the idea of a freeze is illusory." Less than three weeks later, "during the historic meeting at Camp David, on August 14 and 15, 1971, the same Paul W. McCracken . . . was put in charge of the details of the wage–price freeze."[30] So it goes. There is a larger historical curiosity involving the United States and the Soviet Union. New Economic Policy (NEP) seems an unlikely term for the Nixon administration to adopt, for it is the wording used by V. I. Lenin in 1921 for his economic reform program in the Soviet Union. In a sense the two programs are mirror images of each other: Lenin's NEP was a deliberate but temporary step back from socialism toward free markets in order later to advance further toward socialism; Nixon's NEP was a deliberate but temporary step back from free markets toward socialism in order later to advance to a better working capitalism.

The price and wage controls began with a ninety-day freeze, referred to as Phase I, which was followed by three additional phases of various degrees of control until the whole program was abandoned in April 1974. With the adoption of the controls program came more expansionary monetary and fiscal policies.[31] The Federal Reserve System had pressed for an incomes policy in the belief that monetary policy, having carried too much of the burden of limiting inflation, needed help. The existence of an incomes policy therefore permitted a more expansionary monetary policy. Certainly the expansion of M1 during 1972 was unusually high at a 9.2 percent annual rate for the first quarter and over 8 percent for the year as a whole. The economy expanded in 1972, inflation was kept in check at a 3.4 percent increase in the Consumer Price Index—and Nixon was reelected. But then the system "blew up": a recession began at the end of 1973, and the economy did not bottom out until the first quarter of 1975, yet inflation took off at 8.8 percent for 1973 and 12.2 percent for 1974, reaching a 14 percent annual rate at its peak. The worldwide boom in commodity prices, the shock of rising oil prices, crop failures around the world, the ending of controls, the decline of the dollar on the foreign exchange market, and the expansion of the money supply in the early seventies were all contributing factors. With simultaneous double-digit inflation and severe recession the term *stagflation* was widely adopted to describe the combined misery.[32]

By 1974 Arthur Burns, supposedly the stalwart inflation fighter, was under suspicion as having contributed significantly to inflation by excessive monetary expansion, notably in 1972.[33] Between 1970 and 1973 the money stock had grown at the most rapid rate for any three-year period in the post–World War II era, providing fuel for rapid inflation in 1973 and 1974. Criticism came from Congress, the press, and academia, including Milton Friedman. It was said by some critics that for Burns to hold forth in 1974 on the evils of inflation and to charge Congress with irresponsibility for contributing to it through budget deficits was hypocritical. Some charged Burns with politicizing the Fed by excessive money expansion to stimulate the economy and so insure Nixon's reelection. With the 20–20 vision of hindsight, it was generally held that monetary growth in 1972 was clearly excessive. In defense of the Federal Reserve, however, that agency was concerned with overcoming unemployment and stimulating growth as well as with inflation, and, as noted above, there were various causes of inflation beyond the control of the Fed. With the New Economic Policy in place the Fed might have deemed it safe to stimulate the economy substantially. Still, in the year of the Watergate break-in, was there also a Federal Reserve cave-in to political pressure from the White House? A long article in *Fortune* suggested that it was so, and alleged that Burns pressed in the FOMC for stimulus to keep interest rates from rising in the preelection period. A knowledgeable "witness for the defense" who had been a member of the Federal Open Market Committee, Andrew Brimmer, denied that the group had been influenced by politics. This nasty imbroglio seems to have had many facets. Burns had been close to Nixon, had blamed Fed policy in 1960 for Nixon's defeat that year, and so presumably would be very conscious, perhaps overly sensitive, to the possibility that economic conditions might cause his defeat for reelection. But by calling for wage and price controls in late 1970 and 1971, Burns broke with the Nixon White House; it was commonly thought that men close to Nixon—men detested by Burns—had sought to discredit and undermine Burns as leader of the Federal Reserve System. Perhaps the FOMC, trying hard to be seen as neutral, was predisposed to hold short-term interest rates steady in the months prior to the election since they are so "visible" to the press and the public.

Whatever conclusions different observers might draw, a few points seem beyond dispute. Arthur Burns is a distinguished scientific economist with great knowledge of the business cycle. As an "activist" economist and as chairman of the Board of Governors of the Federal Reserve System he significantly influenced short-term economic policy. The fact that the Federal Reserve System is an independent agency of government certainly does not mean that it is hermetically sealed off from political pressure.

One other feature of the New Economic Policy deserves mention here. The long series of U.S. balance of payments deficits had led to the accumulation of foreign debts of huge size. With the rapid depletion of our gold reserve, and the impracticality of a formal devaluation of the dollar, it became necessary to end the system of fixed exchange rates. President Nixon therefore abandoned the Bretton Woods international monetary system by ending the convertibility of the dollar into gold.[34]

Federal Reserve Operating Procedures in Transition

> It is widely understood that monetarist forces in Congress hoped that forcing the FOMC regularly to frame and defend its monetary-growth

> targets relative to a one-year policy horizon would serve as therapy
> against recurrence of FOMC money-market myopia.
>
> Edward J. Kane[35]

New Year's resolutions are made to be broken, and Federal Reserve operating procedures are made to be revised. Broken New Year's resolutions are quickly forgotten, but the results of revisions in Fed operating procedures are meticulously tracked. The Fed has adhered consistently to a policy-making strategy of intermediate targeting ever since the Accord of 1951 was reached. Three elements are involved. There are the (ultimate) goals of low unemployment, stable prices, steady economic growth, and so forth, the stated macroeconomic objectives of the Employment Act of 1946 and the Full Employment and Balanced Growth Act of 1978. To help achieve these the Fed has its policy instruments, principally open-market operations and discount policy. Since the relationship between policy instruments and goals is indirect, the Fed employs a third element, intermediate targets, considered to be linked to the goals and capable of being hit with a reasonable degree of accuracy. "They are conceived as sighting devices that aid policymakers to take indirect aim on hard-to-track goals."[36]

In chapter 8 it was noted that in 1966 the Federal Open Market Committee adopted a proviso clause designed to alter its directive, which continued to be stated in terms of money market conditions, by requiring that secondary targets based on the growth of reserves (or bank deposits) be added. Nothing much happened as a result, but further changes were adopted in the seventies. It is to these developments that attention is now turned.

The Federal Open Market Committee took a significant step in January 1970 by adopting a directive emphasizing the monetary aggregates.[37] Monetary policy would now be measured by money and bank credit, not primarily by money market conditions as had been the case since the time of the accord. Monetary policy would not be considered to be tight or easy based upon what happened to the federal funds rate and net borrowed reserves. It is true that money market conditions, although no longer the main concern, were also to be considered. The change in targeting resulted from the work of a committee on the directive, a subcommittee of the FOMC created in October 1968 by Chairman Martin and now bearing fruit just as Chairman Burns took over the FOMC chair in February 1970.[38]

The FOMC members who promoted the shift from a target based on money market conditions to one based on the monetary aggregates had difficulty in persuading the other FOMC members to make the change, in part because the latter reacted against anything smacking of monetarism. Certain perceived weaknesses in the monetarists' position plus the monetarists' relentless criticism of the system induced a strong negative reaction on the part of some FOMC members. The most convincing arguments in favor of the adoption of monetary aggregates as a target: in the past the money stock had expanded too much at times; the relationship between money and spending is better understood than that between interest rates and spending. Under the new arrangements the basic target was monetary aggregates with M1 emphasized, yet the manager was to operate in terms of money market conditions as before. The procedure might be described as the designation of a different intermediate target but with an unchanged operating guide. The manager of the open-market account would still receive his instructions from the FOMC in terms of money market conditions—federal funds and net borrowed reserves. The money market conditions would be chosen as appropriate to the desired path for monetary aggregates. Approximately two years later the FOMC again revised its directive. When the monetary target was chosen, an operating guide consisting of a certain amount of total reserves would follow, but with adjustments to be made if necessary to keep the federal funds rate within a stipulated range.[39]

In retrospect the decade of the seventies was a transition period for Federal Reserve operating procedures. The system that evolved from 1970 to 1979 combined monetary aggregates as intermediate targets with reserves and interest rates as operating targets. The change introduced in 1970 was prompted by rapid money growth and inflation during the late sixties. At that time monetarist critics attacked the Fed's use of interest rate targets and argued for dropping interest rates entirely and shifting completely to controlling money and bank reserves. The Fed combined the two approaches in "an uneasy compromise between the objectives of monetary control and financial market stability."[40] The problems of inflation and control of the money stock were not solved, however, but became more severe during the seventies, resulting in the next major change in Federal Reserve operating procedures in October 1979. At this time a reserve operating target was adopted (almost) without regard to interest rates. This turning point in Federal Reserve history will be dealt with a little later in the context of the emergency conditions then prevailing.

The shift in emphasis by the Fed toward a money target was a long time coming. Apparently the first explicit reference to changes in the money stock made in Federal Reserve annual reports occurred in 1948. It suggests that changes in the money stock are important per se and not only as indicative of credit market conditions. In the 1952 and subsequent annual reports, and in statements made regularly over the years by Chairman Martin, the impression was given "that providing an average rate of growth of the money stock matching or appropriate to the secular rate of growth of output, though not dominant in short-term policy, has become a background aim of the System."[41] Friedman and Schwartz view statements of this type to be almost revolutionary for the reason that their examination of published documents and the papers of Federal Reserve officials indicated that the system had never before considered the behavior of the money stock itself as a directly relevant policy criterion. The system had been concerned almost entirely with interest rates and the cost and availability of credit; in short, it focused on the credit aspects of its operations and not on the money stock. It is true that the system was very much concerned about the expansion of the money supply during the two world wars; it certainly was not oblivious of the link between the money stock and the price level. But it had been able virtually to ignore the money supply as an explicit target because its guiding principle had been that if the money market were managed correctly in the sense of providing credit for productive use and denying it for nonproductive use, then the money stock would look after itself. Comprehensive money stock data on a monthly basis were not even published by the system until 1944. In the fifties and sixties under Chairman Martin, short-term policy was to lean against the wind, avoiding inflation and deflation, a traditional approach that was developed as early as the *Tenth Annual Report* (for 1923). The policy was stated in very general terms without explaining how to determine wind direction and force or when to start leaning.[42] So in the fifties and sixties the money supply was not ignored but was on the back burner. Money market conditions were considered primary, and the system continued to define its policies in very general terms.

In the late 1960s attempts were made by congressional committees to prod the Federal Reserve System into adopting explicit money supply targets. In 1967 the Joint Economic Committee urged the monetary authorities to aim for moderate and relatively steady increases in the money supply, and specified a range of 3–5 percent per year as desirable. The next year the same position was taken, except that a range of 2–6 percent was given, along with a request that whenever the actual rate was outside the targeted range the Federal Reserve should explain the reasons to Congress. Also in 1968 the committee "urged the Federal Reserve authorities to set forth publicly at the beginning of each year, as specifically as possible, their judgment as to the monetary policy that would be appropriate during the year, given the state of the economy."[43] Representative Henry Reuss, fed up with the Fed for creating money much faster than the Joint Economic Committee recommended without explaining why, observed:

> In recent years, dialog between the Joint Economic Committee, in its annual reports, and the Federal Reserve System, in the minutes of the Open Market Committee, might well have been conducted in Urdu on the one side and Swahili on the other. . . . Our "advice" is obviously not being followed.[44]

In the view of Federal Reserve officials it would be a serious mistake for Congress to lay down detailed rules for the Federal Reserve System; the world in which the Fed operates is too complex and changes too fast.

In the 1970s Congress forced the Fed's hand on monetary targets. In 1975 a Congressional Resolution called for semiannual consultation with Congress on "the ranges of growth . . . of monetary and credit aggregates."[45] When Congress speaks in a firm tone, the Federal Reserve listens. On May 1, 1975, the Board of Governors reported money growth targets for the next year to the Senate for the first time. The requirements were made more definite and detailed by legislation in 1977 and 1978. In November 1977 the Federal Reserve Reform Act directed the Federal Reserve System "to maintain long-run monetary and credit aggregates commensurate with the economy's long-run potential to increase production so as to promote effectively goals of maximum employment, stable prices, and moderate long-term interest rates," and it requires the board "to testify concerning the ranges of monetary and credit aggregates for the upcoming 12 months."[46] Then in 1978 the Full Employment and Balanced Growth Act ("Humphrey–Hawkins") established requirements for reporting and consultation which, while preserving Federal Reserve "independence," attempts to make the Federal Reserve System more accountable to Congress and to integrate monetary policy more deliberately than in the past with the policies of the president and Congress.

> [The Act] Provides that the Board of Governors transmit to the Congress, not later than February 20 and July 20 of each year, independent written reviews and analyses of recent developments affecting economic trends, the objectives and the plans of the Board of Governors and the Federal Open Market Committee with respect to the ranges of growth of the monetary and credit aggregates for the calendar year, and the relation of such objectives and plans to the short-term goals set forth in the most recent Economic Report of the President and to any short-term goals approved by the Congress. The July 20 report is also to include a statement of objectives and plans with respect to the ranges of growth of the monetary and credit aggregates for the next calendar year. The Board is to consult with the appropriate committees, which will then submit their views and recommendations with respect to the Board's intended policies.
>
> While nothing in the act requires the Board to fulfill its plans for the monetary and credit aggregates set out in its reports, if the Board and the Federal Open Market Committee determine that the plans cannot or should not be achieved because of changing conditions, the act does require the Board to explain any revisions of that kind in subsequent consultations.[47]

The Ongoing Struggle to Control Inflation

> The Great Stagflation, like the Great Depression, may with the passage of time prove to be *sui generis*—an unhappy episode caused by

a rare conjunction of events. However, there is every reason to think
that stagflation, which has been with us before, will be with us again.
—Alan S. Blinder[48]

Reference has been made to the buffeting of the economy during the 1970s.
It is time to examine the causes and extent of the disturbances more closely
and to see what was done in response. There was a wavelike movement of
the price level: first consumer prices rose from an annual rate of increase of
3.4 percent in 1972 to a crest of 12.2 percent in 1974; the recession that
bottomed out in the first quarter of 1975 brought inflation down to 4.8
percent in 1976; then a new inflationary wave drove it up again to 13.3
percent in 1979. The unemployment rate hovered in the 5 percent area during 1972–1974, went to 8.5 percent in 1975, and slowly subsided to 5.8
percent in 1979. The discomfort index was double-digit after 1972. Table
9–1 provides annual data for 1972 through 1979.

In reaction to its overly stimulative monetary policy of 1972, the Fed
moved to restraint early in 1973, and the growth rate of M1 then trended
downward until the economy touched its recessionary low point in 1975.
The inflation rate behaved much more erratically than can be explained
convincingly by monetary policy alone, and caused much consternation in
1974 as it reached a level previously associated with less sophisticated economies. Temporary factors under the rubric of exogenous supply shocks struck
the economy with a series of price-raising jolts. Four such shocks have been
identified for 1973–1974:[49]

1. The dollar was "devalued" in 1971 and again in 1973 as a result of the
   collapse of the Bretton Woods system of fixed exchange rates.

Table 9–1
Comparative Price and Unemployment Data, 1972–1979
(percent)

	Change in Consumer Price Index December to December (1)	Unemployment Rate (2)	Discomfort Index (1) + (2)
1972	3.4	5.6	9.0
1973	8.8	4.9	13.7
1974	12.2	5.6	17.8
1975	7.0	8.5	15.5
1976	4.8	7.7	12.5
1977	6.8	7.1	13.9
1978	9.0	6.1	15.1
1979	13.3	5.8	19.1

Source: *Economic Report of the President, 1983*, pp. 201, 225.

2. Worldwide bad harvests began in 1972 and continued in 1973; natural scarcity brought steeply rising food prices.

3. The Organization of Petroleum Exporting Countries (OPEC) cartel reacted to the Arab–Israeli war in October 1973 with a contrived scarcity of oil and steeply rising prices for it.

4. Wage and price controls were removed in April 1974 at the very time that the food and energy prices were pressing upward strongly. After suppressing inflationary forces somewhat, their removal permitted prices rapidly to catch up to their "equilibrium" levels.[50]

The year 1974 was unusually distressing in politico–economic terms. In August Richard Nixon admitted complicity in the Watergate cover-up, took off in a helicopter from the White House grounds, and was succeeded by Gerald R. Ford as president of the United States. No longer following a game plan, policymakers were anxiously scrambling to avoid an economic rout, for not only were prices rising rapidly but real output was falling. A severe recession of sixteen months' duration ran from a cyclical peak in November 1973 to a trough in March 1975, with real GNP declining for five consecutive quarters. The unemployment rate peaked at 9 percent and recovered slowly, for it was down only to 7.8 percent in December 1976. Understandably impressed by double-digit inflation, President Ford labeled it "domestic enemy number one," and there was widespread fear that inflation was getting out of control. In these circumstances macroeconomic policy was not employed during 1974 to arrest the slump. Such forbearance, however understandable and "politically necessary" given the unsettling context of the time, may well have been overdone in view of the role of temporary exogenous supply shocks as causal factors driving inflation sharply above its then "basic" rate. This recession, the longest and steepest of the six post–World War II contractions experienced up to that time, unmistakably confirmed that the business cycle was not extinct and called in question the effectiveness of economic expertise which had a decade earlier seemed so praiseworthy.

For the five years 1975–1979 the economy expanded.[51] In each succeeding year, as real GNP grew, the unemployment rate fell and the inflation rate rose until by 1979 double-digit inflation again appeared and a climate even more panicky than that of 1974 existed. The monetary growth rate increased moderately after the first quarter of 1975—Arthur Burns said he was determined to avoid an "explosion" of money and credit—but then more rapidly. Year-to-year increases in M1 were 6.7 percent for 1976, slightly over 8 percent for 1977 and 1978, and close to 7 percent for 1979. On January 31, 1978, after eight years at the helm, Arthur Burns was replaced as chairman of the Board of Governors by President Carter's nominee, G.

William Miller.[52] As a prominent and community-minded business leader, Miller was viewed as reassuring to the business sector while understanding of social and economic problems. Arthur Burns had become a major irritant to the Carter administration in 1977 by his one-man campaign against the administration's proposal of a $50 income tax rebate, and he continued to view inflation as the paramount danger. Miller, a pragmatic businessman with a law degree to whom no ideological label was attached, did not give primacy to inflation but held that inflation and unemployment should be dealt with simultaneously. Although he had been a director of the Federal Reserve Bank of Boston for six years, Miller's education and experience in monetary affairs provided rather unimpressive preparation for the role of the nation's chief central banker. Like a relief pitcher who only throws to a few batters, Miller's tenure at the Fed was brief. A year and a half later, midway through the tumultuous year 1979, Carter chose Miller as his new secretary of the Treasury and nominated Paul Volcker as the twelfth chairman of the Board of Governors. Volcker took the oath of office on August 6, 1979. Exactly two months later the Federal Reserve took its most important decision since the Accord of 1951.

The Monetarist Flag over the Federal Reserve

> A special October 6, 1979 meeting of the FOMC reoriented the focus of subsequent policy directives as dramatically as a fateful trip to Damascus long ago altered St. Paul's attitude toward Christians.
> —Edward J. Kane[53]

For about a year prior to October 1979, concern over a worsening of the financial situation gradually increased until suddenly there was the fearful perception that the financial system had reached a point beyond which (in the words of W.B. Yeats) "things fall apart; the centre cannot hold; mere anarchy is loosed upon the world." The rate of inflation in the United States accelerated steadily during the expansion that began in 1975, leading to a sharp fall in the value of the dollar in the foreign exchange market late in 1978. President Carter had already appealed for voluntary wage and price restraint. Now the Administration entered the foreign exchange market to support the dollar with huge amounts of borrowed foreign currencies, and Carter openly encouraged the Federal Reserve to be more restrictive in its monetary policy. The monetary growth rate fell in the fourth quarter of 1978 and was even negative in the first quarter of 1979, but then increased again sharply during the summer. Inflation raced ahead at more than a 13 percent per annum rate by mid-1979, and although interest rates surged, the demand for credit was not dampened. The dollar plunged on the foreign exchange market and the price of gold, which more than doubled from $250 an ounce in June to over $500 an ounce at year's end, rose by $100 an ounce in just six weeks as summer turned to fall: confidence in the dollar was fading fast. The Fed seemed unable to control the money supply—"One can make a reasonable case that the Fed faced disaster."[54]

How did this situation develop? As table 9–2 shows, between 1975 and 1979 the M1 money supply and prices rose at about the same rate. The velocity of M1 increased also, at about 56% of the M1 rate of increase. As noted earlier, price increases were gaining momentum with the passage of time.

It was generally thought that the U.S. economy would experience a slow-down ("growth recession") during 1979, and the first half of the year seemed to confirm this expectation, even to suggest the onset of a recession. Thus inflation would be kept at bay. But the revolution in Iran that made the Ayatollah Khomeini a household name disrupted oil production from that country and triggered a series of price increases—the second (since 1973) OPEC "oil shock"—that raised U.S. oil import prices by 87 percent between the end of 1978 and the end of 1979.[55] Prices of other primary commodities increased also as global demand strengthened. Then aggregate demand in the United States rebounded sharply in the second half of the year, confounding consensus forecasters. Under the combined circumstances of rising domestic and world demand, exogenous supply shock, and falling value of the dollar, the price level surged. Inflation psychology, the product of a decade of experience with persistent inflation, was an important factor in spending and borrowing behavior. M1 had increased by 89 percent over the decade, or about 2.5 times the 36 percent growth in real GNP. With the financial markets in turmoil, Paul Volcker rushed home from the annual meeting of the International Monetary Fund in Belgrade before its conclusion. In an extraordinary meeting of the Federal Open Market Committee

Table 9–2
Changes in Output, Prices, Money Stock, and Velocity of Money, 1975 to 1979
(percentage increase)

GNP (current dollars)	56
GNP (constant dollars)	20
Consumer price index	35
GNP price deflator	30
M1	32
Velocity of M1	18

Adapted from *Economic Report of the President, 1985*, pp. 232, 234, 238, 295, 303.

on Saturday night, October 6, 1979, quickly deemed "historic" by financial writers, the Federal Reserve adopted a new policy stance.

The Federal Reserve's October actions were traditional central bank defensive moves to halt inflation and defend the value of the national currency unit vis-à-vis other currencies. The discount rate was raised to 12 percent, and reserve requirements were increased on any increase in various bank liabilities, notably Eurodollar borrowings. What was taken to be of much greater significance was the announcement of a change in operating procedures by shifting away from the federal funds rate to controlling unborrowed bank reserves. The objective was to exercise greater control over the monetary aggregates, even though this would permit much larger fluctuations to occur in the federal funds rate. The Fed committed itself to targeting the money supply. In effect the Federal Reserve admitted that the weakness of the dollar was due to its failure to control the money supply, and it wanted the world to know that it was now determined to exercise effective control over the expansion of money and credit.

> The principal reason advanced for shifting to an operating procedure aimed at controlling the supply of bank reserves more directly was that it would provide greater assurance that the Committee's objectives for monetary growth could be achieved. In the present environment of rapid inflation, estimates of the relationship among interest rates, monetary growth, and economic activity had become less reliable than before, and monetary growth since the first quarter of 1979 had exceeded the rates expected despite substantial increases in short-term interest rates. . . .
>
> Committee members suggested that the shift in operating techniques, along with the other actions being contemplated by the Board of Governors, would tend to increase confidence at home and abroad in the System's determination to achieve its objectives for monetary growth and to avoid further deterioration in the inflationary outlook. Partly because it would increase uncertainty about the near-term course of interest rates, the new operating technique should induce banks to exercise greater caution in extending credit and might dampen speculative behavior by increasing its risks and costs. Altogether, the System's action would tend to moderate inflationary expectations, thereby exerting a constructive influence over time on decisions affecting wages and prices in domestic markets and on the value of the dollar in foreign exchange markets.[56]

The wild behavior of financial and commodity markets in an atmosphere of grave uncertainty had called for some dramatic and definitive gesture. Since the central policy message of monetarism is control of the money stock, it clearly appeared that the Federal Reserve had committed itself to monetarism. As we have seen, the Fed had been tending in this direction for a decade. In speeches and congressional testimony, its leaders had repeatedly voiced their belief in the necessity of adhering to money supply targets to restrain inflation, and they were required by the Humphrey–Hawkins Act of 1978 to tell Congress every six months what their target ranges were for the monetary and credit aggregates. Evidence of an unequivocal determination actually to arrest inflation was what the October 6, 1979, policy change was meant to provide. The question was: Can Volcker stand up to inflation?[57] Volcker had to do something striking to be convincing, for his predecessors at the helm of the Fed had all talked a strong anti-inflation game. His experience and expertise in government and the fact that he was known and respected by central bankers abroad are factors generally thought to have made him especially well qualified for the role he now assumed.

The quotation at the head of this section indicates how radical the policy switch of October 6, 1979, appeared when it was made. The adoption of a strategy based on narrow monetary aggregate growth rates with wide limits on the federal funds rate was a reversal of the previous strategy. Immediately following the adoption of the new monetary program, the growth of the money supply slowed, interest rates rose rapidly, and the dollar was stabilized on the foreign exchange market. Yet the inflation dragon had not yet been subdued, as the events of 1980 soon showed. To those of the monetarist persuasion the new policy gave "a lovely light," but like Edna St. Vincent Millay's candle, it did "not last the night."

A certain poignancy was added to the queasy mood of October 1979 by reminders that it was the golden jubilee of the start of the stock market collapse of 1929. At that time too the Federal Reserve raised interest rates, but with less determination than in 1979. The economy continued to grow right through to year's end, contrary to forecasts, prompting *The Economist* to observe that the U.S. economy had a boom with nine lives.[58]

Financial Innovation

Innovation in the field of banking was relatively minor for the first fifteen years following World War II, but as noted in chapters 7 and 8, there were important new developments during the 1960s. The chief catalyst was the rising rate of interest in an environment of government regulation, notably the interest rate ceilings applied to deposits in banks and thrift institutions. Banks developed the new strategy of liability management and presto, the new corporate time deposits known as negotiable CDs achieved instant success in attracting funds to banks. The banks also discovered organizational innovations in the form of one-bank holding companies and overseas branches (Eurobanks), and took a leaf from the security dealers' book by adopting repurchase agreements as yet another way of borrowing funds.

The incentive to innovate accelerated during the 1970s as interest rates shot up to much higher levels in 1974 and 1978–1979 than they had reached in the 1960s. A graph of interest rates from the end of World War II to 1980 resembles in a rough-and-ready way a geological profile showing first a gradually rising elevation from coastal plain to piedmont and then a steep rise to towering mountain ranges in the late 1970s. (The continental divide was reached in 1980–1981.) Under these conditions, further major innovations appeared. In 1972 the money market mutual fund, a mutation of the well-established common stock mutual fund, appeared. It grew rapidly in 1974 and phenomenally at the end of the 1970s and early 1980s when short-term interest rates reached skyward. Such funds gather money from depositors who can't afford the price of money market instruments by permitting them in effect to invest in such instruments indirectly through ownership of shares in the fund itself. Thus sums were drained from accounts in banks and thrifts paying low, regulated interest rates, and loaned at high money market rates to government, corporate and bank short-term borrowers.

> They are modern-day Robin Hoods who protect the public from a coalition of government and depository institution barons; as in the days of old, they increase social welfare by taking risks. The risks do not appear to be very great. Although there is no protection corresponding to deposit insurance, monetary authorities seem reluctant to allow a major bank to default on its certificates of deposit.[59]

In the wake of money market mutual funds, and no doubt stimulated by them, came several innovations in bank and thrift liabilities. One of these, the negotiable order of withdrawal (NOW account) appeared as quite a surprise to a generation accustomed to an "East is East and West is West" distinction between demand (checking) deposits paying no interest and savings/time deposits paying interest but not subject to withdrawal by check. The fusion of them into NOW accounts began in thrift institutions in Massachusetts and New Hampshire in 1972; thereafter they were permitted to be offered by banks in those states in 1974, after which they reached out like vines through New England and the Middle Atlantic states until finally at the end of December 1980 they were sanctioned for all fifty states.

A variety of time accounts (savings certificates) bearing higher interest rates the longer the maturity were also permitted by the regulatory authorities. Then on June 1, 1978, banks and thrift institutions were allowed to offer a new type of instrument called a money market certificate. These six-month time deposits were designed to give financial institutions greater flexibility in competing for funds, thus enabling them to provide a flow of funds to industries that tend to be deprived of them in times of tight money, notably housing; in other words, to avoid the now familar problem of disintermediation. The feature that made them a true innovation was the tying of their interest rate to the auction rate on the six-month U.S. Treasury bills. Money market certificates were enthusiastically received—within nine months the total outstanding reached $136 billion—and they helped in avoiding disintermediation. They did carry a high price to the nonbank thrift institutions, however, for the spread between their cost and the return on new mortgages was cut by 75 percent over the nine-month period. A few years later in 1982 depository institutions were given permission to offer money market accounts on which an unregulated rate of interest can be paid and which enable these institutions to compete very effectively with money market funds.

Whenever monetary policy and regulation inhibit financial institutions from the revenue-producing activities and aspirations that drive them, they can be counted on to find new ways of conducting their operations and to pursue them unless and until they are checked. "The one clear lesson from recent history is that financial institutions innovate whenever customer relationships are jeopardized by slow monetary growth."[60] The result of these changes in financial practices on the liabilities side of the combined balance sheet for all insured commercial banks is quite striking, as indicated in Table 9–3.

Attempts at Financial Reform

Two major studies of the financial system were sponsored by the federal government during the 1970s. First came the Commission on Financial Structure and Regulation appointed by President Nixon in 1970 (generally called the Hunt Commission after its chairman, Reed O. Hunt, a retired business executive). The motivation for the study was the belief that defi-

Table 9–3
Changes in Percentage Composition of the Liabilities of All Insured
Commercial Banks, 1970, 1980

	Percentage of Total Liabilities and Capital	
	1970	*1980*
Demand deposits	43 } 60	28 } 41
Passbook savings deposits	17	13
Time deposits	19	21
Large-size negotiable CDs	5 } 33	15 } 52
Miscellaneous liabilities[a]	9	16

Adapted from Lawrence S. Ritter and William L. Silber, *Principles of Money, Banking, and Financial Markets,* Fourth edition. New York: Basic Books, 1983, pp. 125, 127.

[a]Includes borrowings from the Federal Reserve and in the federal funds market, borrowing from bank parent holding companies and foreign branches, and repurchase agreements.

ciencies had been revealed in the financial system during the 1960s as a result of inflation and drastic shifts in the flow of funds. There was concern over the reduced liquidity of financial institutions which led them to restrict loans to certain groups of borrowers, notably residential mortgage borrowers, small businesses, and state and local governments. Sharply fluctuating interest rates meant greater risk and uncertainty. Total savings were viewed as inadequate to meet the combined heavy demands of the public and private sectors. The attitude behind the creation of the Hunt Commission was that desirable changes in the system were being prevented by government regulation.

The Hunt Commission's report (1971) recommended many reforms based on the general position that less regulation of financial intermediaries would produce more competition among them, thereby contributing to a more stable monetary/financial structure. To achieve the goal of greater competition, the Regulation Q interest rate limits needed to be eliminated and thrift institutions given freedom to acquire a greater variety of assets and to conduct business over a wider geographic area. Legislation was proposed in 1973 to give effect to several of the Hunt commission recommendations, but failed to be adopted.

In 1975 a second study was commissioned, this one by Congress. In due course it produced the Financial Institutions and the Nation's Economy (FINE) report, and again legislation was proposed based upon the report's recommendations for the removal of regulatory constraints, including the elimination of ceilings on deposit interest rates. Congress did not adopt these recommendations either.

The two attempts to bring reform during the 1970s very likely failed because the degree of concern had not yet become acute enough to generate the political force needed to overcome the objections of interest groups opposed to change. By 1980 the sense of crisis reached the boiling point, and comprehensive legislation was adopted. While the Hunt and FINE reports failed to bring legislative results in direct response to their recommendations, they may well have performed some spadework for the reforms of the early 1980s.

10
Charting a New Course? 1980–1985

> The decade of the 1980s resembles the 1930s in being a crucial watershed for determining the structure of the economy and the role of government. . . .
>
> As in the 1930s, the current financial system of the 1980s is experiencing significant structural change . . . [Complex changes] have recently occurred both in the financial system and in the conduct of monetary policy by the Federal Reserve.
> —Thomas F. Cargill and Gillian G. Garcia[1]

Strong winds blew across the economic/political landscape in the early 1980s. The economy suffered its deepest recession since the Great Depression. This painful experience succeeded in arresting inflation, but unemployment remained abnormally high even in the third year of the subsequent recovery. The strongest shift in half a century of the political winds brought into office a national administration dedicated to the proposition that the role of government in the economy must be shrunk and the role of market forces increased. This shift in political philosophy brought about two highly publicized developments. One of these, supply-side economics, was promoted as a rediscovery of an old idea with remarkable curative powers for the economy. It soon came generally to be viewed as less potent than advertised. The second was the appearance of a budget deficit of enormous size and persistence. How to evaluate and cope with the deficit became the dominant economic policy issue of the mid–1980s. These topics will be reviewed as background for the main concerns of this penultimate chapter: financial reform, the state of banking, and the unsettled state of monetary policy.

Macroeconomic Overview

The expansion that began in March 1975 reached a peak in January 1980. After drifting downward for six months to July 1980, the economy resumed its expansion for a year to July 1981. Then came the most pronounced slump since the 1930s—unemployment reached 10.8 percent—until the low point was reached in November 1982. For 1983 and the first half of 1984, real GNP growth was very strong, after which it tapered off to a much slower pace through 1986. What stands out is the sharpness of the recession and the vigor of the recovery between 1981 and 1984. By 1984 the inflation rate was only one-third that of 1980, while the unemployment rate was slightly higher. Table 10–1 shows output, price, and unemployment data annually, 1975 to 1984, as well as five-year annual averages comparing the last half of the seventies with the first half of the eighties.

Supply-side Economics

A half-dozen years ago, the term "supply-side economics" hadn't even been coined; last Aug. 13, the theory became enshrined in national economic policy when President Reagan signed a three-year, 25% cut in personal income tax rates.

—*The Wall Street Journal*[2]

The supply-side movement began in the mid–1970s among a small group of conservative economists, journalists, and politicians.[3] It was spawned by the perception that Keynesian demand management was unable to rescue the economy from rapid inflation and low real growth. Its advocates observed that inflation was pushing income receivers, particularly those in the upper and middle income strata, into increasingly higher tax brackets thereby

Table 10–1
Comparative Output, Price, and Unemployment Data, 1975–1984
(percent)

	Real GNP Growth (1)	Change in Consumer Price Index December to December (2)	Unemployment Rate (3)	Discomfort Index (2) + (3)
1975	− 1.2	7.0	8.5	15.5
1976	5.4	4.8	7.7	12.5
1977	5.5	6.8	7.1	13.9
1978	5.0	9.0	6.1	15.1
1979	2.8	13.3	5.8	19.1
1980	− .3	12.4	7.1	19.5
1981	2.5	8.9	7.6	16.5
1982	−2.1	3.9	9.7	13.6
1983	3.7	3.8	9.6	13.4
1984	6.8	4.0	7.5	11.5
Average 1975–1979	3.5	8.2	7.0	15.3
Average 1980–1984	2.1	6.6	8.3	14.9

Source: *Economic Report of the President, 1985*, pp. 235, 271, 295.

allegedly sapping incentives to work, save, and invest. A reduction in marginal tax rates would bring about a greater willingness to provide labor and capital, which would increase economic growth and restrain inflation. Say's Law had been discredited by Keynes, but now the supply-siders wanted to discredit Keynes and resurrect Say's Law. A simple diagram called a Laffer curve, drawn on a restaurant napkin by Professor Arthur B. Laffer, became a symbol of supply-side economics. It shows that as tax rates rise from zero, government revenues also rise from zero until eventually a further increase in tax rates discourages production, causing tax revenues to stop rising and eventually to fall. If tax rates rose to 100 percent, no (legal) production would occur and government revenue would return to zero. The main point is that tax *rates* may be so high that when they are reduced government *revenues* may rise or at least hold steady.

The economics profession was certainly not overwhelmed by the supply-side approach. Granted that tax reduction could increase incentives, there was the question of degree. Statistical studies suggested that rather modest results would ensue.[4] In addition to doubt about the extent of increased output, there were other complicating questions concerning demand effects, the distribution of income, and the size of budget deficits.

> Now, the heart of the supply-side argument is the conviction that the American economy is at a point on the curve far too high from the optimum point. Lowering taxes will give the supply side of the economy such a shot in the arm that the United States will slide down the Laffer curve. As a result, tax revenues eventually will rise enough to take care of increased funding of the military; stagflation will end; dynamic growth will begin, and the budget will be balanced.
>
> The trouble with the Laffer Curve is that . . . it is too simple to be of any service except as a symbol of a concept. In the case of the Laffer Curve, the concept is not new, and it is obvious—when taxes are too high they are counterproductive. The problem, of course, is to define *too high*. Few if any economists have any notion of what the Laffer Curve looks like except in the neighborhood of its end points. Even if they did know, few would be willing to say where to put the economy on it.[5]

Concern with the supply side of the economy, that is, with the ability of the economy to produce greater abundance over time, was the primary focus of classical economics beginning with Adam Smith. Keynes shifted attention to the demand side during the 1930s because Western economies were failing to realize their output potential. After World War II, growth theory explicitly examined the question of how to achieve optimal economic expansion over time. As noted in an earlier chapter, the record of growth performance was very good by historical standards for much of the post–World War II period. By the 1970s, however, a slowdown in gains in productivity combined with high inflation led to disenchantment with the existing state of economic theory and policy, and to a renewed emphasis on the question of how to generate increased output and gains in real income. It is hard to imagine economists going to the barricades over so reasonable a matter. What sent them to the barricades was the specific connotation that supply-side economics came to have as a result of its extreme proponents: lower tax rates would so galvanize the economy through more work, saving, and investment that the budget deficit would fall. Eighteen months after the Reagan administration began implementation of the highly touted tax cuts, the economy was severely depressed and the country faced deficits of $200 billion. Many tax-cut supporters must have felt duped.

The disappointing macroeconomic performance of the United States during the 1970s opened the way for the new administration to make its diagnosis of what was wrong. Ronald Reagan had no hesitation in identifying the trouble and pronouncing the remedy: the main cause of the nation's economic problems was the federal government itself, and the remedy was to have considerably less of it. Tax cuts were one of several components of the Reagan administration's program to deal with the troubled economy. In addition the money supply was to grow more slowly and steadily, government regulation would be reduced, and the federal government would spend relatively less. This policy mix was expected by administration savants not only to have salutary long-term results but to reduce inflation and raise output quickly. How could inflation-free prosperity be expected in the short-run instead of the painful adjustment predicted by critics? The magic additive was the newly prominent rational expectations (or "new monetarist") approach, according to which economic actors, including workers, make good use of economic information to forecast future price changes. Once the new administration had made clear its firm commitment to reducing inflation, expectations of high inflation would vanish, workers would lower their wage demands, and interest rates would fall without an increase in unemployment. Rational expectations theorists view the economy's aggregate supply curve as vertical, so that government policy altering aggregate demand does not affect the levels of output and employment. The supply curve would begin shifting to the right as incentives increased and regulatory controls decreased. A balanced budget was projected for 1984. The steep recession of 1981–1982 conspicuously and emphatically failed to confirm the rational expectations view that if the monetary authority presented a clearly articulated policy of monetary contraction, inflation would fall without curtailing economic activity or raising unemployment.[6]

The Reagan administration's diagnosis of and prescription for the economy were amply challenged. Some of the arguments of one carefully reasoned study are presented here in condensed form.

From the 1950s to the 1970s total government expenditures (federal, state, and local) rose from 26 percent to 32 percent of GNP. However, those expenditures that involve government claims on real resources grew by only 1.5 percentage points and those of the federal government fell by 3.8 points. The reason overall government expenditures grew substantially was due to transfer payments for social security and other social insurance programs. Compared with other industrialized countries, total government spending as a percent of GNP in the United States is relatively low. It may nevertheless be true that supply-siders are correct in that the more generous transfer programs, higher taxes, and increased regulations had harmful incentive effects on work effort, saving, investing, and productivity. If so, how serious were these effects?

The labor force grew substantially during the 1970s, and the saving rate of both households and businesses also rose, so that "there is no prima facie evidence to support the view that either work or saving was discouraged." While it is true that studies conclude that taxes and transfers reduce work effort and may reduce saving, the extent and degree of certainty fall well short of expectations raised by some supply-side advocates.

As a share of GNP, investment in the 1970s was on a par with the earlier postwar years. "The slower growth in the amount of capital per worker that occurred during the 1970s was due to the dramatic expansion in the labor force, not to less investment."

Up to 25 percent of the slowdown in productivity growth has been attributed to increased social regulation. During the 1970s businesses had to spend more to comply with regulations designed to provide environmental, health, safety, and consumer protection. Clearly society benefits from cleaner air and greater safety. Yet these benefits escape measurement in GNP, with the perverse result that measured productivity may fall while social welfare is rising.

"All in all, the Reagan administration properly focused on slower productivity growth as a major cause of the disappointing growth in living standards during the 1970s; but it probably placed too much blame on past government policies as the cause of the problem and thus too much hope in its own policies as the solution. Taxes do not appear to have had a major impact on work, saving, or investment, and only a modest portion of the productivity slowdown is related to increasing social regulations."[7]

By 1984, after supply-side economics (Reaganomics) had been in effect for three years, it clearly had failed to accomplish the overly ambitious results claimed for it by its ardent proponents. The tax cuts did, however, stimulate investment spending as expected according to standard neoclassical economics.[8]

The Big Budget Deficit

There is no painless way to reduce a large deficit.
—Alice M. Rivlin[9]

Following the 1981–1982 recession, output and employment revived and inflation dropped to the lowest rate in a decade, but federal government deficits became a source of consternation and reiterated expressions of dire consequences to follow if corrective action were not taken. Deficits have been common since the 1930s, but those of the 1980s have been inordinately large. They doubled in size relative to GNP from about 2.8 percent in 1980–1981 to 5.3 percent in 1985–1986. Budget data for fiscal years 1980 through 1986 are shown in table 10–2.

Economists regularly use the ratio of federal debt to the gross national product to judge the importance of the national debt, for GNP measures the capacity of the economy to save and provide taxes. As national output expands, the economy can service a larger debt, but if the debt rises at a faster rate than output, the ability of the economy to handle the debt is reduced. The ratio of federal debt to GNP followed a declining trend from the end of World War II until the 1970s. This trend was sharply reversed during the first half of the 1980s: federal debt held by the public rose from 28 percent of GNP in Fiscal Year (FY) 1980 to 37 percent in FY 1984. To James Tobin, the change in policy that occurred in 1981 was a fiscal revolution with long-term implications:

> With present spending programs and existing tax and transfer legislation, the (debt-GNP) ratio will rise to 46 percent before the end of the decade and will still be rising, with no stopping place in sight. This outlook holds even in optimistic scenarios in which the economy completes its recovery in another couple of years and settles down without recession into a path of sustained growth with 6 percent unemployment.[10]

Net interest, the cost of servicing the national debt, rose from 2 percent of GNP in 1980 to 3 percent in 1984, and whereas in 1980 net interest

Table 10–2
Federal Budget Data, 1980–1986
($ billion)

Fiscal Year	Total Receipts	Total Outlays	Deficit
1980	517	591	74
1981	599	678	79
1982	618	746	128
1983	601	808	208
1984	667	852	185
1985	734	946	212
1986	769	990	221

Source: *Economic Indicators*. Washington, D.C.: U.S. Government Printing Office, November 1986, p. 32.

absorbed 10 percent of total federal receipts, by 1984 it took 17 percent. In 1984 the interest on the debt was equal to 37 percent of total individual income taxes collected. The interest cost on the national debt has grown rapidly, not only because of the mounting size of the debt but also because of the very high rates of interest to be paid. High deficits entail high interest rates as a result of very heavy borrowing by the Treasury in the money and capital markets to finance the deficits. The real interest rate—the market rate less the rate of inflation—is what matters. Although nominal interest rates fell very substantially from their 1981 highs, the persistence of high real interest rates during the first half of the 1980s is one of the most notable features of the period.

There are multiple reasons for the widely held view among orthodox economists that the large deficits constitute a danger for the economy. Foremost is the contention that deficits on the order of $200 billion will absorb a large share of net private savings, "crowd out" private investment spending, and therefore inhibit economic growth. The portion of savings left over for capital formation is very likely to be inadequate to sustain healthy economic growth. Conceivably private saving could increase to compensate for the huge federal dissaving, but there is not much evidence on which to base such an outcome. Instead whenever the economy does get close to capacity, there is likely to be a scramble by government, business, and consumers for the relatively scarce flow of savings, thus driving up interest rates until they threaten to trip the economy into recession. Even if recession is avoided for a considerable period of time, the deficits are likely to take a heavy toll in reduced economic growth.

> High deficits and high interest rates do not necessarily mean immediate disaster for the economy. The deficits will continue to stimulate the economy generally, while the high interest rates will tend to slow particular types of spending, especially housing and business investment. High deficits and high interest rates affect the *mix* of total spending—with more resources going to consumption and less to housing and investment than would be the case if we had lower deficits and lower interest rates. A low level of investment in plant and equipment is likely to reduce productivity increases and hamper economic growth in the longer run. Penalizing investment is borrowing from the future to increase consumption now.[11]

During previous periods of economic expansion the federal budget moved steadily toward elimination of the deficit. As the economy approached cyclical peaks in 1973 and 1979, for example, the budget was essentially balanced. But after the deficit quadrupled from an annual rate of $50 billion early in 1981 to $200 billion at the end of 1982 it stayed at that level for the next three years while the economy recovered. In just five years, from the end of FY 1980 to the end of FY 1985, the gross federal debt doubled. Unless a miracle occurs, sooner or later recession will strike again. To ask what, then, would happen to the deficit and to the economy seems a little like asking Pandora to open a box. That the deficit might rise to $300 billion or more seems quite likely. The cost of servicing interest on the national debt would then rise, perhaps to 25 percent of total federal spending. Several consequences might well follow: (1) high real interest rates could choke off a substantial recovery; (2) massive monetary expansion could be used to break the log jam with the potential for serious inflation later; (3) the safety of financial securities—perhaps even Treasury bills—might be called into question. Any comfort that might be taken from this scenario seems cold indeed.[12]

In addition to the threat to economic growth and stability posed by high real interest rates on domestic investment spending and to the problems that might come with the next recession, there are several ominous international economic effects attributable to the budget deficits. The high interest rates have acted as magnets drawing capital from abroad. Such net capital inflows provide funds to finance the budget deficit and private investment, but the demand for dollars raised the exchange value of the dollar so much that the competitiveness of American industry and agriculture in world markets was seriously impaired. By the mid–1980s, with the nation experiencing enormous balance-of-trade and current account deficits, a sense of alarm developed over the plight of industries facing foreign competition, and this in turn has fostered a demand in Congress for trade protectionism.

The huge net capital inflows have led to concern that the United States has become too dependent on foreign capital. There is the prospect that eventually foreigners will have their fill of dollar assets as their portfolios become saturated with them. At such time their reluctance to acquire more dollar claims could precipitate a drastic fall in the value of the dollar in the foreign exchange markets. The drying up of the capital inflow might well put severe upward pressure on interest rates. Furthermore the continuation of large net capital inflows would tend to reduce our future standard of living. During 1985, after seventy-one years as a net creditor nation, the United States again became a net debtor. The significant point is that in the future, net interest payments will have to be made to service the foreign net dollar claims. The larger these interest obligations become, the greater the necessity eventually for an export surplus of goods and services, thereby leaving less output for U.S. consumption. We as a nation have been spending more for consumption, investment, and military purposes than we produce, drawing on the savings of the rest of the world. Since this pattern must in the future be reversed, it follows that the large net capital inflows amount to mortgaging our economic future.[13]

High interest rates in the United States tend to cause high interest rates in other countries, inhibiting their growth. They also make it difficult for third world countries to repay their debts to American banks. As a result the banks and the international monetary system are put at risk, and third world borrowing countries have had to adopt restrictive domestic economic policies to deal with their balance of payments problems.

The pessimistic interpretation of the large budget deficits summarized above is disputed by supply-side economists and Reagan administration officials. In its Annual Report in 1985 the Council of Economic Advisers attributes only minor importance to the demand effects of fiscal policy on the economy and gives primacy to the supply-side. Its interpretation of the high real interest rates and high exchange value of the dollar over the past few years attributes them to the economic recovery after 1982 rather than the deficit. As the council explains it, lower taxes and reduced inflation raised the after-tax rate of return on new investment projects. The increased profitability of U.S. corporations in a context of vigorous recovery and favorable long-term prospects for the economy raised the demand for dollars. While the council recognizes the negative effects of the strong dollar on U.S. exports, it sees these balanced by favorable effects.

> In many respects, however, the dollar's rise in value has been beneficial. The strong dollar has stimulated production and investment in sectors less involved in international trade. In other industries, competition from imports has prompted more expenditure on plant and equipment as well as greater attention to controlling wages and other costs. Prices of traded goods and close substitutes have been kept lower than they would have been otherwise, thereby benefiting both U.S. consumers and U.S. producers who use imported inputs. Undoubtedly, the dollar's rise since 1980 has made the task of bringing inflation under control considerably easier. In addition, because of the shift in demand toward dollar assets, U.S. interest rates have been lower and real investment higher than would have been the case otherwise. Stronger U.S. investment will ultimately mean higher productivity and faster potential growth.[14]

The council agrees, however, that the prospective budget deficits are too large. This conclusion is based mainly on the effects of the deficit on the budget in the future: increased future interest payments will have to be met by cutting back on noninterest expenditures or by raising taxes. The council dismisses budgetary effects on the economy (apart from long-run supply-side effects) with the statement that "Changes in Federal expenditure, tax receipts, and the deficit appear to have little effect on total demand, as measured by nominal GNP, except in times of war."[15]

The huge budget deficits have not, as of 1986, had disastrous consequences. Economic expansion has been in progress since the last quarter of
1982. Supply-siders see this as confirmation of their approach, while the
Keynesian interpretation is that it shows the effectiveness of the stimulative
fiscal policy coming to the rescue of a sick economy in tandem with an
expansionary monetary policy. But the true time of testing is yet to come,
according to the arguments outlined above. There has been a widespread
belief for several years that the deficit should be brought under control, but
the political consensus necessary for this may require the onset of an acute
economic problem.[16] Meanwhile, like Edgar Allan Poe's "grim, ungainly,
ghastly, gaunt, and ominous" raven, month after month and year after year
the deficit "still is sitting, *still* is sitting."

Big budget deficits were never advocated by policymakers, so how did
it happen that policies were adopted to create them? As noted in the previous
section, some prominent supply-siders sold the idea that tax cuts would
"unleash" such a great expansion of productive activity that the budget
would quickly be balanced by an enlarged flow of federal revenues. But there
is another explanation of a political nature. A strategy was allegedly designed
that began with the major tax cut. Then, when a large deficit appeared, the
congressional budget process would be used to cut back nondefense spending
programs to an extent politically impossible without the deficit. The prime
objective of the Reagan administration—substantially to reduce nondefense
spending—would be "forced" on Congress by the necessity of dealing with
the alarming deficit. When Congress refused to make sufficiently drastic
nondefense spending cuts, the strategy failed. Professor Martin Feldstein,
who served from mid-1982 to mid-1984 as chairman of the Council of
Economic Advisers, spoke out clearly against the deficits and recognized the
need for additional tax revenues, but his forthright stand only served to
offend leading members of the administration that he served.[17]

Financial Reform

Deregulation in banking is part of a broader movement begun in the late
1970s during the Carter administration. In his final Economic Report, President Carter pointed with pride to accomplishments made after "decades of
inaction."

> In these 4 years we witnessed more progress in economic deregulation than
> at any other time in the century. In the face of great skepticism and initial
> opposition, the executive branch, the Congress, and some of the indepen-
> dent regulatory agencies have deregulated or drastically reduced regulation

in the airline, trucking, and railroad industries, and in banking and other financial institutions.[18]

The theme of economic deregulation has obviously been consistent with the laissez-faire philosophy of the Reagan administration, although the actual movement in this direction was relatively small during the first five Reagan years.

> Since deregulation of some markets began several years ago, the experience has been almost uniformly encouraging. My Administration has supported these step-by-step efforts to reduce these regulations in markets that would otherwise be competitive. It is now time to consider broad measures to eliminate many of these economic regulations especially as they affect the natural gas, transportation, communications, and financial markets.[19]

It was observed at the end of chapter 9 that financial reform was a subject of study and discussion but not of federal legislative action during the 1970s. The 1980s, however, have been a decade of deregulation in the financial industry. Two major national laws have been adopted, the Depository Institutions Deregulation and Monetary Control Act (1980) and the Garn–St. Germain Act (1982), and many changes have occurred in state regulations also. As a result, banking activities are permitted that were previously off limits. The inflation of the 1970s gave increased incentives to financial institutions to evade the regulations and, in the case of Federal Reserve member banks, to drop out of the Federal Reserve System. Pressure for change that had been building since the 1950s finally overcame many regulatory restrictions on the range, pricing, and marketing of financial products. Just as the financial reforms of the 1930s resulted from the Great Depression, the reforms of the 1980s were precipitated by the crisis atmosphere involving inflation, high interest rates, disintermediation, speculation, currency market fluctuation, and fears of financial collapse which had the effect of concentrating the minds of legislators and administrators.

The Depository Institutions Deregulation and Monetary Control Act (1980 act) is considered the most significant legislation in its field since the 1930s. It is an omnibus law dealing with a whole collection of problems pertaining to the structure of financial institutions.[20] Its numerous provisions fall under two main headings, deregulation and monetary control. Selected items are presented here in summary form to indicate the main features of the 1980 act.[21]

Deregulation—to increase competition—took three forms:

1. *Elimination or modification of interest rate ceilings.*
   a. Regulation Q interest ceilings on time/savings deposits at all depository institutions to be reduced gradually and finally eliminated by

March 31, 1986. (The prohibition of interest on demand deposits was left unchanged). The Depository Institutions Deregulation Committee (DIDC) consisting of the chairman of the Board of Governors of the Federal Reserve System, the chairman of the Federal Deposit Insurance Corporation, the secretary of the Treasury, the chairman of the Federal Home Loan Bank Board, the chairman of the National Credit Union Administration, and the comptroller of the currency was created to supervise the phasing out of interest rate ceilings.

    b. Elimination of state government usury ceilings on residential mortgage loans (although a state could keep a limit if it acted by April 1, 1983).

    c. Elimination of state government usury ceilings on business and agricultural loans in excess of $25,000, provided the ceiling was less than 5 percentage points over the discount rate of the Federal Reserve plus any surcharge (although a state could retain such a limit if it acted by April 1, 1983).

2. *Expansion of sources of funds for depository institutions*— to increase the competitive ability of the several types of institutions by enabling them to attract funds more effectively. In particular the nonbank depository institutions gained in their ability to compete with banks.

    a. Thrifts as well as banks were permitted to issue NOW accounts as of January 1, 1981, thus making NOW accounts available nationwide. The NOW accounts must be held by natural persons or nonprofit organizations. (The accounts are known as share draft accounts at credit unions).

    b. Federal deposit insurance was raised to $100,000 per account (from $40,000).

3. *Expansion of uses of funds by depository institutions*—primarily to enable savings and loan associations to diversify by reducing their dependence on mortgage loans.

    a. Percentage-of-asset limitations were removed from certain categories of assets of S&Ls.

    b. S&Ls were permitted to make commercial real estate and consumer loans and to acquire commercial paper up to 20 percent of assets.

Monetary control modifications—to increase Federal Reserve control over the money supply—took two main forms:

1. *Extension of federally imposed reserve requirements.* Reserve requirements administered by the Federal Reserve System were made applicable to nonmember banks and nonbank depository institutions as well as to member banks, a major transfer of regulatory authority from state to

federal jurisdiction. By ending the historic dual set of reserve requirements set separately by the Federal Reserve and state regulatory agencies, Congress met the problem of declining Federal Reserve membership
due to the more stringent requirements of the system. The new uniform
structure, to be phased in gradually during the 1980s, is also simpler
than the old reserve requirement structure.

a. Uniform reserve requirements are to be set up by the Fed nationwide
   for all depository institutions regardless of type, charter, or size.

b. Transactions (checkable) deposits are subject to a reserve set within
   an 8 to 14 percent range (3 percent on deposit balances up to $25
   million initially but with allowance for a gradually rising deposit base).
   Nonpersonal time deposits are subject to a reserve set within a 0 to
   9 percent range.

2. *Extension of Federal Reserve power in other ways.* Instead of interacting
   only with member banks, the Federal Reserve acquired a relationship
   with all depository institutions. The latter have the same borrowing privileges at the Fed, may obtain Federal Reserve services at the same fee
   schedule, and must furnish financial reports to the Fed. In effect, though
   not in name, the depository institutions not previously member banks
   have been drafted into the ranks of the member banks.

Developments in the financial markets following the 1980 act made it
clear that further changes would be necessary. Immediately following the
(March) 1980 act, short-term interest rates fell, but later in 1980 and on
through mid–1982 they were extremely high.[22] Under these conditions it
was not feasible to implement with any speed the phasing out of Regulation
Q ceilings, since the higher market rates would be a crushing burden to
depository institutions, especially to the S&Ls and mutual savings banks.
S&Ls were already under severe pressure as a result of paying market rates
on money market certificates and because of depositors shifting from passbook savings accounts to NOW accounts against which reserves of 12 percent were required. In 1981 on average the S&Ls paid a higher rate to their
depositors than they earned on their mortgages. Furthermore, while disintermediation had slowed from earlier years, the depository institutions were
still unable effectively to compete for funds. In contrast the money market
mutual funds tripled their assets over two years beginning at the end of 1980,
reaching the $240 billion level by late 1982. The plight of the depository
institutions was aggravated by the onset of the severe recession of 1981–
1982. The deteriorating condition of the thrift industry reached a crisis stage
characterized by declining earnings and an increasing failure rate, thereby
providing the stimulation for another financial reform law.

The Garn–St. Germain Depository Institutions Act (1982 act) was a direct response to the problems of the thrifts in general and the S&Ls in particular. Its leading features follow in summary form.[23]

1. *Sources of funds for depository institutions.*

   Depository institutions were authorized to offer money market deposit accounts (MMDAs) designed specifically to be equivalent to and competitive with money market mutual funds (MMMFs). In December 1982 they became available for accounts of $2,500 or more with no interest ceiling, limited transactions features, and no reserve requirement on personal accounts. In addition, in January 1983 Super-NOW accounts (SNOWs) were authorized which permitted unlimited transactions but required a $2,500 minimum balance and were subject to the reserve requirement for transactions balances.[24]

   Regulation Q ceiling differentials between banks and nonbank depository institutions were required to be removed by the beginning of 1984. Thus thrifts would no longer offer a rate ¼ percent above that of commercial banks as they had been permitted to do on most types of deposits subject to ceiling regulation.

2. *Uses of funds for depository institutions.*

   The ability of thrifts to acquire assets was significantly broadened. Federally chartered S&Ls and savings banks were given the power to make commercial loans and to invest in the accounts of other insured institutions, invest in state and local government obligations, and make consumer and educational loans.

   Thrifts may easily change their charters from state to federal (and federal to state, if state law allows). Variable rate mortgages, already in use by federally-chartered institutions, could be offered by state-chartered institutions.

3. *Emergency powers.*

   The 1982 act gave the Federal Deposit Insurance Corporation and the Federal Savings and Loan Insurance Corporation extraordinary powers to deal with the severely troubled thrift industry. These powers could provide aid to meet the needs of institutions that are insolvent, in default, or in peril of collapse. They were made available to meet threats to the stability of the financial system. A half-dozen types of steps were authorized, including acquiring the assets or liabilities of institutions, giving guarantees, and issuing net worth certificates. Emergency acquisitions were authorized permitting institutions to acquire other institutions in cases otherwise prevented by rules against cross-industry and cross-state-line acquisitions. The emergency powers were granted for a three-year period.

The 1982 act continued the process of deregulation begun by the 1980 act. Competition among depository institutions and between them and the MMMFs was significantly increased. The effect of the 1982 act was to "accelerate the movement toward a more efficient and flexible intermediary sector."[25] The success of the MMDA and SNOW accounts was quite remarkable. Within just a few months of their introduction they surpassed the peak level of the MMMFs reached in November 1982, and the rapid growth of the MMMFs turned into decline. The problem of disintermediation, an issue for many years, had been laid to rest as a result of the acts of 1980 and 1982.

The State of Banking

Pressure for change from within and without the banking industry is presently very great. While much uncertainty exists about the configuration to which the process is leading, there is little doubt that "American banking is in a state of flux."[26]

The nation is accustomed to reports on the state of the union, the budget, and the economy which provide focal points for discussion and the formation of policy. If a report on the state of banking were prepared, what would it contain? The purpose of this section is to provide an indication of the main features of such a hypothetical report by identifying the issues that have concerned policymakers in the mid–1980s. The state of banking is of particular interest and importance because rapid changes have occurred in recent years, posing questions for regulators, legislators, and the general public. Between World War I and World War II (especially as a result of the chaotic conditions during the early 1930s), a regulatory framework was established that placed distinct limits on the activities of banks and other financial institutions. The limits were designed to provide a safe and sound system, to prevent excessive concentration of financial power, and to preserve a well-established policy of Congress that there should be a clear separation between banking and "commerce," that is, activity unrelated to banking. For about a third of a century after World War II the regulatory limitations were, on the whole, kept intact, but in the 1970s and especially during the 1980s the regulatory restraining walls have been breached. Financial innovation together with regulatory and legislative changes have already substantially modified the system and, if unchecked, may transform it in ways that may or may not be in the public interest.

Legislation of the late 1920s and mid–1930s partitioned the financial system: each institutional category—commercial banks, investment banks, thrifts, and so on—was limited to a separate set of products, thus limiting competition among categories. Banks concentrated on accepting deposits and making loans, for they were largely excluded from the securities, real estate, and insurance businesses. Competition was also limited among banks, and between them and the other types of financial institutions, by ceilings on the rate of interest that could be paid on deposits. Furthermore, there were geographic restrictions prohibiting interstate banking and requiring national banks to abide by the geographical rules set by state law for state-chartered banks.

In recent years the barriers to competition have been crumbling. Some of the reasons for the increased competition, both among banks and between them and other financial institutions, have previously been discussed. Price competition results from the elimination of interest rate ceilings under the 1980 act. Product competition has increased as a result of the spread of NOW accounts by thrifts and banks, by the creation of money market mutual funds and money market deposit accounts, and by the expanded powers for thrifts granted by the 1982 act. Other competitive developments include the recent entry of large organizations such as Merrill Lynch and Sears, Roebuck as providers of various financial services, and by rule changes that permit banks to enter the securities business by offering brokerage services. Changes in technology have also been a spur to competition, and some states are giving banks under their jurisdiction the right to practice nonbanking activities that are denied under federal law.

The most prominent of the areas of change and of potential change is interstate banking. In a formal, legal sense, interstate banking is essentially prohibited in the United States, but in fact it has become widespread and is likely to grow much more. Federal law shut the door against interstate banking but left several windows open, and the financial community has been breaking and entering through others as well. It was not until the 1920s that national banks were permitted to have any branches. In 1927 the McFadden Act permitted national banks to establish branches in the city where their head office was located, provided state banks had branches there. In 1933 the law was amended to allow national banks to have whatever branching privileges were accorded by the various states to state banks, so that the branching privileges might be state-wide or limited to a smaller area, but did not extend across state lines. The principle of the McFadden Act was retained in the Douglas Amendment of the Bank Holding Company Act of 1956—again the federal government played follow-the-leader behind the states by deciding that whether or not a bank holding company might acquire an out-of-state subsidiary bank would depend upon state law. Since the laws pertain to banks, it is vital to know what a bank is from a legal standpoint. As defined since 1970 when the Bank Holding Company Act was amended, a bank is any institution that does two things: (1) accepts demand deposits, (2) engages in the business of making commercial loans. If an institution does not perform both of these activities, it is not a bank but a "nonbank" able to perform on an interstate basis almost any type of financial service.

Methods by which financial institutions have made interstate banking "a reality today in everything except name" are now summarized.[27]

1. *Grandfathered activities.*
   When Congress acted to restrict interstate bank holding company operations it exempted ("grandfathered") a number of banking organizations already engaged in such operations.

2. *Loan production offices and Edge Act corporations.*
   Banking organizations control hundreds of loan production offices on an interstate basis from which they can reach potential customers in different parts of the country. "Edge Act corporations," although limited to financing international trade, are able to operate on an interstate basis also.

3. *4(c)8 subsidiaries.*
   Section 4(c)8 of the Bank Holding Company Act as amended in 1970 permits holding companies to engage in so-called nonbank activities. A holding company may acquire shares of a subsidiary company engaged in bank-type activities. Since such organizations are not legally banks, once established they are free to open offices in any number of states. The result of this legal loophole is that holding companies provide on an interstate level many of the same financial services as banks. A survey by the Federal Reserve Bank of Atlanta in December 1982 identified 382 such subsidiaries with more than 5,500 offices, each providing financial service across state boundaries.

4. *Reciprocal and nonreciprocal interstate banking laws.*
   A wave of state legislation involving twenty-two states during 1981–1984 makes possible entry by out-of-state banking operations. Some are on a reciprocal basis while others are not. The legality of regional interstate banking was upheld by the Supreme Court in 1985, giving impetus to regional mergers in New England and the Southeast where legislation already permits them. Other parts of the country are likely to follow their example quite soon.

5. *Nonbank banks.*
   The inelegant oxymoron *nonbank banks* has been coined for institutions chartered as banks but which fall outside the bounds of federal law. One type, called special-purpose banks, results from state legislation permitting out-of-state institutions to operate a bank confined to certain services such as credit card operation or wholesale banking. Two other basic types, consumer banks and commercial lending banks, do not meet the legal definition of a bank because they do not engage in both re-

quired activities (accepting deposits, making commercial loans) and therefore are not subject to interstate restrictions. Firms in different lines of business that have many accounts, such as Merrill Lynch (securities), Prudential (insurance), and Sears, Roebuck (retailing), have the potential for establishing consumer banking. They can quite readily realize this potential by acquiring a nonbank bank which will offer demand deposits (but not commercial loans) and which will have deposit insurance and access to the payments system. The acquiring (holding) company is not subject to regulation as a bank holding company. Some states have reacted to the recent trend toward creating nonbank banks by enacting legislation barring them.

What does all this mean for the safety, stability, and competitiveness of the American banking system? What costs and benefits may result? Are the changes bringing a high quality of services at low cost? Are serious dangers inherent in the process that call for renewed legislative and regulatory control?

The favorable results of the weakening of artificial boundaries to competition, and of innovation, come as greater efficiency. As greater competition improves the intermediation process through which funds are gathered and distributed, the operation of the real economy also improves. The financial system becomes more diversified and flexible. Savings depositors benefit from higher rates, customer services are increased, and the bane of disintermediation, with its discriminating impact on the housing industry, is eliminated. The ability of banks and thrifts to offer a greater range of debt obligations paying market rates and with a variety of maturities allows them to match rates and maturities on loans with those on deposits to a greater degree. Proponents of further deregulation anticipate generally lower rates on loans and better service for small businesses.

The other—unfavorable—side of the ledger provides abundant reason for concern about the present and future state of banking. Bank failures have become much more numerous in recent years, and loan losses have been high. Questions have been raised about excessive risk taking by financial institutions, about the prospects of excessive concentration of financial resources as the division between banking and commerce erodes, and about the future of banks in rural areas.

The problem of bank safety seemed well under control after the reforms of the 1930s until the 1980s. On average about 6 banks failed per year in 35 years ending in 1981 out of a banking population of some 14,000 banks. Since then the toll of failures has risen rapidly: 1982—42, 1983—48, 1984—79, 1985—120, 1986—138. It is not just the number of bank failures that has caused concern, but that some very large banks have failed or been in trouble, and unsound, even scandalous banking practices have been disclosed. The failure of the United American Bank of Knoxville, Tennessee, was followed by a rash of bank failures in 1983–1984, 12 of which were linked to wheeler-dealers at UAB.[28] The most dramatic, and frightening, case was the virtual collapse of Continental Illinois National Bank & Trust Company of Chicago. For several months during 1984 desperate resuscitative efforts were necessary to keep this financial giant (sixth largest U.S. bank in 1981) alive.

Even a capsule account of the debacle at Continental Illinois requires mention of the Penn Square Bank of Oklahoma City, which failed in 1982. Penn Square made enormous loans with reckless abandon to oil wildcatters and drillers during the period of acute energy shortage and rising oil prices, especially following the second oil shock in 1979, on the assumption that oil prices would continue to rise. When oil prices headed down and old borrowers began to default, loans were extended to new borrowers on flimsy collateral. Revelations of blatant irregularities, chicanery, and crass behavior by its officers have made Penn Square a case study of how positions of trust can be abused.[29] A large volume of loans generated by Penn Square beyond its own capital capacity were sold to Continental Illinois, which took loans that did not meet its own standards. Continental Illinois acquired loans that were not well-secured and that were not properly documented. When Penn Square failed, Continental Illinois was left holding the bag. In addition to the energy loans, it also held large amounts of doubtful loans it had made to less developed countries (LDCs). Continental Illinois was heavily exposed to risk on its liabilities side as well; nearly 75 percent of its deposits exceeded $100,000, the maximum amount covered by the FDIC. The revelation of extensive problem loans early in 1984 made depositors queasy, and in May a rumor of impending failure led to massive withdrawals. From May to July, sums in excess of $10 billion were pumped into Continental Illinois by banks and federal agencies to keep it afloat. But even after the FDIC broke precedent by guaranteeing the full amount of deposits, not just the first $100,000, the depositors were not impressed enough to stay on board what they considered the financial equivalent of the *Titanic*. Finally, when the FDIC was unable to arrange a merger with a healthy bank, it took over a large chunk of problems loans, put in additional capital, and assumed ownership of 80 percent of the bank, thereby nationalizing it in all but name. The alternative was to let it fail and risk international financial havoc. The FDIC removed the top management of the bank, as it regularly does when a bank fails. Some chief officers of Continental Illinois who were in charge when the problems developed, and therefore were responsible for the success or failure of the enterprise, took early retirement a few months before the bank's demise, laden with munificent pensions, an arrangement that leads to reflection on the rewards and punishments of capitalism.

The high rate of bank failures and considerable number of "problem banks" in the 1980s is largely explained by economic adjustments from rapid inflation in the 1970s to disinflation in the 1980s.[30] Three main categories of loans, energy, LDC,[31] and agricultural, have suffered as borrowers experienced declining prices and high real interest rates. What about deregulation as a cause of what some observers consider a banking crisis? It is generally thought that while deregulation has been constructive in important ways, it has also contributed to the system's problems. There is recognition that the banking system today requires further reform, and that deregulation needs to be evaluated in the context of the requirements for stability.

Deregulation means greater freedom for bankers to venture into risky activities in search of growth and profit.[32] When a bank is in trouble the FDIC traditionally has protected all deposit balances, not just the insured balances, by keeping the bank from failing. The only large bank to be liquidated (with large depositors suffering large losses) was Penn Square in 1982 when the FDIC chairman was William Isaac, an avid deregulator and exponent of "market discipline." According to this approach, banks that overextend themselves or behave imprudently would be led to correct their mistakes and mend their ways by the actions of corporate treasurers and money managers, who would bring pressure on them, in the absence of FDIC protection, by withdrawing deposits gradually. It would not be necessary for Big Brother to intervene because peer brothers would give errant bankers the needed message. These sophisticated depositors would have an incentive to monitor the banks' performance and the ability to act as the policemen of the free market. When Continental Illinois came under fire, the large depositors did not behave so benignly but took their money the old-fashioned way—they ran on the bank.[33] This conjured up the danger of runs on other banks and an international financial panic as foreigners rushed to withdraw their U.S. balances. Under these ominous circumstances the FDIC returned to its previous policy of protecting large depositors, but its credibility had been shattered by the Penn Square experience, with the result that eventually the U.S. government became the majority shareholder in the restructured Continental Illinois Bank. It is clear (1) that the public interest demands that the money supply and therefore the banking system must be kept stable, (2) that the private sector cannot be entrusted unaided to maintain this stability, (3) that the government must protect the system by bearing some of the risks of bank failure, and therefore (4) that government must exercise supervision and regulation of banks to an extent commensurate to the risks it assumes. Banks can hardly expect to be free to make high-risk investments on the implicit assumption that they can keep high profits if successful but will be bailed out by the government if unsuccessful. Shortly before Chairman Isaac departed from his FDIC post in 1985, still an ardent proponent of deregulation, he recommended to the Senate Banking Committee that the Glass–Steagall Act, the Bank Holding Company Act, and the McFadden–Douglas Act should all be repealed, a position that moved the senators—to uproarious laughter.[34] If not over, the drive to deregulate has been stalled as of 1985.

The thrust of the thinking of our leading central bankers is favorable toward further deregulation provided it is properly conducted, but also strongly in favor of new legislation to prevent abuses. In his first public address as president of the Federal Reserve Bank of New York, E. Gerald Corrigan spoke of progress that banks had recently made in strengthening their capital positions and in adopting more conservative attitudes toward loan provisions and reserves. He advocated allowing banks a new range of activities such as underwriting and distributing revenue bonds and broker/ agency activities in insurance and real estate. With respect to interstate banking, he favored further extension with the proviso that some date be set when all federal geographic restrictions would be abolished except as necessary to preserve safety and avoid excessive concentration. At the same time he cautioned banks to use more "prior restraint" in the credit decision-making process, that is, to forgo overextension of loans that might result in loan losses. His "compelling" call for legislative reform referred to the "compulsion of institutions to seize every loophole in law and regulation [which] threatens to reach a point of *de facto* restructuring of the financial marketplace such that even the most basic of doctrines—such as the separation of banking and commerce—may be irreversibly breached." In summation he called for prompt action: "Our Federal banking laws are in desperate need of reform."[35]

Chairman Volcker could hardly have been more emphatic in calling on Congress for banking reform than his statement of May 8, 1985, before the Senate Committee on Banking, Housing, and Urban Affairs. He spoke of the need for a "sense of urgency to reform the existing statutory framework governing 'banking' organizations [for] there are real dangers in permitting the financial system to evolve, as it is now, in a haphazard and a potentially dangerous way."[36] Below are some specific reasons taken from Volcker's statement showing the need for strong and early action by Congress to clarify and strengthen the goals of public policy toward banking:

1. Changes have been occurring pell–mell.
   a. Legislative action is needed on the definition of a bank. Nonbank banks have been proliferating as many commercial companies as well as bank holding companies have applied for and received approval for them.
   b. States have been moving to greatly expand the powers of state-chartered banks and thrifts. They seem to be engaged in a bidding process to attract depository institutions, increase revenues, and expand employment without regard for a coherent banking philosophy. The result may be contrary to the requirements for a sound banking system.

2. The separation of banking and commerce is endangered by the use of nonbank banks by commercial firms prepared to exploit legal loopholes.
3. The rush into new kinds of activities has resulted in much complex litigation, making banking policy the subject of judicial review. The courts and the regulators of financial institutions are in the dilemma of applying old laws to a new set of circumstances. Without comprehensive new legislation, the banking system changes haphazardly.

A proposal for shoring up the banking system that has gained support is an increase in the FDIC's insurance fund. Its size relative to the kind of run experienced by Continental Illinois is a source of concern. It would be easy to increase the annual revenue flow to the fund because for many years the FDIC has been rebating to the banks about half of the one-twelfth of 1 percent of domestic deposits that the law requires them to pay. This policy, adopted as early as 1950 when the risks of failure were low, bears reexamination. Another approach that has been much discussed concerns risk-related premiums for deposit insurance. Under the present flat-rate premium, some depository institutions take excessive risks because their cost of insurance is unrelated to the potential for failure and the likelihood of losses that the deposit insurance fund would be required to pay. There have been several proposals to remedy this, such as adopting a schedule in which the premium rate is made a function of the risk level. Practical problems make this approach difficult to implement, but support for it has been considerable. One additional avenue of reform that has been given prominence is the establishment of higher levels of bank capital.

At the risk of overgeneralization, the state of banking might be summed up in these terms: considerable deregulation of banking has occurred which provides the advantages of competition but which poses a threat to the safety and soundness of the system. To achieve an appropriate balance between market forces and legislative restraint, new legislation seems required; a system in or near a state of disarray needs rules of behavior in the public interest. Net result: fewer regulatory shackles on product and area competition but strong supervision and regulation to enforce redefined rules of a more coherent system.

Monetary Policy: Improvisation at Work

> Judgments about the economic situation require some perspective; a sense not only of where we are, but also a sense of from where we have come and where we are going.
>
> —E. Gerald Corrigan[37]

To have an effective policy concerning anything, it is necessary to define the "thing." Most people probably think that this presents no problem concerning money, since money has been used for more than two and a half millennia, as a nation we have had two centuries to work out our money supply, and as individuals we use money every day. Yet the problem of defining money has bedeviled U.S. monetary policy in the 1970s and 1980s as new assets with the attributes of money have been introduced and more institutions have come to issue them. The prominence of monetarism circa 1979–1980 was based on firm control of the money supply, but unfortunately for the implementation of monetary policy the content of the money supply has been in transition. In 1982 an acute difficulty for monetary policy appeared: the recession of 1981–1982 put monetary policy under so severe a strain that three years after the famous FOMC meeting of October 1979 the Fed found it necessary to suspend its quasi pledge of allegiance to monetarism. The tentative step away from monetarism taken in 1982 took on the appearance of a gulf over the next three years as events rendered monetarism less and less plausible as a policy guide. In short, there was a shift of monetary policy away from monetarism toward eclecticism during the 1980s through 1986.

The question of how to define the money stock of the United States has been of much concern and attention for the last fifteen years, as indicated by the following thumbnail account of the development of money stock measures by the Federal Reserve System.[38] Extensive studies of the monetary measures by the Federal Reserve during the 1970s were prompted by financial developments that changed the significance of the measures then in use. Refinements began to be adopted as close substitutes for money were introduced, such as NOW accounts and telephonic transfers of funds, as more data became available, and as banking practices changed, so that by the mid-1970s five measures were being published instead of only one in 1971. The narrow money stock measure, M1, composed of currency and demand deposits, was supplemented by successively broader measures, M2, M3, M4, and M5. As noted earlier, innovations in financial instruments continued to be introduced. In February 1980 two narrow transactions measures were adopted (M-1A and M-1B), M2 and M3 were redefined, and a very broad measure of liquid assets known as *L* was added. In January 1982 the M-1A measure was discontinued and M-1B became simply M1, a change motivated largely by the slowing of shifts of balances from demand and savings deposits into NOW accounts after they were made available nationwide in January 1981. Further revisions were made in February 1983 in the broader monetary aggregates.

The heart of the difficulty over defining money is that the features which previously differentiated money from other liquid assets have become indistinct. Until recently, transactions balances were clearly different from short-term investment funds. Payments were made only by demand deposits and currency; the payment of interest was prohibited by law on demand deposits. Under these conditions there was a strong financial incentive for demand deposits to be kept no larger than necessary for carrying on transactions. To shift into money from other highly liquid assets (near money) involved a cost. By the early 1980s, payments could be made by check on a variety of accounts in addition to demand deposits, including NOW and Super-NOW accounts, money market mutual funds, money market deposit accounts, and cash management accounts maintained at brokerage houses. There is no longer much of an incentive to minimize balances to amounts needed for transactions purposes. In addition the computerization of the financial system has made the cost of shifting from near money to money insignificant. The Federal Reserve has tried to meet the problem by changing the way the monetary aggregates are defined, but inherent difficulties prevent a satisfactory resolution. The new accounts are part fish and part fowl—they combine transactions and short-term investment elements. Furthermore the changing nature of the narrowly defined aggregate means that the definition of M1 is not constant over time.

The implications of the difficulty of measuring the money stock for monetary policy purposes have been clearly delineated by Frank E. Morris, president of the Federal Reserve Bank of Boston. Morris noted that a great body of theory and much empirical work provided the basis for the decision of the Federal Reserve to target transactions balances with the expectation that the money balances would be predictably related to the nominal GNP. The ability to measure transactions balances accurately, that is, to have a measure of M1 that is consistent over time, is essential. "This we cannot do. We, therefore, have no scientific basis for expecting that the new M1 of the latest redefinition is going to have the same behavioral characteristics relative to the nominal GNP as the M1 of earlier years." The conclusion is far-reaching:

> We are approaching a critical watershed in the formulation of monetary policy. The policy structure of recent years, which has been oriented toward controlling the growth rate of the money stock, is being eroded by a wave of financial innovation which is making it more and more difficult to measure the money stock, i.e. to differentiate money from other liquid assets. We are left with three alternatives: to go back to managing interest rates, to continue the present course of redefining the money supply as best we can to reflect the latest innovations, or to shift from controlling money to controlling the growth of liquidity and/or debt.[39]

Let us recall the circumstances of the October 1979 decision of the Federal Open Market Committee to achieve money growth targets by managing the growth rate of bank reserves. Inflation had been getting more troublesome for over a decade and threatened to get out of control. The Fed saw the necessity of making itself credible as an inflation fighter, for tough talk with little result had cast doubt on its effectiveness. As the Fed implemented its new policy through 1980, 1981, and 1982, the rate of inflation fell sharply (the dragon of inflation had been badly wounded if not slain), but the economy stumbled into a severe recession. In the summer of 1982 the Fed was faced with a moment of truth. For the first half of 1982 the growth rate of M1 was 7 percent (compared with a policy range of 2.5 to 5.5 percent), yet real GNP fell at an annual rate close to 3 percent. Economic forecasts generally predicted an upturn in the third quarter, and one could be expected to occur, along monetarist lines, as a result of the above-target rate of M1 during the previous six months. But when it became clear that the recession was worsening in the third quarter, the Fed found it expedient to abandon its adherence to the monetarist faith. The Fed's long-run strategy called for a gradual reduction in the monetary aggregates, especially M1, over several years to wring inflation out of the economy with minimum effects on output and employment. This approach required the velocity of M1 to be stable. But in 1982 the velocity of M1 unexpectedly dropped sharply and so "compelled" the Fed to depart from its long-run strategy by abandoning M1 as a target.[40]

> Over the year the income velocities of the monetary aggregates (defined as the ratio of nominal gross national product to money) declined at the sharpest rates of the postwar period.
> [T]he FOMC at its meeting in early October decided to deemphasize M1, at least temporarily, as an operating guide for monetary policy, and instead, to place greater emphasis on M2 and M3 in the expectation that these measures would be less affected by developments in the fourth quarter.[41]

The aberrant behavior of velocity was unsettling to monetarist thinking, but perhaps was due to a one-shot disturbance and would soon settle down. In July 1983 the FOMC, reluctant to abandon its M1 range and unwilling to stay within it, adopted a new monetary range for M1 for the last half of the year based on the average money stock for the second quarter of 1983, instead of the fourth quarter of 1982. This device allowed the Fed to overshoot its original target range without abandoning the concept of a target range.

> The decision to adopt a new base for monitoring M1 growth reflected a judgment that the recent rapid growth of M1 would appropriately be treated as a one-time phenomenon that was expected to be neither reversed nor extended. It appeared, in retrospect, that the surge in M1 might largely have reflected an adjustment by the public of its cash balances in response to the

pronounced drop in the opportunity cost of holding low-yielding demand deposits and regular NOW accounts.[42]

By 1984 the Federal Reserve was hopeful that M1 could soon be restored to the preeminent place that it held in monetary policy from 1979 to 1982, although it was not yet ready for full restoration.

> Over the year, the evidence increasingly suggested that M1 was in fact behaving more in line with historical experience. As a result, this aggregate was given more weight in policy implementation than had been the case during the latter part of the cyclical downswing and early phase of the economic recovery. However, all of the monetary and credit measures continued to be evaluated in light of the outlook for the economy and for domestic and international financial markets.[43]

The attempt to remain loyal to M1 targeting was disrupted again in July 1985. In February a 4–7 percent target range of growth was set from a fourth-quarter 1984 base. By June the actual growth rate was nearly 12 percent. Instead of trying to slow M1 growth to keep within the target range, the Fed took two steps: (1) it widened the range to 3–8 percent; (2) it made the second quarter of 1985 the new base period thus "validating" the rapid money growth of the first half of the year.[44] Milton Friedman compared this to a farmer who had numerous targets on his barn door, each with a bullet hole in its center. The secret of this accuracy was that the farmer first shot at the door and then painted the targets.

The hope and expectation that monetary policy might soon again be keyed to M1 growth has faded with the passage of time. It is clear that M1's velocity has been remarkably different during the 1980s from the 1970s. From the early to the late 1970s the ratio GNP/M1 increased from roughly 4.5 to 6.5, or about 3.5 percent per year, but has been virtually flat during the first half of the 1980s. Furthermore there has been a remarkable increase in its volatility. The predictability of the velocity of M1 is crucial to a strategy of monetary targeting.

Some of the reasons for the changing behavior of velocity could well be of a temporary nature. It has been argued that the surprising drop in 1982 was due to the rapid fall in inflation and nominal interest rates and not to a shift in the demand for M1. The public wanted to hold more money at the lower nominal interest rates.[45] The introduction of NOW accounts nationwide in 1981 is another factor that could be expected to be less disturbing as the public becomes accustomed to these new accounts. But a more comprehensive analysis that also takes into account swings in inventories and the deteriorating trade balance of recent years is pessimistic. A study conducted by the Federal Reserve Bank of New York gives little hope for future predictability of velocity.

[I]t is very difficult to predict swings in inventories, net exports, interest rates, and the split in M1 growth among its components. Moreover, there has not been enough experience with M1 in this more deregulated environment to estimate very precisely the interest elasticity of the demand for M1. Hence, even though some of the reasons for the instability of velocity in the 1980s (measured in terms of GNP) can be identified *ex post,* velocity is not likely to be more predictable as a result.[46]

Still another case has been developed challenging the belief that, after a period of adjustment, the money stock will again serve as a good guide for monetary policy. It starts with the introduction of MMDAs in December 1982 and Super-NOWs in January 1983, and concludes that as a result the relationship of GNP to the money stock has become less reliable. The reason is that the financial strategies of depository institutions are important determining factors in the growth of the money stock. In the expectation of rising interest rates, banks and thrifts may tend to promote large denomination CDs more vigorously than the accounts that are part of M1, with the result that M1 increases relatively slowly compared with the growth of GNP. But when the outlook favors declining interest rates, the depository institutions may switch aggressively to promoting transactions accounts, so that the growth of M1 is faster than warranted by economic growth. The result is that "the growth of M1 and M2 now could depend more on interest rate forecasts and funding strategies of depository institutions and their borrowers."[47]

Monetarism has clearly been under heavy criticism in the mid–1980s. Many long-standing opponents remained adamant in their resistance to it during its rise to prominence among policymakers. In Britain, for example, Lord Kaldor viewed the swing toward monetarist policy with disdain: "The distinguishing mark of this new wave of monetarism is its extreme dogmatism and complete lack of intellectual coherence."[48] James Tobin, while readily admitting that much of the influence of monetarism on economic thought and government policy of the past twenty years is durable, widely understood, and accepted, maintains that central banks still have a great range of choice regarding operating procedures, targets, and short-term goals in discharging their duty, a duty that encompasses countercyclical demand management. The influence of strict monetarism is on the way out.

> Mechanical monetarism, stressing targets for intermediate monetary aggregates, is waning in professional opinion and in central-bank practice, especially in the United States. History since 1979 has not been kind to the monetarist prescription of stable policies blind to actual events and new information. In the United States the Fed appears to have subordinated monetary targets and rules, and oriented its month-to-month decisions to macroeconomic performance.[49]

By 1984–1985 the attacks on monetarism had become almost a popular pastime, sometimes expressed with great bluntness.[50]

Professor Friedman, long accustomed to criticism and renowned for his dialectical skills, is probably not surprised or disturbed by most of the recent criticism of his position. He might, however, have felt the sting of an editorial in so close a philosophically kindred spirit as *The Wall Street Journal*. Late in 1985 the *Journal* came to view the money supply as passive, responding to economic activity at home and abroad, with the dynamic variable recently being velocity rather than the money stock. Thus: "It's sad to say, but instructive to relate, that at the moment the monetarists are the principal intellectual opposition to what we would consider progress in economic policy."[51] Friedman has continued to defend his position and to criticize the Federal Reserve's performance. He holds that if the Fed had given the country stable money growth by consistently achieving the explicit numerical targets for the money aggregates that it specified to Congress since 1975, then inflation and recession would have been much less severe. The principal fault lies in the execution of monetary policy which has resulted in highly variable rates of money growth. For example, there was a monetary explosion April 1980–April 1981, retardation April 1981–October 1981 and again January 1982–July 1982, followed by another explosion July 1982–July 1983. Such inconstancy is intolerable to Friedman, who would substitute his monetary rule. He argues that to really make it effective, it should be stated in terms of the monetary base and perhaps enforced by a constitutional amendment.[52]

The rise of monetarism in the years before 1979–1980 occurred largely because of the perception that the post–World War II Keynesian orthodoxy was unequal to the task of providing stable, noninflationary growth. Monetarism seemed to many to be more relevant. But in recent years monetarism has seemed less relevant. In mid-1983 Professor Friedman foresaw a resurgence of inflation that subsequently failed to show up on schedule. An oracle whose prediction is not borne out must expect some loss of credibility.[53]

The quantity theory—monetarism—rests on the proposition that the income velocity of circulation of money is largely invariant to changes in the money stock. The erratic behavior of velocity in the 1980s means that the case for monetarism falls. Defenders of monetarism have been on the defensive, trying to explain away these velocity changes. That monetarism is down should not, however, be taken to mean that it is down for the count. A theory with its intellectual lineage has proven survival power and a core of thought that will persist to some degree. That money is one of the important factors determining spending, if not always the most important factor, is hardly in dispute. While the usefulness of monetarism as a guide has been shown wanting for short and not-so-short periods, its long-term significance may well be very great. Keynes reminded us that we live in the short-run and Friedman that we face long-run consequences of what we do in the short-run. Thus we may find it necessary or desirable to reject monetarism in the short-run only to suffer a hangover later. If the choice were easy, the policy dispute would have faded away long ago.

Where does this leave us? The view that a monetary rule tempered by discretion might be the best approach has a core of reasonableness around which a consensus might coalesce. This is certainly not strict monetarism, but it accepts the control of the money supply as an essential element in monetary policy.

> There is no simple solution to the problem of guiding monetary policy in a time of rapid institutional change. . . . [T]he monetary authorities should be guided by the principle of keeping money growth within a prespecified target range while adjusting those targets when a careful consideration of the evidence indicates that sustained shifts in asset demands have occurred.
>
> The combination of monetary rules and discretion must be applied with great care and judgment. The observance of rules must not become a doctrinaire attachment to arbitrary standards, and the exercise of discretion must not degenerate into unprincipled fine tuning.[54]

> I conclude, therefore, that monetary policy should be one of rules, tempered by discretion. This is not a neat solution but the world is, unfortunately, too complex for neat solutions.[55]

Effective policy-making depends on a realistic interpretation of the role of the monetary system in the economy. Any theory used to provide such an interpretation identifies certain variables and explains how they are related in a cause-and-effect manner. It is important, however, to keep in mind that we live in a changing environment. New practices and attitudes may well be significant enough to disrupt the relationships that comprise a prevailing system of thought, and an awareness of this danger may account for the reluctance of policymakers to embrace a given doctrine. Policy-making based on experience as interpreted by theoretical understanding, yet aware of institutional changes and open to correction in the light of new knowledge, may be the best approach. Because it is eclectic and relies on judgment, such an approach seems to lack the certainty and rigor associated with science, but by avoiding a doctrinaire position it also avoids intellectual hubris and is receptive to relevant information that might not fit an existing pattern of thought. A narrow focus on a particular theoretical view may interfere with peripheral vision and result in avoidable accidents.

11
Summing Up

> No policy can be successful unless it recognizes the constant drift of
> evolutionary change. . . .
>
> —Kenneth E. Boulding[1]

The evolutionary perspective, as Kenneth Boulding has convincingly shown,
is "extremely illuminating in explaining the ongoing processes of economic
life."[2] For the segment of economic life chosen for examination in this book,
the monetary system of the United States over the past ninety years, evolutionary change is obviously great. It is the role of this final chapter to high-
light the striking shifts in structure, theory, and policy that have, time and
again, transformed the monetary institutions of the country. To realize this,
one only has to imagine studying money and banking as of any given date,
say 1910, 1925, 1940, 1955, and then consider how inadequate such knowledge would have been twenty years later. Even more important is the real-
ization that what was known as of a given date did not provide much foresight
of what was to come. How well does our present wisdom prepare us for the
world of 2005? After the following summation, some concluding observations will be offered on this point.

The American monetary system before World War I was structurally
unsound. It was subject to periodic monetary stringency which at times resulted in collapse: bank failures, widespread bankruptcy, general economic
depression. This state of affairs finally became recognized as intolerable as
a result of the Panic of 1907, and led to the establishment of a "central
bank," the Federal Reserve System, in 1914, an institution based on European experience adapted to American conditions.

The Federal Reserve System was designed to provide the nation with a
supply of money and credit appropriate to its needs over time and to be
ready, in the event of a developing liquidity shortage, to be a "lender of last
resort," able to create new money quickly. The system was not intended to

manage or control the money stock on its own initiative according to its assessment of what was good for the country. Instead it was to carry out its functions by *responding* to the needs of the productive units in agriculture, commerce, and industry, and doing so within the rules of the international gold standard.

In the pre–World War I era there was a trinity of highly regarded guiding principles to govern monetary policy. One was the gold standard, to which the country was firmly committed by law—in the long run the money stock of the nation was automatically determined by the size of the monetary gold stock. The second was the quantity theory of money that inexorably linked the price level to the money stock over the long run. The dependence of the price level on the money supply was essential for the gold standard to be workable internationally by preventing an overconcentration of gold in a few nations. The third principle, of lesser stature than the other two, was the real bills doctrine, according to which banks could safely expand loans in their own interest and to the economy's benefit by concentrating on short-term loans for productive purposes. The new Federal Reserve Banks would in turn lend to the commercial banks by rediscounting eligible commercial paper for the banks, paper which had been acquired by the banks as a result of their loans to the public. Enveloping the whole system was a belief in laissez-faire, according to which the market mechanism, allowed to work its will, would automatically bring about the best possible results. The new central bank was viewed as a kind of financial gyroscope needed to prevent an otherwise successful system from veering off course for technical reasons. Once the new mechanism was put in operation, it was expected that the flawed monetary system would be "fixed."

The Federal Reserve System made a somewhat cautious and hesitant entry on the national economic stage. It faced several difficulties: its officers lacked experience as central bankers; many commercial bankers viewed it with suspicion and disapproval; authority was unclearly divided between the Federal Reserve Board and the twelve Federal Reserve Banks; appropriate lending policies needed to be worked out to give practical effect to its new money creating role. Much more important, the timing of the arrival of the central bank coincided with the outbreak of World War I, as a result of which economic conditions changed drastically. Thus the Federal Reserve System began life in an environment that precluded it from working out a modus operandi under the type of conditions that had been assumed by its founders.

Between the time when World War I began and the date of American participation in it, heavy gold inflows led to more money and higher prices. The gold-losing countries of Europe left the gold standard. After U.S. entry into the war, gold stopped flowing in, and for a time this country also suspended the gold standard. The money stock continued to rise after the gold inflow ceased as the Federal Reserve Banks expanded the monetary base. The financial requirements of the Treasury were of paramount importance, and the Federal Reserve System contributed to the war effort by its support of the Treasury in two ways. First, it served as fiscal agent for Treasury financing operations, a role that it has continued to play to the present. Second, as the source of credit it made certain that the Treasury could sell all of the bonds necessary to meet its needs. The method by which the Fed made credit available was by lending to commercial banks with Treasury securities as collateral. Under these conditions the gold standard was inoperative and the real bills doctrine irrelevant. Wartime financing resulted in a rapid expansion of the money supply and inflation.

The immediate postwar years 1919–1921 brought an inflationary boom followed by a shattering collapse of the economy, a painful experience for which the Federal Reserve System was largely blamed. The Federal Reserve was criticized for failing to restrict monetary expansion during the boom. It claimed extenuating circumstances in the form of a continuing need to support the Treasury, as well as the fact that it was in a subservient position due to wartime legislation still in effect under which the president could transfer its powers to the Treasury. After boom turned to bust, the Fed kept interest rates high for a long time as the economy plunged into deep depression. This perverse tight money policy was explained as necessary to protect the gold stock, although the Federal Reserve could have suspended the gold reserve requirement. This excuse did not save the system from being roundly condemned for persisting in a mistaken policy. The original need for the central bank was just as urgent as before the war, however, so it was allowed to continue with the hope that in a "normal" environment it would develop the skills and judgment required for success.

From 1922 to 1929 the American economy enjoyed prosperity with price stability, a happy combination for which monetary policy could claim considerable credit. Over these years the Federal Reserve System redefined its role and operating methods. Changes in economic conditions, attitudes, and behavior resulting from World War I and its aftermath created an environment quite different from the prewar world; in responding to the new conditions the central bank contributed to the shape of the new order and seemed to have mastered the art of central banking. Early in the twenties the Federal Reserve System took upon itself the role of manager of the monetary system. The original concept of a central bank responding automatically to gold flows and legitimate credit needs was no longer tenable. The international gold standard had not been sufficiently restored. As a practical matter the Fed kept inflows and outflows of gold from changing the monetary base. The real bills doctrine lost credibility as a safe way to expand the money supply—it was now considered necessary to regulate the quantity of credit, not to rely on its quality alone. The lesson drawn from the harsh experience of inflation followed by deflation immediately after the war was that the system should exercise control over credit to promote domestic stability. Keynes in 1923 pointed out that regulated monetary systems had become a fact. The shift from an automatic to a regulated system was clearly a significant transformation of the social organism known as central banking.

In 1922 the discovery was made that the Federal Reserve Banks possessed a powerful credit policy instrument in the form of open-market operations and led to the creation of a coordinating group, the Federal Open Market Investment Committee, under the supervision of the Federal Reserve Board. This was not the only way that authority was concentrated in the Federal Reserve Board, for in 1927 the board asserted authority over the setting of discount rates by the banks. The system used open-market operations and discount policy to steady the economy during the twenties.

In addition to economic stability, the Fed had two other important objectives. One was to help in the slow process of restoring the international gold standard. In 1927 the system adopted an easier money policy to assist foreign countries in getting on or keeping on the gold standard. Unfortunately this step conflicted with the objective of denying credit for speculative purposes just as the stock market was beginning to ascend to its dizzy 1929 peak. By the end of the decade, the Federal Reserve lost control of the situation. It wanted to deny credit for stock market speculation but provide it to keep the national economy rolling, and found itself in a dilemma. Furthermore it became apparent that a fundamental conflict existed between the goals of adherence to the gold standard and national stabilization.

During the 1920s commercial banks shifted the composition of their assets as investments rose relative to loans, and security and real estate loans rose relative to commercial loans. Money center banks, using affiliates, underwrote and distributed securities including many foreign securities of poor quality. The number of banks fell from about 30,000 to 24,000, mainly because of changes in the economic landscape that left many small banks in small towns to wither on the vine.

From 1929 to 1933 the economy descended into deep depression. Its recovery was marred by a slump in 1937–1938, after which powerful expansionary forces stemming from the onset of World War II took it to high ground. The Great Depression had drastic effects on the banking system, brought major institutional reforms, and fundamentally changed monetary theory. Over some two and a half years, from the fall of 1930 to the spring of 1933, the economy was wracked by three waves of bank failures. The money stock declined sharply, especially between March 1931 and March 1933. The Federal Reserve System, put to the test by the first liquidity crisis since 1907, failed to meet the challenge. Spending on output fell much more than the money stock as the velocity of money also fell very sharply. The Federal Reserve System reduced the discount rate from 6 percent in 1929 to

1.5 percent in mid-1931 but raised it to 3.5 percent late in 1931, after Britain left the gold standard, because of concern over gold requirements. The Federal Reserve System made little use of its power to expand the monetary base by open-market operations. It bought substantial amounts of government securities for some months in 1932 but did not persist for long. Interest rates dropped to very low levels in nominal terms but not in real terms.

In response to the traumatic experience of the early thirties, the nation adopted extensive banking and monetary reforms soon after the Roosevelt administration came into office in 1933. The Federal Reserve System was given increased powers in the belief that it had not previously been adequately equipped. The system was restructured to centralize policy control in the hands of a new Board of Governors and a new Federal Open Market Committee in Washington. The Board of Governors could vary member bank reserve requirement percentages and regulate credit for the purchase of securities, the latter a "selective" control resulting from the inability of the Fed to cut off the flow of funds to the stock market in the late twenties. The Federal Open Market Committee was given exclusive control over Federal Reserve open-market operations.

The failure of the Federal Reserve System to prevent the epidemic of bank failures led Congress to create a new institution, the Federal Deposit Insurance Corporation, to provide deposit protection and so end the contagion of runs on banks. Although the power in the Federal Reserve System shifted to the board and the FOMC in Washington, the Federal Reserve Banks were given permanent authority to lend to commercial banks on any security deemed satisfactory to them. Thus reliance on eligible commercial paper, once the key feature of the real bills doctrine, came to an end.

By the end of 1933 the number of commercial banks had fallen to about 15,000, compared with twice that number in the early twenties. Unlike the Federal Reserve System, which was given more power and freedom of action, the commercial banks were circumscribed by new controls. The payment of interest on demand deposits was prohibited, and a maximum rate of interest payable on time deposits was set for the banks by the Board of Governors. Commercial banking and investment banking were legally divorced, thereby prohibiting the commercial banks from continuing to have investment affiliates.

The conflict between domestic objectives and adherence to the international gold standard that became apparent in the years following World War I was resolved by changing the way the dollar was linked to gold. A limited international gold-bullion standard was adopted, with the dollar devalued in terms of gold by 41 percent, thereby abandoning the effort to reestablish a full-fledged international gold standard. While the money stock would not be controlled by gold, gold flows would continue for several decades to influence the Federal Reserve System as it exercised control over the money supply.

From 1933 to 1937 the money stock rose rapidly. The Treasury's gold stock was greatly enlarged: devaluation of the dollar plus a major inflow of gold tripled the nation's gold stock. The monetary base rose at a faster rate than M1 as banks accumulated a large amount of excess reserves. The anomoly of huge excess reserves was generally taken as evidence that extremely easy money conditions existed at a time when the demand for loans was low. The strong liquidity preference of banks was apparent also in their holdings of short-term government obligations with yields of just a small fraction of 1 percent. During the economic recession of 1937–1938 the money stock fell.

From 1933 to the end of the decade, Federal Reserve credit was essentially unchanged. During this period the Federal Reserve System played a minor role, and discounting, originally considered the main link of the system to the financial system, was insignificant. In 1936 and 1937 the Federal Reserve raised reserve requirement percentages to soak up a large amount of the banks' excess reserves and so make Federal Reserve open-market operations a feasible option when needed. The banks, however, reacted to the loss of excess reserves by a more restrictive lending policy. The result was that the Federal Reserve was criticized for unintentionally bringing on monetary restriction which contributed, along with a concurrent shift toward restriction in federal fiscal policy, to the 1937–1938 recession.

Monetary theory was transformed in the thirties as John Maynard Keynes presented his income–expenditure analysis to explain changes in national income as an alternative to the quantity theory of money. His liquidity preference theory of interest was used to argue that when the rate of interest was at a very low (depression) level, the demand for money balances would be so highly elastic that an increase in M would have a negligible effect on interest rates and spending. Monetary policy was therefore viewed as ineffective in generating demand for output, and fiscal policy was elevated to the prime policy role. Marriner Eccles and his close associate at the Federal Reserve Board, Lauchlin Currie, were congenial to Keynes's ideas, and as a result the Federal Reserve became a medium for the transmission of Keynesian thought to Washington. Thus in response to the economic breakdown, a revolution in thought occurred that sanctioned a more interventionist role in the economy.

For decades economists have looked back on the events and policies of the thirties to interpret that momentous era of change. The monetary (monetarist) explanation makes the money stock the prime mover of shifts in aggregate demand; changes in velocity in the same direction follow. According to this view, if the Federal Reserve authorities had done their job properly by expanding the money supply, the situation would never have gotten out of hand. An alternative approach holds nonmonetary causes responsible for the economic collapse. This interpretation makes autonomous declines in spending on output the key causal factor; velocity decreased and a fall in M followed. An eclectic view holds that neither the quantity theory nor the income–expenditure theory is sufficient. Whether changes in money causing changes in the economy (monetary hypothesis) or changes in the economy causing changes in money (spending hypothesis) is the more important is a question still waiting for a definitive answer.

All-out war for nearly four years (1941–1945) required the Treasury to finance an unprecedented national mobilization of resources. As in World War I, the Federal Reserve System provided reserves to the banks to insure the success of Treasury debt financing. The method chosen was open-market operations, by which the Fed supported (pegged) the market price of Treasury obligations, not, as in World War I, by discounting. By committing itself in this way, the central bank relinquished control over the money supply. Efforts were made to finance the war with already existing funds, but the money stock more than doubled during the war. Inflation was repressed by direct control over resources, rationing of scarce goods, and price and wage controls. Shortly after World War II, the nation, still preoccupied by the long depression, adopted legislation declaring that the federal government had the responsibility of managing the economy so as to achieve desired macroeconomic goals.

A pleasant surprise occurred after World War II: a severe postwar depression, such as occurred in 1920–1921 or worse, was anticipated but not realized. The large amount of money and other highly liquid assets accumulated as a result of the financing of the war, and now available for peacetime spending, fueled an inflation during 1946–1948. Although a matter of concern, inflation was less severe than might have been expected under the circumstances. Over this two-year period there was only a marginal increase in the money stock, and the increase in velocity was not very large. The relative restraint in aggregate spending was probably due to sizeable government cash surpluses and a lingering fear of hard times ahead that prompted people to spend cautiously so as not to deplete liquid assets that might be sorely needed.

Federal Reserve support of the government securities market was continued after World War II until early 1951. With the passage of time the Federal Reserve System gradually but increasingly wanted to dissolve its "partnership" with the Treasury so that it might regain its powers as an independent central bank to exercise control over the supply of credit. Treasury officials insisted that the pegging policy be continued to hold down the interest cost on the national debt and to ease its problem of rolling over the debt. The Federal Reserve tried to separate itself by tiny steps from the pegging policy: its hesitancy is explained by fear that if it withdrew support prematurely the government securities market might fall, precipitating a financial collapse and tight credit and possibly bringing on the feared economic depression. In 1949 a lull in the economy temporarily eased the tension between the two agencies, but the outbreak of the Korean War in June 1950 set them on the path to a clean break. The Federal Reserve authorities—their duty more clearly defined by the inflationary circumstances—resolved to free themselves of the pegging policy which had so long subordinated monetary policy to the needs of the Treasury. A struggle between the two agencies that spilled into a bitter political fracas ended with a pact, the Accord of March 4, 1951, which ended the Federal Reserve System's support of the government securities market at pegged prices and restored monetary control powers to the system.

The decade and a half from 1951 to 1965 was a generally successful and relatively smooth portion of the journey through the twentieth century. Economic growth in the 1950s was interrupted by three mild recessions, and there was some concern that other countries, notably the USSR, were growing faster than the United States. Disputes over U.S. monetary policy revolved around the question of whether the Fed was providing too little or too much money for the economy to function optimally.

Following the Accord of 1951 the Federal Reserve gradually phased out its support activity in the securities market. As a result the Fed was able to operate in the market as it deemed necessary for monetary control purposes. Under William McChesney Martin, Jr., who chaired the Board of Governors for almost two decades beginning in 1951, the Federal Reserve adopted a "bills only" doctrine in 1953. The idea was that the system should exercise credit control (almost) exclusively by buying and selling Treasury bills so as to minimize its interference in the credit market. Critics maintained that "bills only" did not in fact result in an improved government bond market and had the disadvantage of making monetary policy more difficult to implement because of the need alternately to flood markets with liquidity to ease credit and then later to draw off excess liquidity to restrict credit. The policy was viewed by many as unnecessarily restrictive of central bank power. The "bills only" doctrine was laid to rest in 1961 as a result of a gold outflow while economic activity was slack. To encourage the domestic economy, the Federal Reserve decided to buy long-term Treasury securities to lower long-term interest rates, while simultaneously it kept short-term rates high to deter holders of dollars from shifting to liquid assets abroad.

As a result of the unexpected tendency of the price level to rise during recession in the 1950s, a fresh interpretation of inflation was developed. Cost-push or sellers' inflation was presented to explain inflation that could not be attributed to excess aggregate demand. A consequence of cost-push inflation was to put the monetary authorities in a dilemma: to stop inflation they had to discourage output and employment; to increase output and employment they had to accept inflation. To try to resolve the dilemma, the concept of an incomes policy was developed to supplement a sound monetary/fiscal policy mix. The central proposition of the new approach was to get labor and management to behave in the national interest, labor by accepting average wage increases in line with productivity increases for the economy (to keep labor cost per unit of output stable), and management by keeping the average price level steady. Incomes policies were applied in a variety of forms and degrees during the sixties and seventies.

In the 1950s, as a result of rising interest rates, corporate and individual depositors transferred funds from bank accounts paying zero or low rates of explicit interest to short-term securities and accounts at thrift institutions which yielded a higher return. Faster growth by nonbank competitors stimulated commercial banks into a new strategy of liability management as a way of obtaining additional funds to meet liquidity needs created by faster growing bank assets. The financial instrument adopted for this purpose was the negotiable certificate of deposit (CD), which attracted corporate deposits in huge amounts. The federal funds market became another source of lendable funds for banks.

From 1961 to 1965 the economy enjoyed rapid growth with low inflation. Economic policy was shaped by Keynesian thinking, and the glowing results strongly suggested that an excellent combination of fiscal and monetary policies had been forged. It was a time when economists in general and Keynesian economists in particular enjoyed high respect.

The escalation of U.S. military action in Vietnam in 1965 caused a serious demand-pull inflation for the first time since the Korean War in the early fifties. Federal taxes were not raised until 1968, so for several years the Federal Reserve had macroeconomic policy largely to itself. Monetary restraint in 1966 brought on a severe credit squeeze; the Federal Reserve departed from its free market philosophy by resorting to moral suasion to influence bank behavior when market pressure peaked in the summer. Tight money gripped some sectors of the economy, such as housing, much tighter than others. High market interest rates diverted funds away from savings and loan associations, a phenomenon called disintermediation that was to be repeated from time to time until the eighties. The pace of economic activity eased in late 1966 and 1967. The tax increase of 1968 was adopted in an atmosphere of concern over inflation and the danger of an outflow of gold. Higher taxes, contrary to the expectations of many, including the Federal Reserve, failed to restrain the overheated economy; the Fed therefore added its own measure of restriction. In 1969 money growth was low, interest rates high, disintermediation hurt the thrifts as market interest rates rose above legal ceiling rates, and inflation reached its highest level since the Korean War. At the end of 1969 the long economic expansion that began in 1961 came to an end.

The one-bank holding company began to be used in 1966 as a device by which banks could elude Regulation Q ceilings on negotiable CDs. In 1970 Congress responded to the proliferation of one-bank holding companies by empowering the Federal Reserve to regulate them.

During the fifties and sixties the Federal Reserve System employed a money market strategy in which the net reserve position of the banks and associated interest rate levels were targeted. In accordance with a goal for the net reserve position of the banks by the FOMC, the manager of the Open Market Desk in New York would buy or sell securities. Under these circumstances, as banks expanded their loans to the public they needed additional reserves, which drove up the federal funds rate and led to borrowing from the Federal Reserve Banks. In response, the manager of the open-market account had to buy securities to achieve the targets of the FOMC. While the Fed could control the level of net free or borrowed reserves and the federal funds rate, it could not control the total amount of reserves and the money supply. This mode of operation proved vulnerable to inflationary pressures in the latter half of the sixties, causing the Federal Open Market Committee to reevaluate its targeting procedures. Discussion within the FOMC resulted in a change designed to incorporate control over monetary aggregates in the instructions of the FOMC. Although little practical effect was felt at the time, the groundwork was laid for basic changes to come.

In January 1970 Arthur Burns succeeded William McChesney Martin, Jr., as chairman of the Board of Governors of the Federal Reserve System. In June the Penn Central Railroad collapsed, demoralizing the commercial paper market and touching off a rush for liquidity. The Federal Reserve opened its discount window wide so that banks could readily obtain funds to support lending to borrowers unable to roll over their commercial paper. By stepping in quickly as lender of last resort and providing an abundance of reserves for the banks, the Federal Reserve may have kept the financial system from going over the brink of a financial collapse.

The Nixon administration intended to avoid the use of an incomes policy of any kind when it came into office in 1969. It hoped to bring inflation under control while avoiding a rise in unemployment by relying heavily on a gradual reduction in money growth. By mid-1971 a combination of recession and slow progress on inflation led to public pressure for intervention and the imposition of a price and wage freeze. Arthur Burns contributed to this policy shift by taking the position that monetary and fiscal policies were inadequate alone to meet the nation's demand for results. The freeze was replaced by less rigid controls in several steps until the whole interventionist experiment was abandoned in April 1974.

The wage–price freeze of mid-1971 was part of President Nixon's New Economic Policy. Another major feature of the NEP was termination of the convertibility of the dollar into gold for official foreign holders of dollars.

The Treasury's gold reserve was being depleted, and the system of fixed exchange rates of the Bretton Woods international monetary system set up after World War II broke under the strain of imbalances in international accounts. Thus the departure from gold begun in 1933 was completed.

The money stock grew fairly rapidly from 1970 to 1973, especially in the election year of 1972, and raised questions concerning the Fed as a contributing factor to inflation. A severe recession set in at the end of 1973, with recovery beginning early in 1975, yet double-digit inflation was experienced in the recession year 1974. In addition to the rise in the money stock, contributing factors to the high rate of inflation included rising oil prices (the first "oil shock"), a worldwide boom in commodity prices, crop failures in various parts of the world, the end of domestic price–wage controls, and the fall of the dollar on the foreign exchange market.

What came to be called monetarism, the latter-day version of the quantity theory of money, had been nurtured under Professor Milton Friedman's tutelage in the academic community since the 1950s as a challenge to the post–World War II orthodoxy. A running intellectual battle, the "Keynesian–monetarist debate," was a leading if not the dominant feature of the economic scene in the sixties and seventies. By the 1970s monetarism began to exert an effect on policy, for it was generally accepted by President Nixon's economic advisers and to some extent it influenced the behavior of the Federal Reserve System. In 1970 the Federal Open Market Committee adopted a directive emphasizing the monetary aggregates instead of money market conditions, a step taken in reaction to the rapid money growth and inflation of the late sixties. The system that evolved from 1970 to 1979 combined monetary aggregates as intermediate targets, with reserves and interest rates as operating targets. Despite the new approach, little effects were realized and the problems of inflation and control of the money supply were not solved. In 1975 a congressional resolution called for the setting of explicit money and credit targets and the furnishing of periodic reports to Congress; legislation in 1977 and 1978 made the reporting requirements more specific.

After 1975 the economy expanded and the unemployment rate fell, but the inflation rate rose until in 1979 it exceeded 13 percent. A sense of crisis devloped as a result of a surging price level accompanied by a sharp fall in the foreign exchange value of the dollar, a steep rise in the price of gold, and the second OPEC oil shock. Inflation psychology, the product of a decade of persistent inflation, introduced a potentially dangerous factor into decision-making. Early in 1978 Arthur Burns departed as chairman of the Board of Governors of the Federal Reserve System and was replaced briefly by G. William Miller. In October 1979, shortly after succeeding Miller, Paul Volcker presided over a most significant and dramatic action by the Federal Reserve System. In order to show its determination to halt inflation, the Federal Reserve committed itself to targeting the money supply even if large fluctuations in interest rates would have to be tolerated. Since the central policy message of monetarism is control of the money stock, it clearly appeared that the Federal Reserve had committed itself to monetarism, the culmination of a slow, decade-long trend. Following the introduction of the new program, and the adoption of a restrictive policy, the growth of the money supply slowed, interest rates rose sharply, and the dollar stabilized on the foreign exchange market.

Extraordinarily high interest rates, especially in 1974 and 1978–1979, in conjunction with regulated interest rate ceilings, spurred financial innovation. Among the newborn instruments the following were prominent: money market mutual funds, negotiable orders of withdrawal, money market certificates.

A brief recession in 1980 was followed in 1981–1982 by the most severe slump since the 1930s. Economic growth resumed in 1983 and continued through 1986.

Reaganomics, as the economic program of the right-wing Reagan administration was labeled, brought in a major federal tax cut, part of a general strategy to try to shrink the role of government in the economy. The rationale for the reduction rested on two major premises: (1) Keynesian demand management had been discredited by the high inflation/low growth record of the economy, and (2) output (the "supply side") would increase so much as a result of more work, saving, and investment that tax revenues would rise enough (despite the tax rate decrease) to reduce the budget deficit. In fact the budget deficit expanded from about $75 billion in 1980 and 1981 to some $200 billion annually from 1983 to 1986, and by mid-decade the very large deficit became the dominant economic/political issue of the day.

For about a third of a century following World War II, American banking was carried on under a regulatory framework established prior to 1940. Distinct limits were placed on the activities of banks and other financial institutions to provide a safe and sound system, to prevent excessive concentration of financial power, and to preserve the traditional separation between banking and commerce. In recent years the system has been in the process of a transformation only partly the result of deliberate public policy. New legislation has encouraged price and product competition among financial institutions. The most prominent of the areas of change and potential change is interstate banking, which is essentially prohibited de jure but running free de facto. Legal loopholes permit "nonbanks" and "nonbank banks" to engage in banking activities outside the purview of federal regulatory control, thereby raising legitimate questions concerning the future safety and stability of the banking system to weigh against the advantages of competition. Bank failures have been on the increase in the 1980s, and some major banks have been among the casualties. Instances of gross mismanagement by bank officials have come to light, undermining confidence in the standards of banking practice and raising doubts about the effectiveness of the supervisory system. Leading spokesmen of the Federal Reserve System have described the need for banking reform legislation as urgent and even desperate to prevent the banking system from evolving in a potentially dangerous way.

The 1980s, like the 1930s, have been years of financial reform, but generally in the opposite direction. As a result of the Great Depression, the theme of reform in the 1930s was regulation; as a result of inflation, high interest rates, disintermediation and general dissatisfaction with the inhibiting effects of regulation on market efficiency, the major theme of the 1980s has been deregulation. In 1980 the Depository Institutions Deregulation and Monetary Control Act eliminated interest ceilings on deposits at all depository institutions and expanded the sources and uses of funds by depository institutions to increase competition and provide greater diversification of assets. In the area of monetary control it made all commercial banks and nonbank depository institutions subject to reserve requirements administered by the Federal Reserve System, so that in this respect, as in the 1930s, regulatory control was further concentrated in the central bank in Washington. The 1982 Garn–St. Germain Depository Institutions Act was a response to the severe problems of the savings and loan associations. It authorized depository institutions to offer money market deposit accounts (to compete with money market mutual funds) and Super-NOW accounts, and it broadened the ability of thrifts to acquire assets.

By announcing its intention to control the money stock with a firm hand in October 1979, the Federal Reserve was generally perceived to have embraced monetarism. In the minds of monetarists there was less to this than met the eye, for they consider the subsequent implementation of policy to have fallen well short of what was required. In any case, after three years the Fed in 1982 found it necessary to move away from its October 1979 position due to the severe recession of 1981–1982, which was generally viewed as attributable to or at least contributed to by monetary policy.

Monetarism, which requires a clearly defined concept of the money stock, has been rendered suspect for policy purposes because of the changing definition of money. The problem arises from the fact that no clear distinction can be drawn today between money and other liquid assets, and because the narrow definition of money is not constant but varies as a result of innovations in financial assets. A further serious difficulty for monetarism arises from the behavior of the velocity of spending. The quantity theory requires an income velocity that is essentially constant or predictable, but the velocity of M1 in the eighties has departed from its earlier path and has been volatile. Much of the acceptance of monetarism at the end of the seventies and early eighties has dissipated. Neither the Keynesian revolution nor the Friedman counterrevolution has emerged supreme; monetary theory is essentially a duopoly.

In the mid-1980s the Federal Reserve, still without a north star, set monetary targets but did not hold fast to them if economic indicators such as the price level, GNP growth, interest rates, and the foreign exchange value of the dollar seemed to justify departure. Targeting monetary growth went out of style with academic and other economists who give free advice to the Fed. By the end of 1986, mirabile dictu, there appeared to be somewhat of a consensus among Keynesians, monetarists, and rational expectationists that the Federal Reserve would do well to target nominal GNP.

There seem to be good reasons for the Federal Reserve to take an eclectic approach. In the light of experience and the persistence of institutional change, the best approach may well be one of using money growth targets as a first approximation to monetary policy, subject to and tempered by discretion as events unfold. As Boulding has observed, "One of the difficulties of evolutionary theory, both in biology and in social systems, is that it does not have very much predictive power. This is inherent in the nature of the process itself and is not simply a remediable defect of human knowledge."[3] The notion that there are scientifically derivable rules or tools to provide a "correct" solution for every economic problem may be more seductive than attainable. Perhaps a good understanding of how we got where we are plus an awareness of the ongoing changes taking place in our socioeconomic organism are just as important as abstract theory. In one of Solzhenitsyn's novels, history is likened to a river. The question of where to look for the laws to govern the flow of the river is answered with "That's the riddle. It may be that they are unknowable."[4] Economics, a current in the flow of history, is imperfectly knowable.

Notes

Chapter 1

1. Used in recent years to describe policies that enrich the affluent immediately but are expected eventually to benefit the broad lower levels of society.

2. Quoted by Gilbert C. Fite in appendix to "Election of 1896," in *History of American Presidential Elections 1789–1968,* Vol. II, ed. Arthur M. Schlesinger, Jr. (New York: Chelsea House in association with McGraw–Hill, 1971), pp. 1849–1850.

3. Ibid., p. 1828.

4. Ibid., p. 1863.

5. Ibid., p. 1833.

6. "Nominalist and Realist" (1844), in Ralph Waldo Emerson, *Essays, First and Second Series* (New York: Macmillan, 1926), p. 350.

7. *The Purchasing Power of Money* (New York: Macmillan, 1911), p. 323.

8. Milton Friedman and Anna Jacobson Schwartz, *A Monetary History of the United States 1867–1960,* a study by the National Bureau of Economic Research (Princeton: Princeton University Press, 1963), pp. 37–42, 94, 96, 135, 137. Scattered excerpts reprinted with permission of Princeton University Press.

9. This formal differentiation between money and deposits meant little to the general public. "The bank customer, however, thinks of his deposit claim as money, and it really serves him all the purposes of money. The right to have the money when desired is as good as the actual money, is more convenient, and is as readily and as serviceably transferred." Herbert Joseph Davenport, *The Economics of Enterprise* (New York: Macmillan, (1913), 1936), p. 262.

10. "The spirit of free banking is evident in the liberal opportunities available to private banks and to trust companies. Non-national institutions flourished by meeting the various needs which national banks were prevented from fulfilling— needs for small-scale country banking, for mortgage loans, for trust services." Paul B. Trescott, *Financing American Enterprise* (New York: Harper and Row, 1963), p. 266.

11. *The American Crisis*, No. 1, 1776 (London: Daniel Isaac Eaton, n.d.), p. 20.

12. Frederick Lewis Allen, *The Great Pierpont Morgan* (New York: Harper and Brothers, 1949), p. 266.

13. Ibid., p. 265.

14. Friedman and Schwartz, op. cit., p. 167.

15. Edwin R. A. Seligman, "Introduction —The Crisis of 1907 in the Light of History," in *The Currency Problem and the Present Financial Situation* (New York: Columbia University Press, 1908), pp. xix–xx.

16. Frank A. Vanderlip, "The Modern Bank," in *The Currency Problem and the Present Financial Situation* (New York: Columbia University Press, 1908), p. 3.

17. Ibid., p. 14.

18. *The ABC of the Federal Reserve System*, 7th edition (Princeton: Princeton University Press, 1928), p. 2.

19. Friedman and Schwartz, op. cit., p. 169.

20. "It is generally recognized that the collapse of bank credit brought about by loss of confidence is the essential fact of every crisis, be the cause of the loss of confidence what it may." Irving Fisher, *The Purchasing Power of Money*, op. cit., p. 66.

21. Edwin Walter Kemmerer, *The ABC of the Federal Reserve System*, op. cit., p. 11.

22. *The Purchasing Power of Money*, op. cit., p. 296.

23. Mark Blaug, *Economic Theory in Retrospect*, 3rd edition (Cambridge: Cambridge University Press, 1978), p. 645.

24. Joseph A. Schumpeter, *History of Economic Analysis* (New York: Oxford University Press, 1954), p. 872. Milton Friedman concurs, calling Fisher America's greatest economist by far.

25. Maurice Allais, "Irving Fisher," in *International Encyclopedia of the Social Sciences*, Vol. 10 ed. David L. Sills (New York: Macmillan and Free Press, 1968), p. 478.

26. Irving Fisher, *The Purchasing Power of Money*, op. cit., p. 71.

27. Ibid., p. 56.

28. Ibid., p. 63–64.

29. Paul M. Warburg, *The Federal Reserve System, Its Origin and Growth*, Vol. 1 (New York: Macmillan, 1930), p. 16.

30. Robert Craig West, *Banking Reform and the Federal Reserve 1863–1923* (Ithaca: Cornell University Press, 1977), p. 138. My discussion of the real bills doctrine draws on this source.

31. Warburg, op. cit., pp. 18–19.

Chapter 2

1. Lester V. Chandler, *Benjamin Strong, Central Banker* (Washington, D.C.: The Brookings Institution, 1958), p. 14.

2. Op. cit., p. 10.

3. Following the establishment of the Federal Reserve System, data for demand deposits separate from time deposits became available, thereby permitting the money stock to be measured as the sum of currency (coin and paper money) plus the public's demand deposits in commercial banks.

4. Friedman and Schwartz, op. cit., p. 193.

5. Ibid., pp. 194–196.

6. Quoted by Chandler, op. cit., p. 105.

7. Ibid., p. 112.

8. Friedman and Schwartz, op. cit., pp. 218–219.

9. Ibid., p. 239.

10. West, op. cit., p. 194.

11. John Kenneth Galbraith, *Money* (Boston: Houghton Mifflin, 1975), p. 169. Professor Galbraith holds the view that central bankers seldom pay for the mistakes they make as long as they conform to orthodox thinking and behavior.

12. Roy F. Harrod, *The Dollar* (New York: Harcourt, Brace, 1954), p. 43.

Chapter 3

1. *Financing American Enterprise,* op. cit., p. 193.

2. Chandler, op. cit., p. 205.

3. Ibid., pp. 238–239.

4. The Conference of Governors was formed after the Federal Reserve Banks were established, for the purpose of coordinating the policies of the reserve banks. The Federal Reserve Board viewed it as a threat to its authority.

5. Chandler, op. cit., p. 188.

6. Thirty years later, Roy Harrod described the *Tenth Annual Report* as "one of the most important documents in world monetary history. . . . [i]t presented a new philosophy of central bank management which was destined to be the background, and to supply the implicit pre-conceptions, of all future discussions of policy." Harrod praised the *Report* for its clear statement that the Federal Reserve would carefully monitor the economy for indications of overexpansion or depression and would seek to maintain steady credit conditions to achieve steady economic growth. Harrod, op. cit., pp. 49–53.

7. Friedman and Schwartz, op. cit., p. 240.

8. John Maynard Keynes, *A Tract on Monetary Reform,* in *The Collected Writings of John Maynard Keynes,* Vol. IV (London: Macmillan St. Martin's Press for the Royal Economic Society, 1971), pp. 137–138.

9. Director's preface to Charles O. Hardy, *Credit Policies of the Federal Reserve System* (Washington, D.C.: The Brookings Institution, 1932), ix.

10. Galbraith, op. cit., p. 174.

11. Benjamin M. Anderson, *Economics and the Public Welfare* (Indianapolis: Liberty Press, 1979), p. 189. (Originally published by D. Van Nostrand Company, Inc., 1949.) Anderson was editor of the *Chase Economic Bulletin* (Chase National Bank, New York) from 1920 to 1937. Later he was professor of economics at the University of California at Los Angeles.

12. Ibid.

13. John Kenneth Galbraith, *The Great Crash* (Boston: Houghton Mifflin, 1954), p. 16; Friedman and Schwartz, op. cit., p. 291; Galbraith, *Money*, op. cit., pp. 173, 178.

14. Frederick Lewis Allen, *The Lords of Creation* (New York: Harper and Brothers, 1935), p. 315.

15. Friedman and Schwartz, op. cit., p. 255.

16. Elmus R. Wicker, *Federal Reserve Monetary Policy 1917–1933* (New York: Random House, 1966), p. 117.

17. Galbraith, *The Great Crash*, op. cit., p. 75.

18. Warburg, op. cit., pp. 823–824.

19. Friedman and Schwartz, op. cit., p. 291.

20. Chandler, op. cit., p. 479.

21. "Judged by the standards that Federal Reserve officials accepted during the period—standards approved by many of their contemporaries and sanctioned at least implicitly by the Federal Reserve Act and accepted prewar central banking practices—Federal Reserve policy during this period of deflation was a success. It did, after all, succeed in maintaining gold payments and in avoiding financial crisis and 'disorderly' liquidation. But the old standards were soon to be rejected, partly because of this painful experience." Chandler, op. cit., p. 187.

22. Ibid., pp. 197–198.

23. "Governor Strong had no fundamental grasp of the problems of central banking. His statements in private discussion regarding his policies indicated that they were short-run policies and, at times, contradictory." Anderson, op. cit., p. 129.

24. Ibid.

25. Galbraith, *The Great Crash*, op. cit., pp. 32–33.

Chapter 4

1. *Growing Up* (New York: Congdon and Weed, 1982), p. 67.

2. *America's Greatest Depression 1929–1941* (New York: Harper and Row, 1970), p. 31.

3. Charles P. Kindleberger, *The World in Depression 1929–1939* (Berkeley and Los Angeles: University of California Press, 1973), p. 128.

4. Friedman and Schwartz, op. cit., p. 167.

5. Gerald Epstein and Thomas Ferguson, "Monetary Policy, Loan Liquidation, and Industrial Conflict: The Federal Reserve and the Open Market Operations of 1932," *The Journal of Economic History* XLIV:4 (December 1984), p. 981.

6. Ibid,. pp. 969–977.

7. Friedman and Schwartz, op. cit., p. 493; Lester V. Chandler, *America's Greatest Depression, 1929–1941*, op. cit., pp. 3–4.

8. Jesse H. Jones, with Edward Angly, *Fifty Billion Dollars* (New York: Macmillan, 1951), pp. 45–46; Arthur M. Schlesinger, Jr., *The Coming of the New Deal* (Boston: Houghton Mifflin, 1959), p. 443.

9. Friedman and Schwartz, op. cit., p. 474.

10. Schlesinger, op. cit., p. 229. One account of Pittman's escapades has him sitting naked in a pantry sink at Claridge's in London while regarding himself as a statue in a fountain. Galbraith, *Money*, op. cit., p. 203.

11. Chandler, *America's Greatest Depression*, op. cit., p. 140.

12. E. Cary Brown, "Fiscal Policy in the 'Thirties: A Reappraisal," *American Economic Review* XLVI (December 1956), p. 863.

13. "Comments and Observations," *History of Political Economy* 10:4 (Winter 1978), p. 542. Reprinted with permission.

14. "Money: Quantity Theory," in *International Encyclopedia of the Social Sciences*, Vol. 10 (New York: Macmillan and Free Press, 1968), p. 438.

15. *The Economist*, June 4, 1983, p. 17. Reprinted with permission.

16. *The New York Times*, May 29, 1983, sec. 3, pp. 1, 6. Copyright© 1983 by The New York Times Company. Reprinted by permission.

17. *The Economist*, op. cit., pp. 17, 19. Reprinted with permission.

18. Blaug, op. cit., p. 646.

19. John Maynard Keynes, *The General Theory of Employment Interest and Money* (London: Macmillan, 1936), p. 293.

20. Keynes, *A Tract on Monetary Reform*, op. cit., pp. 61, 64–65.

21. Blaug, op. cit., p. 646.

22. Richard T. Selden, "Monetarism," Chapter 13 in *Modern Economic Thought*, ed. Sidney Weintraub, (Philadelphia: University of Pennsylvania Press, 1977), p. 255.

23. A. D. Bain, *The Control of the Money Supply*, 3rd edition (Harmondsworth, England: Penguin, 1980), pp. 79–80.

24. Milton Friedman, *The Counter-revolution in Monetary Theory*. First Wincott Memorial Lecture. Occasional Paper 33. (London: The Institute of Economic Affairs, 1970), p. 10. Copyright 1970 by the Wincott Foundation. Reprinted by permission.

25. The discussion of Eccles's role is based mainly on Sidney Hyman, *Marriner S. Eccles* (Stanford: Graduate School of Business, Stanford University, 1976).

26. Ibid., p. 110.

27. Friedman and Schwartz, op. cit., p. 526.

28. Hyman, op. cit., pp. 235–238.

29. Byrd L. Jones, "Launchlin Currie, Pump Priming, and New Deal Fiscal Policy, 1934–1936," *History of Political Economy* 10 (Winter 1978), pp. 509–524; Launchlin Currie, "Comments and Observations," op. cit., pp. 541–548; Byrd L. Jones, "Launchlin Currie and the Causes of the 1937 Recession," *History of Political Economy* 12 (Fall 1980), pp. 303–315; Launchlin Currie, "Causes of the Recession (1938)," *History of Political Economy* 12 (Fall 1980), pp. 316–335.

30. "From the time of the publication of *The General Theory* forward, the center of Keynesian evangelism in Washington was the Board of Governors of the Federal Reserve System." Galbraith, *Money*, op. cit., p. 229. According to Galbraith, central banks are not likely points of entry for new ideas into government. His study of American banking led him to conclude that economists have generally treated the Federal Reserve System with excessive respect.

31. Friedman and Schwartz, op. cit.; Kindleberger, op. cit.; Peter Temin, *Did*

Monetary Forces Cause the Great Depression? (New York: W.W. Norton, 1976); Karl Brunner, ed., *The Great Depression Revisited* (Boston: Martinus Nijhoff, 1981).

32. Friedman and Schwartz, op. cit., p. 695.

33. Temin, op. cit., p. 178.

34. Donald F. Gordon, Review of Peter Temin, *Did Monetary Forces Cause the Great Depression?* in *Journal of Economic Literature* XVI (March 1978), pp. 118–119; Arthur E. Gandolfi and James R. Lothian, Review of Peter Temin, *Did Monetary Forces . . .,* in *Journal of Money, Credit and Banking* IX (November 1977), pp. 679–691.

35. Karl Brunner, "Epilogue: Understanding the Great Depression," in Brunner, op. cit., chapter 17.

36. Charles P. Kindleberger, Review of Karl Brunner, *The Great Depression Revisited,* in *Journal of Economic Literature* XIX (December 1981), p. 1586.

Chapter 5

1. *American Monetary Policy* (New York: McGraw–Hill, 1951), p. 186.

2. Jules I. Bogen, "The Federal Reserve System Since 1940," in *The Federal Reserve System,* ed. Herbert Prochnow (New York: Harper and Brothers, 1960), pp. 338–339; Lester V. Chandler, *Inflation in the United States 1940–1948* (New York: Harper and Brothers, 1951), pp. 183–186.

3. Earlier, at the end of 1940, the board, the presidents of the Federal Reserve Banks, and the Federal Advisory Council joined in asking that the maximum permissible reserve requirement percentages be doubled so that excess reserves could readily be absorbed, but Congress turned a deaf ear to this appeal.

4. *Federal Reserve Bulletin* 28:1 (January 1942), p. 2.

5. Bogen, op. cit., p. 341.

6. A. Jerome Clifford, *The Independence of the Federal Reserve System* (Philadelphia: University of Pennsylvania Press, 1965), p. 178.

7. Chandler, *Inflation,* op. cit., p. 61.

8. Goldenweiser, op. cit., pp. 184–185.

9. Ibid.

10. Clifford, op. cit., pp. 175–176.

11. Chandler, *Inflation,* op. cit., pp. 194–196.

12. Friedman and Schwartz, op. cit., pp. 564–565.

13. Ibid., p. 548.

14. Chandler, *Inflation,* op. cit., p. 6

Chapter 6

1. 15 U.S.C. 1021.

2. Chandler, *Inflation,* op. cit., p. 217.

3. A number of econometric models failed to forecast accurately the economic events immediately following the war. Among the errant prognosticators was the

young Paul Samuelson, who predicted that unemployment would be a serious problem when peace returned. This experience on the part of an acknowledged brilliant mathematical economist demonstrated the vulnerability of the forecasting models.

4. Chandler, *Inflation,* op. cit., p. 216.

5. In 1943 and 1944 personal saving was some 25 percent of disposable personal income, compared with 4.5 percent in 1940 and 3.1 percent in 1947. *Economic Report of the President 1983,* p. 190.

6. Friedman and Schwartz, op. cit., p. 577.

7. Ibid., pp. 581–584.

8. The discussion in this section draws on A. Jerome Clifford, op. cit., chapters VII and VIII.

9. Friedman and Schwartz, op. cit., p. 578.

10. After the war, Marriner Eccles suffered a loss of influence. He supported proposals by the Board of Governors to Congress (which were denied in 1947) for increased reserve requirement limits and permanent direct control over consumer credit, but he placed the blame for the urgent need for restrictive monetary/credit policies on the administration's fiscal program. After being denied reappointment as chairman of the Board of Governors by President Truman in 1948—McCabe succeeded him on April 15, 1948—Eccles continued as a board member until July 1951.

11. As quoted in Clifford, op. cit., pp. 233–234.

12. As quoted in Clifford, op. cit., p. 248.

13. As quoted in Clifford, op. cit., p. 230.

Chapter 7

1. Galbraith, *Money,* op. cit., p. 253.

2. Marshall I. Goldman, *U.S.S.R. in Crisis* (New York: W. W. Norton, 1983), p. 1.

3. William McChesney Martin, "The Transition to Free Markets," *Federal Reserve Bulletin* XXXIX (April, 1953), p. 333.

4. Exceptions were made on three occasions, in 1955, 1958, and 1960. In each case the Fed bought securities other than bills to deal with a problem, that is, stringent money market conditions when the Treasury was engaged in a refunding operation, disorderly market conditions, and an outflow of gold.

5. Daniel S. Ahearn, *Federal Reserve Policy Reappraised, 1951–1959* (New York: Columbia University Press, 1963), p. 62. This is a comprehensive examination of Federal Reserve policy during the 1950s.

6. In fact, the degree of market linkage was shown to be far from perfect.

7. Ahearn, op. cit., pp. 108–109.

8. *Federal Reserve Bulletin* XLVII (February, 1961), p. 165. Although the Fed abandoned the "bills only" doctrine, the bulk of its open-market operations are nevertheless conducted in short-term securities.

9. Friedman and Schwartz, op. cit., p. 634.

10. With the end of the Fed's pegging policy, the banks began to go to the Fed once again for loans. This involved a learning (or relearning) experience on the part

of commercial bankers and Federal Reserve officials alike, since discounting had vanished for seventeen years.

11. Walter Heller, Gardner Ackley, and Arthur Okun, who served in turn as chairmen of the Council of Economic Advisers in the 1960s, were all prominent and influential in this regard.

12. The distinction between demand-pull and cost-push and its implications for policy were summarized in a paper entitled "Wage-Push Inflation" by Professor Walter A. Morton, given at the American Economic Association convention in Chicago in December, 1958 (mimeographed).

13. "All economic interests must be forced to live within the ambit of a stable monetary unit." Ibid., p. 13.

14. Martin Bronfenbrenner and Franklyn D. Holzman, "Survey of Inflation Theory," *American Economic Review* LIII (September 1963), pp. 613–614, 626.

15. *The Conquest of Mexico*, vol. 2 (Philadelphia: Lippincott, 1873), p. 51.

16. Walter W. Heller, *New Dimensions of Political Economy* (New York: W. W. Norton, 1967), pp. 1–2.

17. Arthur M. Okun, *The Political Economy of Prosperity* (New York: W. W. Norton, 1970), pp. 31, 59. The enhanced status of economics at this time is reflected in the establishment of the Nobel Memorial Prize in Economics by the Central Bank of Sweden in 1968. Prizes have been awarded annually since 1969.

18. President Kennedy sent a special tax reduction message to Congress on January 24, 1963, which resulted in the enactment of legislation in 1964 following his assassination on November 22, 1963. The tax cut was considered a bold step because the federal deficit was rising at the time and the economy was on the up-swing. It was an application of Keynesian economics, to which the president had become a convert, with emphasis on maintaining economic growth.

19. Heller, op. cit., p. 61.

20. G. L. Bach, *Making Monetary and Fiscal Policy* (Washington, D.C.: The Brookings Institution, 1971), pp. 101, 117, 121.

21. "Federal Reserve policy in 1961–1963 was not like that of 1952–1960. At the early stages of recovery in the 1950s, the Federal Reserve, overly sensitive to inflationary dangers, aborted recoveries. Whether the explanation was a growing conviction that inflation was no longer a threat, or whether it was an awareness that the Kennedy administration would not tolerate stifling monetary policies, the Federal Reserve made no serious attempts to deflate the economy after 1960. In fact, in 1963, Mr. Martin boasted of the large contributions made to expansion." Seymour E. Harris, *Economics of the Kennedy Years* (New York: Harper and Row, 1964), p. 121.

22. Franco Modigliani and Richard Sutch, "Innovations in Interest Rate Policy," *American Economic Review* LVI (May 1966), pp. 178–197.

23. *Commercial Banking in the Economy*, 3rd edition (New York: Random House, 1979), p. 142.

24. This is not to deny that historically bankers have participated in speculative excesses from time to time.

25. The prime rate charged by banks rose from about 3 percent in 1954 to 5

percent in 1959; the rate on three-month Treasury bills rose from approximately 1 percent to 3.4 percent between those years.

26. This is true for the large and medium-sized banks that are responsible for the bulk of the banking business.

27. Walter Wriston of First National City Bank in New York (Citibank) apparently was chiefly responsible for the CD breakthrough. First National City interested the dealers in government securities in making a secondary market for the instruments. Martin Mayer, *The Bankers* (New York: Weybright and Talley, 1974), p. 192.

28. Bruce J. Summers, "Negotiable Certificates of Deposits," *Instruments of the Money Market,* 5th edition (Richmond: Federal Reserve Bank of Richmond, 1981), pp. 75, 78.

29. Paul S. Nadler, *Commercial Banking in the Economy,* op. cit., pp. 142–145. The power of attracting funds from afar by interest rates recalls an old City (of London) saying, in the days of the gold standard before World War I: "Seven percent will bring gold from the moon." Cited in P. T. Ellsworth, *The International Economy* (New York: Macmillan, 1950), p. 316.

Chapter 8

1. *The Economy: Old Myths and New Realities* (New York: W.W. Norton, 1976), p. 196.

2. "What Vietnam Did to the American Economy," *The New York Times,* January 28, 1973, sec. 3, p. 1, as quoted in Arthur M. Johnson, *The American Economy* (New York: Free Press, 1974), p. 97. Excerpt copyright © 1973 by The New York Times Company. Reprinted by permission.

3. Edwin L. Dale, Jr., ibid., p. 98.

4. Gardner Ackley states that President Johnson realized that a tax increase was needed, but was convinced after widespread consultations that it was politically impossible to enact it. Congress is thus implicated in the blame. Johnson hoped either that the need for it would evaporate or that influential persons would soon see that it was necessary. Ackley adds that some of his political advisers may well have discouraged the idea of a tax increase because even as early as 1966 the war was unpopular. Gardner Ackley, "International Inflation," in *Economic Policies of the 1970's,* ed. Alfred K. Ho (Ann Arbor: Bureau of Business Research, Graduate School of Business Administration, The University of Michigan, 1971) as reprinted in Johnson, ibid., p. 92.

5. *The Political Economy of Prosperity* (New York: W.W. Norton, 1970), p. 81.

6. Some observers considered the stand taken by the central bank at this time as "the Fed's finest hour" for asserting its independence in the face of President Johnson's vigorous opposition. Chairman Martin was summoned to the presidential ranch in Texas for barbecued steaks (presumably smothered in blandishments), but was not persuaded to change his mind. Roger Leroy Miller and Raburn M. Williams, *The New Economics of Richard Nixon* (San Francisco: Canfield Press, 1972), p. 5.

7. Sherman J. Maisel, *Managing the Dollar* (New York: W.W. Norton, 1973), pp. 71–77, 89. The author is an academic economist who served as a member of the Board of Governors of the Federal Reserve System from 1965 to 1972. The book provides an extremely valuable inside view of Federal Reserve policy making.

8. Chairman Martin was widely praised by some and blamed by others for the tight money policy of mid–1966. But things are not always what they seem. Actually Martin was recuperating from an operation throughout the period, and the board did not request his advice until he was ready to return in the autumn. Bach, op. cit., p. 130.

9. *Annual Report*, Federal Reserve Bank of New York, 1966, 1967, p. 8.

10. The erroneous forecasts, like those near the end of World War II, underestimated the strength of aggregate demand.

11. The term *monetarism* began to appear in the late sixties. It was used by Karl Brunner in an article in the *Federal Reserve Bank of St. Louis Review,* July 1968. Thomas Mayer refers to monetarists in his *Monetary Policy in the United States* (New York: Random House, 1968), the preface of which is dated October 1967.

12. "However, the experience of 1968 indicates how difficult it is to slow an economy in which inflationary price and wage expectations are a major driving force. These expectations must change if the economy is to return to a pattern of sustainable growth, but they are now so firmly entrenched that this is likely to prove a difficult task." *Annual Report*, Federal Reserve Bank of New York, 1968, 1969, p. 8.

13. *Managing the Dollar*, op. cit., pp. 62–63.

14. This discussion draws on Gordon H. Sellon, Jr. and Ronald L. Teigen, "The Choice of Short-Run Targets for Monetary Policy," *Economic Review*, Federal Reserve Bank of Kansas City (May 1981), pp. 3–9.

15. Maisel, *Managing the Dollar*, op. cit., p. 78.

16. *Free reserves* are the difference between excess reserves held by the banks and total borrowing by the banks from the Fed. Net free reserves result when excess reserves exceed borrowing. *Net borrowed reserves* means that bank borrowing exceeds the excess reserves.

17. On a week-to-week basis, not over a long period of time.

18. Maisel, op. cit., p. 81.

19. Ibid., p. 86.

20. Ralph C. Bryant, *Controlling Money* (Washington, D.C.: The Brookings Institution, 1983), pp. 67–68.

Chapter 9

1. *Economic Policy and the Great Stagflation* (New York: Academic Press, 1979), p. 2.

2. "Uniting Against Inflation," *The Brookings Bulletin* 16:3 (Winter 1980), p. 1.

3. *The Bankers* (New York: Weybright and Talley, 1974), pp. 421–422.

4. As Assistant Secretary of the Treasury, Martin negotiated with the man he

succeeded as chairman at the Fed, Thomas McCabe, concerning the accord. Indeed Martin was the "chief architect" of the accord. Bach, op. cit., p. 83.

5. When Martin took over at the Fed in the wake of the accord, the question of Federal Reserve independence was of great interest. One writer's view of what happened is unequivocal. "Handling President Eisenhower and Congressional committees with equal Missouri suavity, Martin established for the Fed an independence of political direction that was one of the wonders of American government—he was even able to force a policy of economic restraint in an election year, which almost certainly cost Richard Nixon the 1960 election and saddled the incoming Kennedy administration with 7 percent unemployment." Martin Mayer, op. cit., p. 188.

6. Sherman Maisel found Martin to be either on the side of expansion or in the middle of the spectrum of the FOMC during most of the sixties, and that Martin favored maximum growth with a compatible financial structure. Maisel, op. cit., p. 119.

7. The editor of *The Wall Street Journal* witnessed Nixon's praise of Burns at a White House dinner early in Burns's term at the Fed. Reflecting on the fact that it was not long before they crossed swords, he observed later that "Once in that post with its fixed term, Federal Reserve chairmen are as unpredictable in performance as Supreme Court judges." Vermont Royster, *My Own, My Country's Time* (Chapel Hill: Algonquin Books, 1983), p. 256.

8. *Reflections of an Economic Policy Maker* (Washington, D.C.: American Enterprise Institute for Public Policy Research, 1978), pp. 110–111.

9. Maisel, op. cit., p. 9.

10. "Empirical Evidence on Fiscal and Monetary Models," in *Issues in Fiscal and Monetary Policy,* ed. James J. Diamond (Chicago: De Paul University, 1971), p. 35.

11. "Monetarism: A Historic–Theoretic Perspective," *The Journal of Economic Literature* XV:2 (June 1977), p. 470. Reprinted with permission.

12. From the 1950s through the 1970s, the major macroeconomic controversy involved alternative ways of specifying aggregate demand. Keynesians explained aggregate demand by the addition of consumption, investment, and government spending on output, whereas monetarists retained the traditional multiplication of M times V from the equation of exchange. In policy terms, the debate concerned how much monetary policy really mattered, and then how much fiscal policy really mattered. By the end of the 1970s, the debate had subsided considerably with a recognition that both approaches have explanatory value and that aggregate demand responds to both fiscal policy and monetary policy. If at times the debate was marred by rigidity, extremism, and ill-feeling, the observations of Schumpeter on the nineteenth-century German Battle of Methods (*Methodenstreit*) may apply. He observed that much mutual misunderstanding enters into controversies between scientific parties and that "we must never forget that genuine schools are sociological realities—living beings. They have their structures—relations between leaders and followers—their flags, their battle cries, their moods, their all-too-human interests. Their antagonisms come within the general sociology of group antagonisms and of party warfare. Victory and conquest, defeat and loss of ground, are in themselves values for such schools and part of their very existence." Schumpeter, op. cit., p. 815.

224 · *The American Monetary System*

13. Milton Friedman and Walter W. Heller, *Monetary vs. Fiscal Policy,* Arthur K. Salomon Lecture, New York University Graduate School of Business Administration (New York: W. W. Norton, 1969).

14. For example: Change in the money supply is the only systematic factor determining nominal income, affecting output in the short-run and prices in the long-run.

15. For a decade beginning in 1943 "Warburton truly stood alone against the profession in advocating the monetarist position." Thomas F. Cargill, "Clark Warburton and the Development of Monetarism Since the Great Depression," *History of Political Economy* 11:3 (Fall 1979), pp. 427–428; reprinted with permission. This article is the basis of the present paragraph.

16. "The times were simply not conducive to an examination of old ideas like the quantity theory of money. The Great Depression convinced almost everyone that money and monetary policy played minor roles in determining the level of economic activity." ibid., p. 446.

17. Leland B. Yeager, "Clark Warburton, 1896–1979," *History of Political Economy* 13:2 (Summer 1981), p. 284. In this appreciation of his contribution, Warburton is described as a liberal in the New Deal sense of the term. It seems unlikely that he would have been comfortable with the Chicago monetarists.

18. Friedman and Schwartz, op. cit., p. xxii. Friedman and Schwartz express their indebtedness to many persons in the preface but "owe an especially heavy debt to Clark Warburton." At three other places in this book they express their indebtedness to him again, and the index lists fifteen references to Warburton.

19. Leonard Silk, *The Economists* (New York: Basic Books, 1976), pp. 45, 79.

20. Friedman's eminence is beyond dispute. He has been president of the American Economic Association (1967) and Nobel Laureate (1976). "It can be said by one man: 'Monetarism, that's me.' That man, of course, is Milton Friedman." Paul A. Samuelson, "Reflections on the Merits and Demerits of Monetarism," in *Issues in Fiscal and Monetary Policy,* op. cit.

21. Friedman, *Counter-revolution,* op. cit., pp. 10–22. Friedman cautions that this is a summary of main points and not a complete explanation with all of the qualifications that would be required for a full understanding.

22. Ibid., pp. 8, 17.

23. Ibid., pp. 22–24.

24. In December 1971 Friedman discussed the response to the monetary slowdown of January 1969 to February 1970 and found that inflation did not respond as rapidly as he had expected. Feeling "chastened," he reexamined the data for the postwar period and decided that the typical time lag between changes in M and the subsequent changes in P was considerably longer (eleven to thirty-one months) than he had thought. Milton Friedman, "Have Monetary Policies Failed?" *The American Economic Review* LXII: 2 (May 1972), p. 14.

25. *Reflections of an Economic Policy Maker,* op. cit., pp. 118, 127.

26. Consumer prices rose by 6 percent in 1969, 5.5 percent in 1970, and 3.7 percent per annum in the first eight months of 1971.

27. After the election Mr. Nixon was quoted as saying "I am now a Keynesian" to indicate acceptance of budget deficits when the economy is below full employment.

This discussion relies in part on Leonard Silk, *Nixonomics,* 2nd edition (New York: Praeger, 1972).

28. Drawn from Arthur F. Burns, *Reflections,* op. cit.

29. The decision was certainly "historic" in that it was the first time in our national history that wage–price controls were adopted in peacetime. Public opinion as measured by the Gallup Poll showed clear support for controls for about four years before they were instituted, and continued to favor them even after they lapsed in 1974.

30. Miller and Williams, op. cit., p. 20.

31. The August 1971 package contained some fiscal stimulants.

32. Arthur Okun's invention, a discomfort index, combines the unemployment rate and the rate of change of consumer prices. In 1974 this index easily set a post–World War II record, reaching 17.8. But worse was to come in 1979 and 1980 when the index exceeded 19.

33. This paragraph draws on Paul Lewis, "Challenging the Olympian Fed," *The New York Times,* August 18, 1974, Sec. 3.

34. An attempt was made by the industrial nations to restore fixed rates in December 1971 at the Smithsonian conference, but by early 1973 this arrangement collapsed. It has been plausibly argued that governments in most of the industrial world responded to the release from the fixed exchange rate system by overly expansive monetary policies in 1972–1973.

35. "Selecting Monetary Targets in a Changing Financial Environment." In *Monetary Policy Issues in the 1980s* (Kansas City: Federal Reserve Bank of Kansas City, 1982), p. 189. Scattered excerpts reprinted by permission of the author.

36. Edward J. Kane, ibid., p. 182. The changes in operating procedures that we are concerned with are changes in the priority given to different intermediate targets as the Fed moved toward greater reliance on monetary aggregates and away from money market conditions. The intermediate targets are now usually divided into two groups which Kane has labeled intermediate target #1 and intermediate target #2. His graphic description depicts a policy instrument as a cannon that "aims proximately through the center of an intermediate-target tube that [tracks] a heat-seeking missile (intermediate target #2), which itself follows the tiny goal variable (more accurately, the current flock of goal variables) as it wings through the clouds." Thus, for example, the Fed decides on a certain desired rate of GNP growth, sets the target range for money growth that is expected to generate the GNP growth, sets the target ranges for the growth in reserves and federal funds rate (money market conditions) expected to bring the desired money growth, and uses its open-market operations and discount policy to control the money-market conditions. The money market target(s) is(are) intermediate target #1 and the money target is intermediate target #2 using this nomenclature. Alternative terminology limits the intermediate target to one type of target, the growth of money (or monetary aggregate); money-market conditions would then be called the operating target or guide.

37. The intended shift from emphasis on stable money-market conditions to control of the monetary aggregates was subsequently tested mathematically by a money-market model that indicated "strong evidence that there was a shift in monetary policy toward placing more emphasis on controlling the money supply," and

that "an ancillary interest in stabilizing money-market conditions remains." Edgar L. Feige and Robert McGee, "Has the Federal Reserve Shifted from a Policy of Interest Rate Targets to a Policy of Monetary Aggregate Targets?" *Journal of Money, Credit and Banking* XI:4 (November 1979), p. 396.

38. The change in policy was presented in characteristically bland Federal Reserve language. "In 1970 monetary aggregates came to play a more prominent role in the phrasing of the second paragraph, and references were made to the money supply as well as to bank credit." "[T]he Committee stated more directly its desires with respect to the aggregates rather than referring to them in the form of a proviso clause." *Federal Reserve Bulletin*, February 1971, p. 83.

39. This explanation is derived from the firsthand account of Sherman Maisel, who served as chairman of the Committee on the Directive. Maisel, op. cit., pp. 230, 249–254, 301.

40. Sellon and Teigen, op. cit., p. 10.

41. Friedman and Schwartz, op. cit., p. 629.

42. Ibid., pp. 628–632.

43. Quoted in Bach, op. cit., p. 139.

44. Ibid., p. 140.

45. *62nd Annual Report of the Board of Governors of the Federal Reserve System 1975*, 1976, pp. 260–261.

46. *64th Annual Report of the Board of Governors of the Federal Reserve System 1977*, 1978, p. 397.

47. *65th Annual Report of the Board of Governors of the Federal Reserve System 1978*, 1979, pp. 339–340.

48. Alan S. Blinder, *Economic Policy and the Great Stagflation*, op. cit., p. 4. An excellent analysis and summary of the 1970s.

49. Ibid.

50. According to Blinder, price controls were "the stagflationary shock *par excellence:* their imposition in 1971 and removal in 1974 added an unwanted element of variability to the inflation rate without having much effect on the average inflation rate, and the ill-timed demise of controls helped cause the Great Recession. In sum, and with a degree of discernment that admittedly can be obtained only after the fact, the 1971–1974 controls program constituted a remarkable act of national self-flagellation." Ibid., p. 132.

51. More precisely, the expansion of real GNP went on for fifty-eight months, from March 1975 to January 1980.

52. There are some background similarities between William Miller and the former chairman, William Martin: Miller had been only 35 when he became president of the conglomerate Textron, and he too came from midcontinent (Oklahoma). He exchanged a $380,000 annual salary at Textron for $57,500 at the Fed.

53. "Selecting Monetary Targets in a Changing Financial Environment," in *Monetary Policy Issues of the 1980s* (Kansas City: Federal Reserve Bank of Kansas City, 1982), p. 189.

54. Thomas Mayer, James S. Duesenberry, and Robert Z. Aliber, *Money, Banking, and the Economy,* 2nd edition (New York: W. W. Norton, 1984), p. 465.

55. It also led to spot shortages of gasoline and long lines at gasoline service

stations. The sharply higher price of gasoline brought a change in its retail marketing as self-service became widespread for the first time.

56. "Record of Policy Actions of the Federal Open Market Committee," in *66th Annual Report of the Board of Governors of the Federal Reserve System 1979*, 1980, pp. 202–203.

57. The title of an article by Nicholas von Hoffman in *The New York Times Magazine*, December 2, 1979, p. 57. Copyright © 1979 by The New York Times Company; reprinted by permission. It is observed here that "it almost seems as though Paul Volcker has spent most of his life preparing for the Fed chairmanship." After graduate study at Harvard and the London School of Economics, and early work at the Treasury, Federal Reserve Bank of New York, and The Chase Manhattan Bank, he held high level Treasury positions in the Kennedy and Nixon administrations and was president of the Federal Reserve Bank of New York immediately before his appointment as chairman of the Board of Governors in July 1979 by President Carter. (In taking over the chairmanship of the board he took a cut in pay from $110,000 to $57,500 a year). President Reagan re-appointed him chairman in 1983. In serving under Kennedy, Nixon, Carter, and Reagan, it would seem that Volcker has truly been a monetary man for all seasons.

58. *The Economist*, December 15, 1979, p. 30.

59. Donald D. Hester, "Innovations and Monetary Control," *Brookings Papers on Economic Activity* 1:1981, p. 162. This is a careful examination and evaluation of financial innovation from 1960 to 1980. The author considers the innovations laudable for providing improved efficiency of the money and capital markets by enabling "savers and investors to have a greater opportunity to lend and borrow at a rate close to the real rate of interest" (p. 167). On the other hand he found them to be so disruptive to a monetary policy which tries to control monetary aggregates that he advocates the renunciation of monetary aggregate targets (p. 183).

60. Ibid., p. 183.

Chapter 10

1. *Financial Reform in the 1980s* (Stanford, California: Hoover Institution Press, 1985), p. 2. Reprinted with permission.

2. October 8, 1981, p. 1. Reprinted by permission of *The Wall Street Journal*, © Dow Jones & Company, Inc., 1981. All rights reserved.

3. Jack Kemp, Arthur B. Laffer, Robert Mundell, Paul Craig Roberts, Norman B. Ture, and Jude Wanniski were prominent.

4. In an article in *The Wall Street Journal* of March 19, 1980 (p. 24), Herbert Stein, chairman of the Council of Economic Advisers in the Nixon and Ford administrations, made a "plea for modesty" in discussing supply-side economics as a means of combating inflation. Rather than ideological matters, he considered the propositions of supply-side economics to be "matters of arithmetic" that had been exaggerated by overenthusiastic advocates.

5. George Macesich, *The Politics of Monetarism* (Totawa, New Jersey: Rowman & Allanheld, 1984), p. 82.

6. Martin Feldstein makes the point that while the rational expectations view is logically sound, it is based on the presumption of universal and complete belief in future monetary contraction in making price and wage decisions. Since the conditions required for painless disinflation are not realistic, "the theory is essentially untestable by experience." Martin Feldstein, "Monetarism: Open-eyed Pragmatism," *The Economist,* May 18, 1985, p. 18.

7. Isabel V. Sawhill, and Charles F. Stone, "The Economy: The Key to Success," chapter 3 in *The Reagan Record,* ed. John L. Palmer and Isabel V. Sawhill (Cambridge, Mass.: Ballinger, 1984), pp. 73.–78.

8. "When I say that post–Keynesianism has received some vindications from experience, I am also saying that some of the standard hypotheses of neoclassical microeconomics have been borne out by experience. Thus, good-sense supply-side economics would expect that tax reductions which reduce the wedge between pre-tax and post-tax returns might well strengthen investment demand, *ceteris paribus.* The record, I think, bears this out. Adjusting for cyclical factors and for the height of real interest rates, we do seem to observe stronger demands for equipment than past regressions would call for. The Reagan tax cuts, I would suppose, do explain part of this story." Paul A. Samuelson, "Evaluating Reaganomics," *Challenge* 27:5 (November/December 1984), p. 11. Published by M.E. Sharpe, Inc., Armonk, New York. Reprinted by permission.

9. "Why and How to Cut the Deficit," *The Brookings Review* 2:4 (Summer 1984), p. 3.

10. James Tobin, "The Fiscal Revolution: Disturbing Prospects," *Challenge* 27:6 (January/February 1985), p. 13. Published by M.E. Sharpe, Inc., Armonk, New York; excerpt reprinted by permission. The author is Sterling Professor of Economics at Yale University and was a Nobel prizewinner in 1981.

11. Rivlin, "Why and How to Cut the Deficit," op. cit., p. 4.

12. The observations of several prominent financial forecasters on this point are cited in an article in *The Wall Street Journal* by Alfred L. Malabre, Jr., September 20, 1985, p. 6.

13. A clear discussion of these issues based on both economic theory and empirical evidence is presented in Craig S. Hakkio and Bryon Higgins, "Is the United States Too Dependent on Foreign Capital?" *Economics Review,* Federal Reserve Bank of Kansas City 70:6 (June 1985). The authors conclude that "the increased net capital inflow and associated growing dependence on foreign capital could pose serious risks for the U.S. and world economies. . . . Empirical evidence implies that high government budget deficits have been a major factor contributing to large U.S. net capital inflows. As a consequence, reducing budget deficits would reduce the troublesome U.S. dependence on foreign capital" (p. 36).

14. *Economic Report of the President, 1985,* p. 106.

15. Ibid., pp. 67, 71.

16. Perhaps there is a tendency to take the dubious advice given in Thornton Wilder's play *The Skin of Our Teeth* in 1942 to "just enjoy the ice cream while it's on your plate."

17. David Stockman, director of the Office of Management and Budget from 1981 until mid–1985, made the following statement on June 5, 1985, a month before

it was announced that he would leave his government post to join a Wall Street firm. "The basic fact is that we are violating badly, even wantonly, the cardinal rule of sound public finance: Governments must extract from the people in taxes what they dispense in benefits, services and protections . . . indeed, if the [Securities and Exchange Commission] had jurisdiction over the executive and legislative branches, many of us would be in jail." Quoted in Daniel Patrick Moynihan, "Reagan's Inflate-the-Deficit Game," *The New York Times*, July 21, 1985, sec. 4, p. 21. Copyright © 1985 by The New York Times Company. Reprinted by permission.

Friedrich von Hayek, the prominent conservative (Austrian School) economist, Nobel laureate, and "guru of Reaganomics," wrote in March 1985 that "Reagan thinks it is impossible to persuade Congress that expenditures must be reduced unless one creates deficits so large that absolutely everyone becomes convinced that no more money can be spent." Quoted in Tom Wicker, "A Deliberate Deficit." *The Chattanooga Times*, July 20, 1985. Copyright © 1985 by The New York Times Company. Reprinted by permission.

18. *Economic Report of the President, 1981*, p. 6.

19. *Economic Report of the President, 1983*, p. 6. By 1985 President Reagan maintained that regulatory reform had continued, but at too slow a pace, and complained about the failure of Congress to adopt proposals of his administration for further deregulation of banking.

20. There is a certain piquancy to the term *omnibus* in this context given the fact that the word derives from "Omnes' bus." In 1828 a certain Monsieur Omnes from Nantes initiated in Paris the service of a carriage for all, or omnibus. A host of reform measures had accumulated to board the 1980 legislative "bus" when at last it passed through Congress.

21. Adapted from Cargill and Garcia, op. cit., pp. 57–62.

22. The three-month Treasury bill rate fell from about 16 percent in March 1980 to about 8 percent over the next three months, but went back up to 16 percent by the end of the year, falling gradually after mid–1981 but not reaching single-digit territory until the second half of 1982.

23. Adapted from Cargill and Garcia, op. cit., pp. 67–70.

24. The minimum denomination on MMDAs and SNOWs was reduced to $1,000 as of January 1, 1985, and eliminated entirely on January 1, 1986.

25. Cargill and Garcia, op. cit., p. 70.

26. Henry C. Wallich, "Whither American Banking Reform?" *Challenge* 28:4 (September/October 1985), p. 43. Dr. Wallich was a member of the Board of Governors of the Federal Reserve System when he made this statement.

27. Adapted primarily from David D. Whitehead, "Interstate Banking: Probability or Reality?" *Economic Review*, Federal Reserve Bank of Atlanta (March 1985), pp. 6–17.

28. A study released by the FDIC late in 1985 found that this experience had caught the attention of the Tennessee legislature and the financial community sufficiently to bring about reforms making banks stronger. It was pointed out that banks in the Knoxville area now require good collateral before making loans.

29. The book *Belly Up* by Phillip L. Zweig (Crown, 1985), a study of Penn Square, has been recommended for bankers, bank examiners, and business school

students by a Wall Street investment counselor as a mental inoculation against depravity. See review by John Train, *The Wall Street Journal,* November 4, 1985, p. 22.

30. The number of banks on the FDIC's "problem list" rose steadily from a level of 200 in 1981 to 1,100 in 1985.

31. Finance ministers who had been solicited eagerly by bankers urging them to take more loans later found it extremely difficult to service them. A description by an international financial journalist of the annual meetings of the International Monetary Fund and World Bank circa 1980 has the flavor of a salesmen's convention or "trade fair" as bankers sought clients. "As they pursue their prey down the escalators, up the elevators, along the upstairs corridors into the suites, they cannot conceal their anxiety to do business. For these men who look as if they might have been trained to say No from their childhood are actually trying to sell *loans.* 'I've got good news for you,' I heard one eager contact man telling a group of American bankers: 'I think they'll be able to take your money.' " Anthony Sampson, *The Money Lenders* (New York: Viking, 1981), p. 12. A similarity to the international lending practices of some American banks in the 1920s is evident.

32. During expansionary periods in the 1970s some bankers liked to talk about being "aggressive." The idea refers to making loans faster than their rivals do, so as to outgrow the competition. Since financial rewards and prestige are related to rapid growth, there is a tendency to lower banking standards. This "go for it" psychology may also contain a macho element.

33. The notion that money managers should act to police the banking system is flawed on the practical grounds that they would have a hard time getting the knowledge necessary to judge bank loans, and would violate the law if they did obtain such confidential information.

34. *The Wall Street Journal,* October 30, 1985, p. 60.

35. E. Gerald Corrigan, "A Look at the Economy and Some Banking Issues," *Federal Reserve Bank of New York Quarterly Review* 10:1 (Spring 1985), p. 5.

36. *Federal Reserve Bulletin* 71:7 (July 1985), pp. 517–519.

37. Corrigan, op. cit., p. 1.

38. In 1960, in order to provide a more refined measure of money for analytical purposes, M1 began to be based on averages of daily figures instead of monthly data as of a single date.

39. Frank E. Morris, "Monetarism without Money," *New England Economic Review* (March/April 1983), pp. 5–6.

40. The average *growth* rate in the velocity of M1 from 1960 through 1981 was 2.8 percent. "In 1982, velocity fell sharply at a 4.7 percent rate. This decline is over 3 standard deviations from the average and represents highly unusual behavior for the series." John P. Judd, "The Recent Decline in Velocity: Instability in Money Demand or Inflation?" *Economic Review,* Federal Reserve Bank of San Francisco (Spring 1983), p. 13.

41. *69th Annual Report of the Board of Governors of the Federal Reserve System 1982,* 1983, p. 14.

42. *70th Annual Report of the Board of Governors of the Federal Reserve System 1983,* 1984, pp. 15, 17.

43. *71st Annual Report of the Board of Governors of the Federal Reserve System 1984*, 1985, p. 12.

44. For all of 1985 the growth rate of M1 was 11.7 percent, or almost 50 percent above the upper limit of the target range.

45. Judd, op. cit., pp. 16, 18.

46. Lawrence J. Radecki, and John Wenninger, "Recent Instability in M1's Velocity," *Federal Reserve Bank of New York Quarterly Review* 10:3 (Autumn 1985), p. 22.

47. Richard W. Kopcke, "Bank Funding Strategy and the Money Stock," *New England Economic Review* (Jan./Feb. 1985), p. 14. The author is vice president and economist at the Federal Reserve Bank of Boston.

48. Nicholas Kaldor, *The Scourge of Monetarism* (New York: Oxford University Press, 1982), p. xi.

49. James Tobin, "Monetarism: An ebbing tide?" *The Economist*, April 27, 1985, p. 25. Reprinted with permission.

50. "It is high time to give monetarism the decent burial it so richly deserves." Robert Kuttner in *Business Week*, August 19, 1985, p. 16.

51. *The Wall Street Journal*, December 4, 1985, p. 30. Reprinted by permission, Copyright © Dow Jones & Company, Inc., 1985. All rights reserved.

52. Milton Friedman, "The Case for Overhauling the Federal Reserve," *Challenge* 28:3 (July/August 1985), pp. 5–7.

53. In an editorial page article in *The Wall Street Journal*, September 1, 1983, Friedman, after discussing reasons for velocity changes, made the following statement. "In short, excessive monetary growth over the past year means that we are facing the near-certainty of an overheated economy for the next few quarters at least, which will almost certainly mean a subsequent acceleration of inflation, probably in middle or late 1984." By the end of 1986, no surge of inflation had appeared. Excerpt reprinted by permission of *The Wall Street Journal*, copyright © Dow Jones & Company, Inc., 1983. All rights reserved.

54. *Economic Report of the President, 1983*, p. 25. This statement reflects the position of the Council of Economic Advisers under the chairmanship of Martin Feldstein.

55. Frank E. Morris, "Rules plus Discretion in Monetary Policy—An Appraisal of Our Experience since October 1979," *New England Economic Review* (Sept./Oct. 1985), p. 4.

Chapter 11

1. Kenneth E. Boulding, *Evolutionary Economics* (Beverly Hills: Sage Publications, 1981), p. 121.

2. Ibid., p. 17.

3. Ibid., p. 44.

4. Alexander Solzhenitsyn, trans. by Michael Glenny, *August 1914* (London: The Bodley Head, 1972), p. 430.

Selected Bibliography

Ahearn, Daniel S. *Federal Reserve Policy Reappraised, 1951–1959*. New York: Columbia University Press, 1963.

Allais, Maurice. "Fisher, Irving." In *International Encyclopedia of the Social Sciences,* Vol. 10, ed. David L. Sills, New York: Macmillan and Free Press, 1968.

Allen, Frederick Lewis. *The Great Pierpont Morgan*. New York: Harper and Brothers, 1949.

Anderson, Benjamin M. *Economics and the Public Welfare*. Indianapolis: Liberty Press, 1979. (Originally published by D. Van Nostrand, 1949.)

Bach, G. L. *Making Monetary and Fiscal Policy*. Washington, D.C.: Brookings Institution, 1971.

Bain, A. D. *The Control of the Money Supply*, 3rd edition. Harmondsworth, England: Penguin Books, 1980.

Blaug, Mark. *Economic Theory in Retrospect*, 3rd edition. Cambridge: Cambridge University Press, 1978.

Blinder, Alan S. *Economic Policy and the Great Stagflation*. New York: Academic Press, 1979.

Board of Governors of the Federal Reserve System. *Annual Report. 1975, 1977–1979, 1982–1984.*

———. *Banking and Monetary Statistics*. Washington, D. C., 1943.

———. *Banking and Monetary Statistics 1941–1970*. Washington, D. C., 1976.

Bogen, Jules I. "The Federal Reserve System Since 1940." In *The Federal Reserve System,* ed. Herbert V. Prochnow. New York: Harper and Brothers, 1960.

Boulding, Kenneth E. *Evolutionary Economics*. Beverly Hills: Sage Publications, 1981.

Bronfenbrenner, Martin, and Franklyn D. Holzman. "Survey of Inflation Theory." *American Economic Review* LIII (September 1963).

Brown, E. Cary. "Fiscal Policy in the 'Thirties: A Reappraisal." *American Economic Review* XLVI (December 1956).

Brunner, Karl, ed. *The Great Depression Revisited*. Boston: Martinus Nijhoff, 1981.

Bryant, Ralph C. *Controlling Money*. Washington, D. C.: Brookings Institution, 1983.

Burns, Arthur F. *Reflections of an Economic Policy Maker*. Washington, D. C.: American Enterprise Institute for Public Policy Research, 1978.

Cargill, Thomas F. "Clark Warburton and the Development of Monetarism Since the Great Depression." *History of Political Economy* 11:3 (Fall 1979).

Cargill, Thomas F. and Gillian G. Garcia. *Financial Reform in the 1980s*. Stanford, California: Hoover Institution Press, 1985.

Chandler, Lester V. *America's Greatest Depression, 1929–1941*. New York: Harper and Row, 1970.

———. *Benjamin Strong, Central Banker*. Washington, D. C.: Brookings Institution, 1958.

———. *Inflation in the United States 1940–1948*. New York: Harper and Brothers, 1951.

Clifford, A. Jerome. *The Independence of the Federal Reserve System*. Philadelphia: University of Pennsylvania Press, 1965.

Corrigan, E. Gerald. "A Look at the Economy and Some Banking Issues." *Federal Reserve Bank of New York Quarterly Review* 10:1 (Spring 1985).

Currie, Lauchlin B. "Causes of the Recession (1938)." *History of Political Economy* 12 (Fall 1980).

———. "Comments and Observations." *History of Political Economy* 10 (Winter 1978).

Dale, Edwin L., Jr. "What Vietnam Did to the American Economy." *The New York Times,* January 28, 1973. Reprinted in *The American Economy,* ed. Arthur M. Johnson. New York: Free Press, 1974.

Davenport, H. J. *The Economics of Enterprise*. New York: Macmillan, (1913) 1936.

Diamond, James J., ed. *Issues in Fiscal and Monetary Policy*. Chicago: De Paul University, 1971.

Economic Report of the President. 1981, 1983, 1985. Washington, D. C.: U.S. Government Printing Office.

Epstein, Gerald, and Thomas Ferguson. "Monetary Policy, Loan Liquidation, and Industrial Conflict: The Federal Reserve and the Open Market Operations of 1932." *The Journal of Economic History* XLIV:4 (December 1984).

Federal Reserve Bank of New York. *Annual Report*. 1966, 1968.

Federal Reserve Bulletin. January 1942, February 1961, February 1971, July 1985.

Feige, Edgar L., and Robert McGee. "Has the Federal Reserve Shifted from a Policy of Interest Rate Targets to a Policy of Monetary Aggregate Targets?" *Journal of Money, Credit and Banking* XI:4 (November 1979).

Feldstein, Martin. "Monetarism: Open-eyed Pragmatism." *The Economist,* May 18, 1985.

Fisher, Irving. *The Purchasing Power of Money*. New York: Macmillan, 1911.

Fite, Gilbert C. "Election of 1896." In *History of American Presidential Elections 1789-1968,* Vol. II, ed. Arthur M. Schlesinger, Jr. New York: Chelsea House Publishers in association with McGraw–Hill, 1971.

Friedman, Milton. "The Case for Overhauling the Federal Reserve." *Challenge* 28:3 (July/August 1985).

———. *The Counter-revolution in Monetary Theory*. First Wincott Memorial Lecture. Occasional Paper 33. London: The Institute of Economic Affairs, 1970.

———. "Have Monetary Policies Failed?" *American Economic Review* LXII:2 (May 1972).

———. "Money: Quantity Theory." In *International Encyclopedia of the Social Sciences,* Vol. 10, ed. David L. Sills. New York: Macmillan and Free Press, 1968.

Friedman, Milton and Anna Jacobson Schwartz. *A Monetary History of the United States 1867–1960,* a study by the National Bureau of Economic Research. Princeton: Princeton University Press, 1963.

Friedman, Milton and Walter W. Heller. *Monetary vs. Fiscal Policy.* Arthur K. Salomon Lecture, New York University Graduate School of Business Administration. New York: W. W. Norton, 1969.

Galbraith, John Kenneth. *The Great Crash.* Boston: Houghton Mifflin, 1954.

———. *Money.* Boston: Houghton Mifflin, 1975.

Gandolfi, Arthur E. and James R. Lothian. Review of Peter Temin, *Did Monetary Forces Cause the Great Depression?* In *Journal of Money, Credit and Banking* IX (November 1977).

Goldenweiser, E. A. *American Monetary Policy.* New York: McGraw–Hill, 1951.

Gordon, Donald F. Review of Peter Temin, *Did Monetary Forces Cause the Great Depression?* In *Journal of Economic Literature* XVI (March 1978).

Hakkio, Craig S. and Bryon Higgins. "Is the United States Too Dependent on Foreign Capital?" *Economic Review,* Federal Reserve Bank of Kansas City 70:6 (June 1985).

Harris, Seymour. *Economics of the Kennedy Years.* New York: Harper and Row, 1964.

Harrod, Roy F. *The Dollar.* New York: Harcourt, Brace, 1954.

Heller, Walter W. *The Economy: Old Myths and New Realities.* New York: W. W. Norton, 1976.

———. *New Dimensions of Political Economy.* New York: W. W. Norton, 1967.

Hester, Donald. "Innovations and Monetary Control." *Brookings Papers on Economic Activity* I:1981. Washington, D. C.: Brookings Institution.

Hyman, Sidney. *Marriner S. Eccles.* Stanford, Calif.: Graduate School of Business, Stanford University, 1976.

Jones, Byrd L. "Lauchlin Currie and the Causes of the 1937 Recession." *History of Political Economy* 12 (Fall 1980).

———. "Lauchlin Currie, Pump Priming, and New Deal Fiscal Policy, 1934–1936." *History of Political Economy* 10 (Winter 1978).

Jones, Jesse H., with Edward Angly. *Fifty Billion Dollars.* New York: Macmillan, 1951.

Judd, John P. "The Recent Decline in Velocity: Instability in Money Demand or Inflation?" *Economic Review,* Federal Reserve Bank of San Francisco (Spring 1983).

Kaldor, Nicholas. *The Scourge of Monetarism.* New York: Oxford University Press, 1982.

Kane, Edward J. "Selecting Monetary Targets in a Changing Financial Environment." In *Monetary Policy Issues in the 1980s.* Federal Reserve Bank of Kansas City, 1982.

Kemmerer, Edwin Walter. *The ABC of the Federal Reserve System,* 7th edition. Princeton: Princeton University Press, 1928.

Keynes, John Maynard. *The General Theory of Employment Interest and Money.* London: Macmillan, 1949 (1st edition 1936).

———. *A Tract on Monetary Reform.* The Collected Writings of John Maynard

Keynes, Volume IV. London: Macmillan St. Martin's Press for the Royal Economic Society, 1971 (1st edition 1923).

Kindleberger, Charles P. Review of Karl Brunner, ed., *The Great Depression Revisited.* In *Journal of Economic Literature* XIX (December 1981).

———. *The World in Depression 1929–1939.* Berkeley and Los Angeles: University of California Press, 1973.

Kopcke, Richard W. "Bank Funding Strategy and the Money Stock." *New England Economic Review* (Jan./Feb. 1985). Federal Reserve Bank of Boston.

Lewis, Paul. "Challenging the Olympian Fed." *The New York Times,* August 18, 1974.

Macesich, George. *The Politics of Monetarism.* Totowa, N.J.: Rowman & Allanheld, 1984.

Maisel, Sherman J. *Managing the Dollar.* New York: W. W. Norton, 1973.

Martin, William McChesney. "The Transition to Free Markets." *Federal Reserve Bulletin* XXXIX (April 1953).

Mayer, Martin. *The Bankers.* New York: Weybright and Talley, 1974.

Miller, Roger Leroy, and Raburn M. Williams. *The New Economics of Richard Nixon.* San Francisco: Canfield Press, 1972.

Morris, Frank E. "Monetarism without Money." *New England Economic Review* (March/April 1983). Federal Reserve Bank of Boston.

———. "Rules plus Discretion in Monetary Policy—An Appraisal of Our Experience since October 1979." *New England Economic Review* (Sept./Oct. 1985). Federal Reserve Bank of Boston.

Moynihan, Daniel Patrick. "Reagan's Inflate-the-Deficit Game." *The New York Times,* July 21, 1985.

Nadler, Paul S. *Commercial Banking in the Economy,* 3rd edition. New York: Random House, 1979.

Nobay, A. Robert, and Harry G. Johnson. "Monetarism: A Historic–Theoretic Perspective." *Journal of Economic Literature* XV:2 (June 1977).

Nourse, Edwin G. Director's preface to Charles O. Hardy, *Credit Policies of the Federal Reserve System.* Washington, D. C.: The Brookings Institution, 1932.

Okun, Arthur M. *The Political Economy of Prosperity.* New York: W. W. Norton, 1970.

———. "Uniting against Inflation." *The Brookings Bulletin* 16:3 (Winter 1980).

Radecki, Lawrence J., and John Wenninger. "Recent Instability in M1's Velocity." *Federal Reserve Bank of New York Quarterly Review* 10:3 (Autumn 1985).

Rivlin, Alice M. "Why and How to Cut the Deficit." *The Brookings Review* 2:4 (Summer 1984).

Sampson, Anthony. *The Money Lenders.* New York: Viking, 1981.

Samuelson, Paul A. "Evaluating Reaganomics." *Challenge* 27:5 (November/December 1984).

Sawhill, Isabel V., and Charles F. Stone. "The Economy: The Key to Success." In John L. Palmer and Isabel V. Sawhill, eds., *The Reagan Record.* Cambridge, Mass.: Ballinger, 1984.

Schlesinger, Arthur M., Jr. *The Coming of the New Deal.* Boston: Houghton Mifflin, 1959.

Schumpeter, Joseph A. *History of Economic Analysis*. New York: Oxford University Press, 1954.

Seldon, Richard T. "Monetarism." In Sidney Weintraub, ed., *Modern Economic Thought*. Philadelphia: University of Pennsylvania Press, 1977.

Seligman, Edwin R. A. "Introduction—The Crisis of 1907 in the Light of History." In *The Currency Problem and the Present Financial Situation*. New York: Columbia University Press, 1908.

Sellon, Gordon H., Jr., and Ronald L. Teigen. "The Choice of Short-Run Targets for Monetary Policy." *Economic Review*. Federal Reserve Bank of Kansas City (May 1981).

Silk, Leonard. *The Economists*. New York: Basic Books, 1976.

———. *Nixonomics,* 2nd edition. New York: Praeger, 1972.

Sills, David L., ed. *International Encyclopedia of the Social Sciences*. New York: Macmillan and Free Press, 1968.

Summers, Bruce J. "Negotiable Certificates of Deposit." *Instruments of the Money Market,* 5th edition. Federal Reserve Bank of Richmond, 1981.

Temin, Peter. *Did Monetary Forces Cause the Great Depression?* New York: W. W. Norton, 1976.

Tobin, James. "The Fiscal Revolution: Disturbing Prospects." *Challenge* 27:6 (January/February 1985).

———. "Monetarism: An Ebbing Tide?" *The Economist,* April 27, 1985.

Trescott, Paul B. *Financing American Enterprise*. New York: Harper and Row, 1963.

Vanderlip, Frank A. "The Modern Bank." In *The Currency Problem and the Present Financial Situation*. New York: Columbia University Press, 1908.

von Hoffman, Nicholas. "Can Volcker Stand Up to Inflation?" *The New York Times Magazine,* December 2, 1979.

Wallich, Henry C. "Whither American Banking Reform?" *Challenge* 28:4 (September/October 1985).

Warburg, Paul M. *The Federal Reserve System, Its Origin and Growth,* Vol. 1. New York: Macmillan, 1930.

West, Robert Craig. *Banking Reform and the Federal Reserve 1863–1923*. Ithaca: Cornell University Press, 1977.

Whitehead, David D. "Interstate Banking: Probability or Reality?" *Economic Review*. Federal Reserve Bank of Atlanta (March 1985).

Wicker, Elmus R. *Federal Reserve Monetary Policy 1917–1933*. New York: Random House, 1966.

Wicker, Tom. "A Deliberate Deficit." *The Chattanooga Times,* July 20, 1985.

Yeager, Leland B. "Clark Warburton, 1896–1979." *History of Political Economy* 13:2 (Summer 1981).

Index

Accord of March 4, 1951, 110, 113–117
Ackley, Gardner, 134n4
Ahearn, Daniel S., 121n5
Aldrich, Nelson W., 16, 26
Aldrich-Vreeland Act, 16–17
Allen, Frederick Lewis, 13, 52n14
Anderson, Benjamin M., 48–49, 58, 59n24

Baker, Russell, 61
Bank, defined, 184
Bank failures, 2, 12, 14, 39, 52, 62–65, 186
Banking Act of 1933, 73–75
Banking Act of 1935, 73–76, 92, 104
Bills only, 120–123
Blaug, Mark, 89
Blinder, Alan S., 143, 160
Board of Governors of the Federal Reserve System, 74, 92, 134, 159. *See also* Federal Reserve Board
Boulding, Kenneth E., 199, 212
Brimmer, Andrew, 155
Bronfenbrenner, Martin, 126
Bryan, William Jennings, 3–5, 80
Budget deficit, 173–178
Burns, Arthur F., 143–145, 151–155, 161–162

Cargill, Thomas F., 169
Carter, Jimmy, 161–162, 178
Certificates of deposit (CDs), 131, 135, 138, 146
Chandler, Lester V., 30n1, 42nn2–3, 43n5, 55, 61, 72, 85n11, 104
Cleveland, Grover, 2–3
Clifford, A. Jerome, 104n6, 105n10, 113n8
Commercial banking: before World War I, 10–11, 14–16; 1920s, 51–52; 1930s, 63–65, 81; 1960s, 130–131; 1970s, 146, 165–167; 1980s, 183–190
Continental Illinois National Bank & Trust Company, 187–188
Corrigan, E. Gerald, 189n35, 190
Currie, Lauchlin, 86, 94–95

Dale, Edwin L., Jr., 133
Depository Institutions Deregulation and Monetary Control Act, 179–181
Depressions: 1907–1908, 12; of 1920–1921, 37–40. *See also* Great Depression
Disintermediation, 136, 138, 166
Douglas, Paul H., 114, 117

Eccles, Marriner S., 91–94, 116
Eisenhower, Dwight D., 126
Emergency Banking Act, 76
Emerson, Ralph Waldo, 5
Employment Act of 1946, 109
Epstein, Gerald, 71
Excess reserves, 81, 83–84, 95, 101, 106

Federal Deposit Insurance Corporation (FDIC), 73–74, 76, 187–188, 190
Federal Open Market Committee (FOMC), 74, 83, 93, 102–103, 116, 137, 139–141, 145, 155–159, 162–164, 191–193. *See also* Open Market Policy Conference
Federal Reserve Act, 17–20, 33, 35, 39, 42, 44, 51, 104
Federal Reserve Bank of New York, 48, 54, 56, 63, 66, 69, 137, 140, 194
Federal Reserve Banks, 17–20, 29–38, 42–43, 49, 55–57, 70–72, 74–75, 83–84, 92–93, 136
Federal Reserve Board, 17, 29–30, 33, 36–38, 40, 42–45, 48–49, 53–56,

About the Author

Robert A. Degen is Professor of Economics, Emeritus, at The University of the South, where he taught money and banking, history of economic thought, and comparative economic systems, and was chairman of the Department of Economics for ten years. He holds the B.S. and M.A. degrees from Syracuse University and the Ph.D. from the University of Wisconsin. Prior to his career as an academic economist, the author spent five years in commercial banking in New Jersey. During World War II he served as a statistical control officer with the Air Transport Command of the U.S. Army Air Forces in North Africa.